Digital Content Creation in Schools

DIGITAL CONTENT CREATION IN SCHOOLS

A Common Core Approach

Karen S. Ivers and Ann E. Barron

 LIBRARIES UNLIMITED

AN IMPRINT OF ABC-CLIO, LLC
Santa Barbara, California • Denver, Colorado • Oxford, England

Library of Congress Cataloging-in-Publication Data

Ivers, Karen S.
  Digital content creation in schools : a common core approach / Karen S. Ivers and Ann E. Barron.
    pages cm
  Includes bibliographical references and index.
    ISBN 978–1–61069–629–6 (paperback) — ISBN 978–1–61069–630–2 (ebook) 1. Media programs (Education) 2. Interactive multimedia. 3. Technological literacy—Study and teaching. 4. Educational technology. 5. Computer-assisted instruction. 6. Group work in education. I. Barron, Ann E. II. Title.
LB1028.4.I94   2015
371.33—dc23   2014027765

ISBN: 978–1–61069–629–6
EISBN: 978–1–61069–630–2

19 18 17 16 15   1 2 3 4 5

This book is also available on the World Wide Web as an eBook.
Visit www.abc-clio.com for details.

Libraries Unlimited
An Imprint of ABC-CLIO, LLC

ABC-CLIO, LLC
130 Cremona Drive, P.O. Box 1911
Santa Barbara, California 93116-1911

This book is printed on acid-free paper ∞

Manufactured in the United States of America

Blackline masters may be copied for educational purposes. They may also be used to help educators create their own DECIDE activity and organization sheets, such as a modified survey, computer schedule, or bibliography information sheet.

Contents

Preface

There is nothing more rewarding for an educator to experience than the enthusiasm and joy created by students actively engaged in a learning activity. Students *willingly* seek knowledge, spend extra time on their projects, and take pride in their work. Both the teacher and the students enjoy coming to school!

Digital Content Creation in Schools: A Common Core Approach provides educators with strategies to ensure learning is active, collaborative, and meaningful as students engage in higher-level thinking skills to create digital projects. It is designed as a guide for practitioners, based on the DDD-E model, with a foundation grounded in cooperative learning, multiple intelligences, and constructivism. *Digital Content Creation in Schools: A Common Core Approach* supports 21st-century learning skills and the use of alternative assessments.

Using a Common Core Approach supports teachers' use of a variety of approaches to ensure learning is meaningful and addresses real-world learning opportunities. Students engage in critical thinking, creativity, collaboration, and communication through the development of multimedia digital content. Digital content creation provides students with a powerful communication medium and offers them new insights into organizing, synthesizing, and evaluating information.

Digital Content Creation in Schools: A Common Core Approach begins by discussing the Common Core State Standards, 21st-century learning, and the latest technology standards. Chapter 1 also describes research in the areas of cooperative learning, multiple intelligences, and constructivism and how these theories can be applied to digital content creation. Chapter 2 introduces the DDD-E (DECIDE, DESIGN, DEVELOP, and EVALUATE) model that is used to guide the reader through the rest of the book. Chapter 3 (DECIDE) discusses classroom management issues, grouping alternatives, computer-scheduling options, and other issues related to planning a project. Chapter 4 (DESIGN) introduces the reader to the design stages of digital content creation, including flowcharts, storyboards, and basic design issues. DEVELOP is divided into two chapters. Chapter 5 (DEVELOP: Media Elements) addresses and defines the various media elements that are available for digital projects, including graphics, animations, audio, and video. Chapter 6 (DEVELOP: Digital Content Creation Tools) provides an overview of development tools. Chapter 7 (EVALUATE) discusses alternative assessment techniques and assessment strategies. It also includes information on rubric design and assigning grades.

Following the chapters on DECIDE, DESIGN, DEVELOP, and EVALUATE, five activity chapters provide the reader with ideas for digital content creation projects. The activities focus on various development tools in several content areas, and they address a variety of grade levels and subject areas.

Throughout the book, the emphasis is on a Common Core Approach, student-learning outcomes, and managing the development of digital projects. Each chapter begins with a scenario illustrating the implementation of digital projects in an educational setting. The chapters contain detailed graphics, charts, and tables. In addition, blackline masters are included that can be copied for educational purposes. Teachers, media specialists, and administrators will find this book an invaluable resource for producing, designing, managing, and assessing digital projects.

Digital Content Creation in Schools: A Common Core Approach is designed from the educator's perspective and can be used to facilitate classroom instruction as well as in-service workshops on strategies for developing digital projects. It is appropriate for classroom teachers and for educational technology courses at both the undergraduate and graduate levels.

The Impact of Multimedia and Digital Content Creation on Student Learning

A SCENARIO

Riley and Joya were mesmerized, along with their classmates, as they gathered around Dana to look at her Facebook page. Dana had posted pictures, videos, and text about her recent trip to the local animal shelter. Her dad had taken her there to adopt a dog. Dana shared that it was a "no kill" shelter and people volunteered their time to take care of and foster the animals. She was given a tour and learned that many of the animals had been abused or abandoned, and that the shelter was supported by a variety of charities. She also learned about "puppy mills," large-scale commercial dog-breeding operations that place profit over the well-being of their dogs. "These are often the dogs that are sold in pet stores," Dana shared. "Sometimes the breeder dogs are rescued and taken to shelters, but it can sometimes take more than year before the dogs are relaxed enough to allow human touch."

"People don't care about animals—they care about money!" shouted Matthew.

"Maybe there is something we can do about it," mentioned Tia. "Maybe people need to know why they should support shelters instead of pet stores."

A real-world learning activity was unfolding itself as Mr. Mercer watched his students enter his classroom. His students were engaged with Dana's report, although it was not in any way tied to a current class assignment. His students' ability to capture video, pictures, and enter text with their smartphones was second nature to them. "Why not use these tools to support their formal education?" he asked himself. "I think I've figured out how to speak their language and make learning more meaningful and authentic. I'm going to follow up with Maryann, our media specialist."

OVERVIEW

As technology and media have transformed, it has become easier to create digital content. Digital content is what drives most aspects of our communication—e.g., social networks, blogs, wikis, text, e-mail, tweets, and so on. Just as our students use digital content to share their lives with others, students can create digital content to explain their ideas and what they have learned, using multimedia to convey their understanding of a topic in a variety of ways. Bennett (1996, 16) notes that students "know that they have learned something when they can explain their work and ideas to others or when they can successfully teach others difficult concepts or content." The Common Core State Standards (CCSS) emphasize the importance of students being able to explain their thinking to others (Common Core State Standards Initiative 2012a). Digital content creation provides students with a powerful communication medium and offers them new insights into organizing, synthesizing, and evaluating information. It supports multimodal composition, requiring students to use visual elements to supplement or replace text in a purposeful way. Digital content creation has the potential to change the roles of teacher and learner and the interaction between them by allowing students to create their own interpretations of information.

In addition to content knowledge and skill development, developing digital content offers students the opportunity to work collaboratively; engage in authentic learning experiences, multiple modalities of learning, and reflective thinking; and use a constructivist approach to learning. It supports 21st-century learning skills by helping students use their knowledge to analyze, create, solve problems, communicate, collaborate, and innovate (Cox 2009; Harris 2010; Hersh 2009; International Society for Technology in Education [ISTE], Partnership for 21st Century Skills, and State Educational Technology Directors Association [SETDA] 2007; Pope, Beal, Long, and McCammon 2011; United Nations for Educational, Scientific and Cultural Organization 2008). This chapter defines multimedia and examines research addressing the benefits of developing digital content. Topics include the following:

Definition and history of multimedia in education

- 21st-century learning and digital content creation
- Common Core State Standards
- ISTE's Technology Standards for Students

Research on digital multimedia and student learning

- Howard Gardner's theory of multiple intelligences
- Cooperative learning
- Constructivism

DEFINITION AND HISTORY OF MULTIMEDIA IN EDUCATION

In general terms, *multimedia* is the use of several media to present information. Combinations may include text, graphics, animation, pictures, video, and sound. Educators have been using multimedia for years. For example, it is not uncommon for teachers to support a unit on Ancient Civilizations with digital video and audio from the Internet or DVDs, along with pictures, text, and artifacts. In years past, teachers may have supported the same unit with paper charts and diagrams, bound encyclopedias, and analog video, film strips, or slides. Today's technologies, however, allow educators and students to integrate, combine, and interact with media far beyond what was previously possible.

"Hyper" environments, such as hypertext, hyperlinks, and hypermedia, have added to the complexity and sophistication of multimedia's definition by providing electronic, nonlinear approaches to moving through a body of information. These environments allow users and creators to personalize the delivery, markup, and organization of the content (Baehr and Lang 2012). Hypertext facilitates interaction between readers and texts by organizing and linking information. This can create associations, definitions, examples, and other relationships between the text passages (Rouet, Levon, Dillion, and Spiro 1996; Salmeron and Garcia 2012; Vandendorpe 2009). Hyperlinks connect text in the project to external files or websites. Hypermedia adds video clips, graphics, or audio files to hypertext. Combining these elements results in greater comprehension, recall, and inference (Chambers et al. 2008; Fabio and Antonietti 2012; Jones 2009; Wilson 2008). These multimodal approaches to education effectively accommodate students with diverse learning and cognitive styles (De La Paz and Hernandez-Ramos 2013; Fabio and Antonietti 2012; Kay and Knack 2009; Spence 2009; Wieman, Perkins, and Adams 2008). In addition, hypermedia applications are better suited to transmitting knowledge that is not easily conveyed through print or verbal explanations (Dikshit, Garg, and Panda 2013; Stelzer, Gladding, Mestre, and Brookes 2009; Urban-Woldron 2009).

This book focuses on the creation of digital content using a variety of digital content creation tools, including multimedia documents and apps, presentation and hypermedia programs, web page production, digital video, and eBooks. The purpose of this book is to help teachers and students design, produce, and assess the creation of multimedia using various digital content creation tools. Strategies focus on 21st-century learning and using a "Common Core Approach"—emphasizing such skills as critical thinking, communication, and collaboration—throughout the DECIDE, DESIGN, DEVELOP, and EVALUATE (DDD-E) process of creating digital content. Guidelines are provided for projects that provide authentic learning experiences in the classroom.

21st-Century Learning and Digital Content Creation

Advances in technology have significantly impacted society and global awareness. Even so, the U.S. Department of Education and businesses have noted that "there is a profound gap between the knowledge and skills most students learn in school and the knowledge and skills they need in typical 21st century communities and workplaces" (Partnership for 21st Century Skills 2014, para. 3). In 2002, a coalition of business and educational leaders and policy makers founded the Partnership for 21st Century Skills. Over several years and in collaboration with educators, nonprofits, foundations, and corporate members, the *Framework for 21st Century Learning* was created (see http://www.p21.org/our-work/p21-framework). The *Framework* describes outcomes and support systems designed to ensure students are prepared to succeed in life and meet the demands of the work environment in the 21st century. Outcomes include knowledge and expertise in the Core Subjects and 21st Century Themes (global awareness; financial, economic, business, and entrepreneurial literacy; civic literacy; health literacy; and environmental literacy), Learning and Innovation Skills (creativity and innovation, critical thinking and problem solving, and communication and collaboration—the 4Cs), and Information, Media, and Technology Skills. Support systems include 21st Century Standards, Assessments for 21st Century Skills, 21st Century Curriculum and Instruction, 21st Professional Development, and 21st Century Learning Environments.

Common Core State Standards

In an effort to ensure all students are equally prepared to enter college or the 21st-century workplace, the Common Core State Standards (CCSS) were developed. Previous state standards were unique to each state, which made it difficult to assess student outcomes across the states and to ensure students, no matter where they went to school, were "prepared with the skills and knowledge necessary to collaborate and compete with their peers in the United States and abroad" (Common Core State Standards Initiative 2012b, para. 4).

Similar to the *Framework for 21st Century Learning*, the CCSS were developed in collaboration with teachers, researchers, and leading experts. The initiative for the CCSS began with the nation's governors and education commissioners—the National Governors Association (NGA) and the Council of Chief State School Officers (CCSSO). The Partnership for 21st Century Skills endorses the CCSS, noting that the standards align with the *Framework for 21st Century Learning* in many ways (Partnership for 21st Century Skills 2011). For example, the CCSS focus on higher-order thinking skills, rigorous core academic content mastery, and competencies like reasoning, critical thinking, communication, and collaboration. The CCSS emphasize media, information, and technology literacy across subject areas as well, and require educators to integrate technology into the classroom. The CCSS focus on authentic learning experiences, conceptual understanding, career and college readiness, and what it means to be a literate person in the 21st century. The Partnership for 21st Century Skills (2011) notes that "it is crucial to design curricula and assessment systems that emphasize authentic real world problems, engage students in inquiry and exploration and provide opportunities for students to apply what they know in meaningful ways" (p. 10).

Digital content creation supports the CCSS by emphasizing the 4Cs: creativity and innovation, critical thinking and problem solving, and communication and collaboration. Digital content creation encourages students to work in groups, express their knowledge in multiple ways, solve problems, revise their own work, and construct knowledge. Students have the opportunity to learn and apply real-world skills. They learn the value of teamwork; the impact and importance of different media, including design issues, media appropriateness and validity, and copyright laws; the challenges of communicating to different audiences; the importance of research, planning, and organization skills; the significance of presentation and speaking skills; and how to accept and provide constructive feedback. Digital content creation helps to reinforce students' technology skills and to prepare them for the demands of future careers.

Engaging students in digital content creation also makes effective use of technology in the classroom. It supports a Common Core Approach by promoting

- the integration of technology into the curriculum;

- active learning, inquiry, problem solving, and other higher-order thinking skills;

- environments that engage students in individual and collaborative work;

- the use of technology to present and represent ideas; and

- information and media literacy skills.

ISTE's Technology Standards for Students

The process of creating digital content also addresses the International Society for Technology in Education (ISTE)'s technology standards for students. Focusing on 21st-century learning skills, students use technology to create and innovate; communicate and collaborate; research, assess, and apply information; think critically, problem solve, and make decisions; learn to become a digital citizen; and understand technology concepts (ISTE 2007). The standards profile technology-literate students and provide sample digital learning activities for students in different grade levels. For example, the ISTE standards suggest students in grades PK–2 have opportunities to use digital tools to illustrate and communicate original ideas, work in groups to produce digital presentations, demonstrate the ability to navigate virtual environments such as eBooks, and so on. Sample activities for students in grades 3–5 include creating media-rich digital stories; deciding on, designing, and developing individual and group projects using digital tools with teacher support; and conducting research and experiments using digital tools. In grades 6–8, the standards suggest students create original animations and videos, participate in online learning communities, use authoring tools, and so on. For students in grades 9–12, sample activities include designing, developing, and testing a digital learning game, designing a website, and creating media-rich presentations. Examples emphasize real-world learning, curriculum content, and higher-order thinking skills. To effectively implement technology in schools, ISTE (2009) recommends the following:

- Shared vision

- Empowered leaders

- Implementation planning

- Consistent and adequate funding

- Equitable access

- Skilled personnel

- Ongoing professional learning

- Technology support

- Curriculum framework

- Student-centered learning

- Assessment and evaluation

- Engaged communities

- Support policies

- Supportive external context

RESEARCH ON DIGITAL MULTIMEDIA AND STUDENT LEARNING

Advancements in technology have made it possible for teachers and students to develop elaborate digital content in the classroom. Using Macintosh and PC-based computers, as well as tablets and other mobile devices, students are able to express themselves through a variety of media—text, audio, video, graphics, animation, and sound—in linear and nonlinear formats. Research in the area of multimedia demonstrates that its use can be effective for teaching and learning (Ke 2014; Korat 2010; Magana 2014; Neo, Neo, and Tan 2012) with all levels of students, including second-language learners and those with special needs (Carnahan, Basham, and Musti-Rao 2009; De La Paz and Hernandez-Ramos 2103; Liu 2013; O'Hara and Pritchard 2008; Poobrasert and Cercone 2009; Shamir and Shlafer 2011). Interactive, multimedia learning environments can support higher-order thinking and problem-solving skills (Ke 2014; Neo and Neo 2009; Su 2008), increase students' achievement (Chambers et al. 2008; De La Paz and Hernandez-Ramos 2013; Kingsley and Boone 2008; Tuzun, Yilmaz-Soylu, Karakus, Inal, and Kizilkaya 2009; Ziden and Rahman 2013), increase student motivation (Bertacchini, Bilotta, Pantano, and

Tavernise 2012; Ciampa 2012; Neo and Neo 2010; Papastergiou 2009; Poobrasert and Cercone 2009; Tuzun, Yilmaz-Soylu, Karakus, Inal, and Kizilkaya 2009), and develop more positive dispositions toward learning mathematics and other STEM (science, technology, engineering, and math) related fields (Beier, Miller, and Wang 2012; Bertacchini, Bilotta, Pantano, and Tavernise 2012; Johnson, Ozogul, DiDonato, and Reisslein 2013; Ke 2014; Liu 2013; Piliouras, Siakas, and Seroglou 2011). In addition, creating digital content helps students construct knowledge and makes topics more meaningful and motivating to learn (Wolfe 2010). Bagui (1998, 4) suggests that "multimedia may make it easier for people to learn because of the parallels between multimedia and the 'natural' way people learn."

Howard Gardner's Theory of Multiple Intelligences

Several researchers have developed theories on various ways of knowing, suggesting that students possess several intelligences (Gardner 1983, 1999, 2006, 2011b; Samples 1992; Sternberg 1994). Perhaps the most recognized theory of multiple intelligences is Howard Gardner's theory of multiple intelligences (Gardner 1983, 1999, 2011b). In his book *Intelligence Reframed: Multiple Intelligences for the 21st Century*, Gardner reviews the seven intelligences he introduced in his first book, *Frames of the Mind: The Theory of Multiple Intelligences*, and adds another—the naturalist intelligence. Gardner defines *intelligence* as "a biopsychological potential to process information that can be activated in a cultural setting to solve problems or create products that are of value in a culture" (Gardner 1999, 33–34). He suggests that intelligences are neural conditions that will or will not be activated by opportunities, personal decisions, or values. He also states that everyone possesses these intelligences, noting that people acquire and represent knowledge in different ways. Gardner's proposed eight areas of intelligence include:

1. Linguistic Intelligence: the ability to use words effectively, whether orally or in writing.

2. Logical-Mathematical Intelligence: the capacity to use numbers effectively and to reason well.

3. Spatial Intelligence: the ability to perceive the visual-spatial world accurately and to perform transformations on those perceptions.

4. Bodily-Kinesthetic Intelligence: expertise in using one's body to express ideas and feelings and facility in using one's hands to produce or transform things.

5. Musical Intelligence: the ability to perceive, discriminate, transform, and express musical forms.

6. Interpersonal Intelligence: the ability to perceive and make distinctions in the moods, intentions, motivations, and feelings of other people.

7. Intrapersonal Intelligence: self-knowledge and the ability to act on the basis of that knowledge.

8. Naturalist Intelligence: expertise in recognizing and classifying living and nonliving forms within one's environment. Gardner (1999, 49) notes, "The young child who can readily discriminate among plants or birds or dinosaurs is drawing on the same skills (or intelligence) when she classifies sneakers, cars, sound systems, or marbles."

Gardner identified these intelligences based on a series of tests that included eight different criteria. Gardner has speculated on the possibility of a ninth intelligence, existential intelligence, noting that there is suggestive evidence that it exists (Gardner 2011b). He has also explored the idea of a pedagogical intelligence, as well as considered a digital intelligence (Gardner 2011b). Additional intelligences have been proposed—including spirituality, moral sensibility, sexuality, humor, intuition, and creativity—but it remains to be seen whether these proposed intelligences meet the required criteria (Armstrong 2009; Gardner 1999, 2011b).

There are several important elements to remember about Gardner's theory of multiple intelligences. In his book *Multiple Intelligences in the Classroom*, Armstrong (2009) states that

- Each person possesses all eight intelligences.

- Most people can develop each intelligence to an adequate level of competency.

- Intelligences usually work together in complex ways.

- There are many ways to be intelligent within each category.

Many educators have successfully implemented Gardner's theory of multiple intelligences into their classrooms (Dorfman and Rosenberg 2103; Douglas, Burton, and Reese-Durham 2008; Eksi 2009; Gardner 2011a; Kosky and Curtis 2008; Kunkel 2009; Vermonden and Alcock 2013). Applying Gardner's theory of multiple intelligences can benefit all learners, including students with learning disabilities, gifted students, second-language learners, and students from diverse cultural backgrounds (Bakic-Miric 2010; Chen, Moran, and Gardner 2009; Dorfman and Rosenberg 2103; Perez and Beltran 2008).

Commercial multimedia applications and the development of digital content encourage a multimodal approach to learning. Well-designed multimedia applications present content in several media formats and allow students to use their own individual learning styles. Although multimedia applications can effectively teach content, student-based digital content creation allows students to gain skills beyond content-area knowledge. These skills include finding and interpreting information, articulating and communicating knowledge, and using the computer as a cognitive tool (De La Paz and Hernandez 2013; Jonassen 2008; Ke 2103; Neo and Neo 2009; Su 2008).

Applying the Theory of Multiple Intelligences to Digital Content Creation

One of the many benefits of digital content creation is that it allows students to construct and communicate knowledge in various ways. Digital content creation also encourages group work and social interaction, but it does not require a uniform experience for all students. According to Levin (1994), group work and social interaction are necessary for a multiple intelligences approach, but a uniform experience for all children is not.

When assigning multimedia design teams, students should be placed in groups that provide them with the opportunity to take advantage of their strengths, as well as nurture their weaknesses. For example, students who are identified as spatially intelligent might be responsible for the graphic content and layout of a multimedia project. Students who are identified as logical-mathematically intelligent might be responsible for designing the structure/flowchart of the project and the scripting or programming requirements. Table 1.1 correlates each intelligence with the observed student behaviors and recommended roles when developing digital content.

It is important to note that all students have all intelligences, although one or more may be stronger than others. Placing students in design teams that capture the diversity of their intellectual profiles can provide them with the motivation, skills, and support necessary to learn. Armstrong

Table 1.1. Roles of Multiple Intelligence in Digital Content Creation

Intelligence	Observed Student Behaviors	Leadership Roles in Digital Content Creation
Linguistic	Loves to read books, write, and tell stories; good memory for names, dates, and trivia; communicates well	Gather and develop text for project; provide narration; keep journal of group progress
Logical-Mathematical	Excels in math; has strong problem-solving skills; enjoys playing strategy games and working on logic puzzles	Design flowchart; write scripting and programming code; develop navigation routes
Spatial	Needs a mental or physical picture to best understand things; draws figures that are advanced for age; doodles a lot	Create graphics, animation, and other visual media for project; design layout
Body-Kinesthetic	Excels in one or more sports; good fine-motor skills; tendency to move around, touch things, gesture	Keyboard information; manipulate objects with mouse; operate multimedia equipment
Musical	Remembers melodies; recognizes when music is off-key; has a good singing voice; plays an instrument; hums a lot	Identify works for content integration; create musical score for project; input audio/sound effects
Interpersonal	Enjoys socializing with peers; has leadership skills; has good sense of empathy and concern for others	Coordinate group efforts; help set group goals; help solve group disputes
Intrapersonal	Has strong sense of self; is confident; prefers working alone; has high self-esteem; displays independence	Conduct independent research to share with teammates; pilot test multimedia projects; lead multimedia presentations
Naturalist	Enjoys the outdoors, plants, and animals; easily recognizes and classifies things within his or her environment	Collect outside elements for incorporation into projects; organize project work

(2009) comments that most students have strengths in several areas; hence, students may contribute to projects in multiple ways. For example, one student may lead the group in developing the text and music for the project, another student may lead the group in creating the graphics and flowcharts for the project, and so on.

Intellectual profiles can change over time as intelligences develop in strength. Gray and Viens (1994, 24) note, "The differences among individual intellectual profiles are the result of personal and local factors as well as cultural influences." Working in diverse groups allows students to nurture their weaknesses and capitalize on their strengths. Students are able to make valuable contributions to group projects, as well as augment their intellectual profiles.

Cooperative Learning

Cooperative learning takes place when students work together to accomplish shared goals. Most cooperative conditions use small groups "so that students work together to maximize their own and each other's learning" (Johnson and Johnson 1999a, 5). Johnson and Johnson (1999b, 2009) suggest that a cooperative learning group has five defining characteristics:

1. Positive Interdependence. There is a group goal to maximize all members' learning beyond their individual abilities; members succeed only if the other members in their group succeed.

2. Individual Accountability. Group members hold themselves and each other accountable for high-quality work; students are held accountable for their share of the work.

3. Face-to-Face Promotive Interaction. Group members produce joint products, providing both academic and personal support; students promote each other's learning.

4. Social Skills. Group members are taught social skills and are expected to use them to coordinate their efforts; teamwork and task work are emphasized.

5. Group Processing. Groups analyze how well they are achieving their goals, working together, and learning.

The researchers note that a cooperative group is more than the sum of its parts and state that students often perform better academically than they would if they worked by themselves (Johnson and Johnson 1999b, 2009).

There are a variety of cooperative group techniques, including Student Teams Achievement Divisions, Teams Games Tournament, Team Assisted Individualization, Jigsaw, Group Investigation, and Learning Together (Slavin 1994, 1999, 2011; Vermette 1998), as described below.

Student Teams Achievement Divisions (STAD)—students learn something as a team, contribute to the team by improving their own past performance, and earn team rewards based on their improvements. Students are usually heterogeneously mixed by ability and take individual weekly quizzes. For example, student teams may study about the Westward Movement and take weekly quizzes on the content. Teams earn points based on each student's improvement from previous quizzes. If a student scores 5 out of 10 points on the first quiz and 8 out of 10 on the second quiz, he may earn 8 points for his team, plus 2 bonus points for improving. If a student scores 7 out of 10 points on the first quiz and 5 out of 10 on the second quiz, he may earn 5 points for his team, but no bonus points. If a student scores 10 points on both quizzes, she may earn a total of 12 points (10 points for the second quiz plus 2 bonus points for the perfect score) for her team.

Teams Games Tournament (TGT)—similar to STAD except that weekly tournaments replace weekly quizzes. Homogeneous, three-member teams are formed from the existing heterogeneous groups and compete against similar-ability groups to earn points for their regular, heterogeneous group. As with STAD, high-performing teams earn group rewards. For example, existing heterogeneous groups may contain one each low-, average-, and high-ability student. During weekly tournaments (e.g., a game of Jeopardy), low-ability students form groups of three, average-ability students form groups of three, and high-ability students form groups of three. Low-ability groups compete against each other, average-ability groups compete against each other, and high-ability groups compete against each other. The winning homogeneous groups earn points for their heterogeneous teams.

Team-Assisted Individualization (TAI)—combines cooperative learning with individualized instruction. Students are placed into groups but work at their own pace and level. Team members check each other's work and help one another with problems. Teams earn points based on the individual performance of each member in the group. Team members encourage and support one another because they want their teams to succeed (Slavin 1994). For example, students at different spelling levels may be placed into heterogeneous groups. The group may consist of one low speller, two average spellers, and one advanced speller. Students are responsible for learning their assigned spelling words, but they have their team members to assist and encourage them. Groups earn points based on their team members' performance on weekly spelling tests. Members take responsibility for each other's learning, as well as their own.

Jigsaw—a cooperative group learning method that assigns each of its members a particular learning task. For example, learning about the Civil War may include famous men and women, battles, economic factors, and issues of slavery. Each member chooses a topic and is responsible for teaching his or her team members "all that there is to know" about that topic. Team members meet with members of other groups to form "expert groups" to discuss and research their topic. For example, the team members of the cooperative groups who chose famous women would meet together in a separate cooperative group focused on learning only about famous women of the Civil War. Following research and discussion, the students return to their own teams and take turns teaching their teammates about their topic. Afterward, students take individual quizzes and earn a team score.

Group Investigation—similar to the Jigsaw method, except students do not form expert groups. Students work in small groups toward an overall class project. Each group is assigned a different task or activity. Within each group, members decide what information to gather and how to organize and present their findings.

Learning Together—incorporates heterogeneous student groups that work on a single assignment and receive rewards based on their group product. For example, student groups may be assigned to draw and label the human skeletal system. Each student would receive the same final grade for the group product.

Cooperative learning groups differ from traditional learning groups in that most support positive interdependence, individual accountability, group processing, peer responsibility, and heterogeneous membership (Bertucci, Johnson, Johnson, and Conte 2011; Gillies and Boyle 2008; Johnson and Johnson 1999a, 2009). General findings conclude that:

- Cooperative groups are appropriate for any instructional task.

- Cooperative groups do just as well or better on achievement than competitive and individualistic learning conditions.

- Cooperative conditions appear to work best when students are heterogeneously grouped, although high-ability students do just as well or better in homogeneous groups.

- Group discussion promotes higher achievement.

- Cooperative learning is more likely to have an effect on student outcomes when cooperation is well defined.

- Stereotypes are likely to be reduced when using cooperative groups.

- Using cooperative groups promotes equality among perceived ability and leadership roles among males and females.

- Cooperative learning can reduce anxiety and create more interesting learning.

- Cooperative groups can be more cost-effective than individualistic learning conditions.

- Cooperative learning appears to be effective at all primary and secondary grade levels and with groups of two to five.

- Cooperative conditions can benefit all ability levels.

- Cooperative groups support achievement-oriented behavior and healthy social development.

- Cooperative grouping can increase student self-esteem and foster higher-order thinking skills.

Although researchers report many positive outcomes using cooperative learning (Bertucci, Conte, Johnson, and Johnson 2010; Choi, Johnson, and Johnson 2011; Gillies 2008; Law 2008; Slavin 2013; Tarhan, Ayyildiz, Ogunc, and Sesen 2013), others note that there are pitfalls (Esmonde 2009; Hall and Buzwell 2013; Johnson and Johnson 1999a; Kao 2013; Mastin and Yoon 2013; Slavin 1994; Vermette 1998). Pitfalls include the "free-rider effect" or "social loafing" (members let the more capable members do all the work) and the "sucker effect" (more able members have the less able members do all the work). Individual accountability, peer evaluation, and grades based on the team's average individual scores can help avoid these pitfalls (Epstein 2007; Johnson and Johnson 1999a; Kao 2013; Lee and Lim 2012; Slavin 1994, 2011). Researchers suggest teacher monitoring, randomly calling on group members to summarize their group's progress, or requiring each student to write a concluding summary or a description of his or her group's activity, including a retelling of each individual's role and contribution (Hall and Buzwel 2013; Vermette 1998). Others recommend placing students in smaller groups so it is harder to hide or "free-ride," define individual expectations of group members, and assign roles that focus on the strengths of the students (Aggarwal and O'Brien 2008; Baloche 1998; Bertucci, Conte, Johnson, and Johnson 2010; Gillies and Boyle 2008; Marr 2000). Linnenbrink-Garcia, Rogat, and Koskey (2011) note the importance of affect and social-behavioral engagement in reducing the occurrence of social loafing or the free-rider effect. They suggest teaching students to work effectively with peers prior to placing students in groups, helping students develop strategies for alleviating disagreements and disrespectful interactions, and understanding the needs of others. In the case of chronic absenteeism, Baloche (1998) recommends:

- Group members phone or e-mail peers with what they have missed.

- Chronically absent students be placed in larger groups so that other group members are not as dependent on them.

- Group members have access to the other members' project information and material.

- Assessment is structured so group members are not penalized for work missed by the absent student.

- High expectations must be the norm for all students, with everyone viewed as a valuable member of the team.

Frequent assessments of a team's progress, including peer evaluations, can help teachers gauge the dynamics of the group. When evaluating team projects, Lee and Lim (2012) found that instructors tend to place greater emphasis on the outcome of the product, whereas students focus on social and managerial competencies (e.g., organizing or coordinating abilities to keep the project moving forward) that the instructor may not easily observe. The researchers stress the importance of peer evaluation, noting "peer evaluation can facilitate the authentic goal of team project-based learning" (p. 222). Expected participation and contributions need to be clarified, and instructors should tell students at the beginning of the project that peer evaluation will be included in the final grade.

Applying the Theory of Cooperative Learning to Digital Content Creation

Using cooperative groups in digital content creation has many benefits. These include peer teaching, increased use of metacognitive and elaboration strategies, the accommodation of individual differences, self-reflection, increased motivation and positive attitudes toward learning, and increased performance (Chen and McGrath 2003; De La Paz and Hernandez-Ramos 2013; Gillies and Boyle 2008; Ke 2013; Neo and Neo 2010). The teacher's role is to guide and facilitate the cooperative groups' efforts, as well as encourage group processing (Bertucci, Johnson, Johnson, and Conte 2012). Table 1.2 provides examples of students' roles and responsibilities in different cooperative group settings. Cooperative group methods that require individual accountability, peer evaluation, and grades assigned on the average of the team's individual scores are recommended (see Chapter 7).

Cooperative group digital content creation allows students to develop lifelong learning skills that are important to their future success, including respect, tolerance, and communication skills for working successfully in teams (Neo, Neo, Kwok, Tan, Lai, and Zarina 2012a). It supports small-group interactions, positive socialization, peer teaching and learning, and the development of original projects that reflect the groups' collaboration (Bertucci, Conte, Johnson, and Johnson 2010; De La Paz and Hernandez-Ramos 2013; Ke 2014). In addition, cooperative groups can reduce the complexity and time commitment of creating digital projects by assigning students to specific design roles and responsibilities. Each student contributes to the project as a whole and has the opportunity to share his or her expertise with, as well as learn from, others. Techniques for establishing, monitoring, and assessing group projects are included in Chapters 3 and 7.

Constructivism

Cognitive psychologists believe in the process of learning through the construction of knowledge. They assert that "people learn by actively constructing knowledge, weighing new information against their previous understanding, thinking about and working through discrepancies (on their own and with others), and coming to a new understanding" (Association for Supervision and Curriculum Development 1992, 2). These ideas, combined with social learning, are not new. Kilpatrick (1918) expressed the need to base education on purposeful acts and social activity, which he designed into his project method of instruction. Dewey (1929) stated that "social tools" (reading, spelling, and writing) are best acquired in a social context. Piaget believed that people try to make sense of the world and actively create their own knowledge through direct experience with objects, people, and ideas (Woolfolk 1987). Vygotsky (1978, 88) argued that "human learning presupposes a specific social nature and a process by which children grow into the intellectual life of those around them."

Professional organizations, such as the National Council for Teachers of Mathematics (NTCM), the American Association for the Advancement of Science (AAAS), and the National Council for the Social Studies (NCSS), continue to emphasize the need to engage students in constructivist thinking—decision making, problem solving, and critical thinking. Researchers

Table 1.2. Cooperative Group Settings and Responsibilities in Digital Content Creation

Cooperative Group Method	Digital Content Creation Examples and Evaluation	Student Roles and Responsibilities in Digital Content Creation
Student Teams Achievement Divisions (STAD)	Groups are provided with specific questions for research and content information on the Westward Movement. They display their knowledge through multimedia digital projects. Announced weekly quizzes check individual content learning. A rubric can be used to evaluate final projects for a group grade.	Students learn about the Westward Movement as a team, helping each other understand the content. Groups may alternate project responsibilities to ensure everyone has a chance to explore the content in different ways.
Teams Games Tournament (TGT)	Similar to STAD, except weekly tournaments replace weekly quizzes, and students complete against similar-ability groups to earn points for their heterogeneous group. Responsibilities remain the same.	
Team-Assisted Individu-alization (TAI)	Groups create digital projects on a select genre, such as mystery stories. Groups display information about several books. The project is evaluated based on each student's book report.	Each student is responsible for reading a select book (at the appropriate level) and reporting on it. The team project introduces and links each report.
Jigsaw	Groups create digital projects on the Civil War. Students are evaluated on their group's final product and their individual knowledge of all the content areas researched for the Civil War.	Each member is assigned a particular content area of the Civil War, such as famous men and women, battles, economic factors, issues of slavery, and so on. Members meet with other groups' members assigned to the same content area. For example, members researching famous battles meet together and help each other become an "expert" on the topic. Members return to their groups and share what they have learned. Students design their portion of the group's digital product. (This approach may also be used to learn about different skills, such as creating animation, videos, and so on.)
Group Investigation	Similar to the Jigsaw method except students do not form expert groups. Students work in small groups toward an overall class project. Each has a specific task or assignment.	
Learning Together	Groups decide on a project of interest (e.g., a project about volcanoes) and present their final project to the class. Each student receives the same final grade for the group product.	After deciding on the project, students determine each other's role and responsibilities based on their interests. Responsibilities and roles may change during the project. (Individual accountability may be weak.)

(Gagnon and Collay 2001; Marlowe and Page 2005; Shapiro 2003) define *constructivist teachers* as those who

- Encourage and accept student autonomy and initiative

- Use raw data and primary sources, along with manipulative, interactive, and physical materials

- Use cognitive terminology such as *classify, analyze, predict,* and *create*

- Allow student responses to drive lessons, shift instructional strategies, and alter content

- Inquire about students' understanding of concepts before sharing their own understandings of those concepts

- Encourage students to engage in conversations with the teacher and with one another

- Encourage student inquiry by asking thoughtful, open-ended questions and encouraging students to ask questions of each other

- Seek elaboration of students' initial responses

- Engage students in experiences that might create contradictions to their initial hypotheses and then encourage discussion

- Allow wait time after posing questions

- Provide time for students to construct relationships and create metaphors

- Nurture students' natural curiosity through frequent use of the learning cycle model (discovery, concept introduction, and concept application)

These teacher practices can help guide students in their understanding and intellectual and reflective growth. Creating multimedia digital content provides an ideal forum for a constructivist approach.

Applying the Theory of Constructivism to Digital Content Creation

Research has demonstrated that digital content creation can help students learn how to develop concepts and ideas, design plans, apply what they learn, refine questions, make predictions, collect and analyze research, communicate findings, and solve problems (Bertacchini, Bilotta, Pantano, and Tavernise 2012; Neo and Neo 2009; Neo, Neo, Kwok, Tan, Lai, and Zarina 2012b). Creating digital content can provide a concrete and meaningful context for developing higher-order thinking skills, engaging students in the learning process, and inviting them to use technology as a cognitive tool (Ke 2014; Neo and Neo 2009, 2010; Piliouras, Siakas, and Seroglou 2011).While creating digital content, students begin to see themselves as authors of knowledge, collaborators, and active participants in the learning process (Connors and Sullivan 2012; Neo and Neo 2009; Piliouras, Siakas, and Seroglou 2011).

According to Simons (1993), constructivist learning includes at least five components: active, cumulative, integrative, reflective, and goal directed. Their definitions and relationship to the construction of digital projects are presented in Table 1.3. Gagnon and Collay (2001) describe similar elements but include a sixth—grouping—noting that "small groups are necessary for

Table 1.3. Constructivist Components and Their Relationships to Digital Content Creation

Constructivist Learning Component	Definition	Relationship to Digital Content Creation
Active	Students process information meaningfully.	Digital projects allow students to be active learners by defining the content and creating the media components.
Cumulative	Learning builds on prior knowledge.	Digital projects allow students to connect current knowledge to new ideas through a variety of formats.
Integrative	Learners elaborate on new knowledge.	Digital projects offer environments in which students can create increasingly complex programs, as well as present current and new knowledge in new ways.
Reflective	Students assess what they know and need to learn.	Digital projects incorporate multiple levels of assessment at various phases throughout the design and development process.
Goal-directed	Learners engage in purposeful learning activities.	When assigning digital projects, the teacher and students work together to define specific learning outcomes.

students to move from personal meaning to shared meaning in the social construction of knowledge" (p. 36). Design teams allow students to work in small groups.

Herman, Aschbacher, and Winters (1992) also discuss the implications of aligning instruction and assessment with constructivist learning. Table 1.4 (p. 16) presents cognitive learning theories and their implications for instruction, assessment, and digital content creation.

Digital content creation can provide ideal learning environments for implementing a constructivist approach to learning. Digital content creation encourages divergent thinking, multiple modes of expression, goal setting, critical-thinking skills, teamwork, opportunities to revise and rethink, and more. Students are active participants, constructing knowledge that is meaningful, applicable, and memorable. In addition, creating digital content provides educators with multiple ways to assess students' progress. Assessment strategies are discussed in Chapter 7.

SUMMARY

Multimedia combines several media to present information. Digital multimedia uses technology to present multiple media formats that convey information in a linear or nonlinear format. Creating digital content reinforces students' technology skills and invites them to work cooperatively and use a variety of media to express their understanding. It is a process approach to learning, encouraging students to think differently about how they organize and present information. Digital content creation supports 21st-century learning skills and a Common Core Approach, focusing on creativity and innovation, critical thinking and problem solving, and communication

Table 1.4. Cognitive Learning Theories' Relationships to Digital Content Creation

Cognitive Learning Theory	Implications for Instruction/Assessment	Relationship to Digital Content Creation
Learning is a process of creating personal meaning from new information and prior knowledge.	Encourage discussion, divergent thinking, multiple links and solutions, varied modes of expression, critical-thinking skills; relate new information to personal experience; apply information to new situations.	Digital projects encourage knowledge construction and group efforts, stimulating discussion, and divergent thinking. Media elements provide various modes of expression.
Learning is not necessarily a linear progression of discrete skills.	Engage students in problem solving and critical thinking.	Developing flowcharts and storyboards requires problem-solving and critical-thinking skills to "chunk" and organize information into linear and nonlinear formats. Students see how data relate to each other.
There are a variety of learning styles, attention spans, developmental paces, and intelligences.	Provide choices in task, varied means of showing mastery and competence, time to think about and do assignments, opportunities for self-evaluation and peer review.	Design teams offer task options, allowing students to demonstrate their skills in many ways. The process of developing projects requires students to revise and rethink and provides students with hands-on, concrete learning experiences.
Students perform better when they know the goal, see models, and know how their performance compares to the standard.	Discuss goals and let students help define them (personal and class); provide and discuss examples of student work and allow them to have input into expectations; give students opportunities for self-evaluation and peer review.	Rubrics, goals, and expectations for projects can be decided as a whole class without sacrificing the teacher's basic objectives. Sample projects can help clarify project expectations. The process of developing projects encourages self-evaluation and peer review.
It is important to know when to use knowledge, how to adapt it, and how to manage one's own learning.	Provide real-world opportunities (or simulations) to apply or adapt new knowledge; provide opportunities for students to think about how they learn and why they like certain work.	Digital projects support real-world learning experiences, plus they have the potential to enhance students' communication and metacognitive skills.
Motivation, effort, and self-esteem affect learning and performance.	Motivate students with real-life tasks and connections to personal experiences; encourage students to see the relationship between effort and results.	Digital projects provide students with real-life tasks that they can connect to their personal interests and experiences. Digital projects serve as a visual outcome of students' efforts.
Learning has social components. Group work is valuable.	Provide group work; establish heterogeneous groups; enable students to take on a variety of roles; consider group products and group processes.	Digital projects encourage cooperative grouping techniques.

and collaboration. It supports self-reflection, authentic learning, and the use of technology as a cognitive tool. In addition, digital content creation offers an effective alternative for assessing student learning and provides students with a real-world learning environment.

Research demonstrates that multimedia development tools provide students with opportunities to show greater descriptive detail, unique perspectives, and diverse interests and skills. Opportunities to explore concepts and express understanding through multimedia may create positive turning points in the development of a student's intelligences. Students report a desire to learn, feel more confident, and consider themselves producers of knowledge rather than consumers when creating digital content. By working cooperatively and constructing knowledge, students become empowered learners and are better prepared to meet the needs of our global society.

REFERENCES

Aggarwal, P., and O'Brien, C. (2008). Social loafing on group projects: Structural antecedents and effect on student satisfaction. *Journal of Marketing Education*, 30(3), 255–264.

Armstrong, T. 2009. *Multiple intelligences in the classroom* (3rd ed.). Alexandria, VA: Association for Supervision and Curriculum Development.

Association for Supervision and Curriculum Development. 1992. Wanted: Deep understanding "constructivism" posits new conception of learning. *ASCD Update*, 34(3), 1–5.

Baehr, C., and Lang, S. M. 2012. Hypertext theory: Rethinking and reformulating what we know, Web 2.0. *Journal of Technical Writing and Communication*, 42(1), 39–56.

Baloche, L. A. 1998. *The cooperative classroom: Empowering learning*. Upper Saddle River, NJ: Prentice-Hall.

Bagui, S. 1998. Reasons for increased learning using multimedia. *Journal of Educational Multimedia and Hypermedia*, 7(1), 3–18.

Bakic-Miric, N. 2010. Multiple intelligences theory—a milestone innovation in English language teaching at the University of NIÅ Medical School. *Acta Medica Medianae*, 49(2), 15–19.

Bennett, D. T. 1996. Assessment through video. *Electronic Learning*, 15(4), 16–17.

Bertacchini, F., Bilotta, E., Pantano, P., and Tavernise, A. 2012. Motivating the learning of science topics in secondary school: A constructivist edutainment setting for studying chaos. *Computers & Education*, 59(4), 1377–1386.

Bertucci, A., Conte, S., Johnson, D., and Johnson, R. 2010. The impact of size of cooperative group on achievement, social support, and self-esteem. *Journal of General Psychology*, 137(3), 256–272.

Bertucci, A., Johnson, D., Johnson, R., and Conte, S. 2012. Influence of group processing on achievement and perception of social and academic support in elementary inexperienced cooperative learning groups. *Journal of Educational Research*, 105(5), 329–335.

Beier, M., Miller, L., and Wang, S. 2012. Science games and the development of scientific possible selves. *Cultural Studies of Science Education*, 7(4), 963–978.

Carnahan, C., Basham, J., and Musti-Rao, S. 2009. A low-technology strategy for increasing engagement of students with autism and significant learning needs. *Exceptionality*, 17(2), 76–87.

Chambers, B., Slavin, R., Madden, N., Abrami, P., Tucker, B., et al. 2008. Technology infusion in success for all: Reading outcomes for first graders. *Elementary School Journal*, 109(1), 2008–2015.

Chen, J., Moran, S., and Gardner, H. (Eds.). 2009. *Multiple intelligences around the world.* San Francisco: Jossey-Bass.

Chen, P., and McGrath, D. 2003. Moments of joy: Student engagement and conceptual learning in the design of hypermedia documents. *Journal of Research on Technology in Education*, 35(3), 402–422.

Choi, J., Johnson, D., and Johnson, R. 2011. Relationships among cooperative learning experiences, social interdependence, children's aggression, victimization, and prosocial behaviors. *Journal of Applied Social Psychology*, 41(4), 976–1003.

Ciampa, K. 2012. Improving grade one students' reading motivation with online electronic storybooks. *Journal of Educational Multimedia and Hypermedia*, 21(1), 5–28.

Common Core State Standards Initiative. 2012a. [online]. Available at: http://www.corestandards.org/. Retrieved on August 2, 2014.

Common Core State Standards Initiative. 2012b. Frequently asked questions [online]. Available at: http://www.corestandards.org/about-the-standards/frequently-asked-questions/. Retrieved on August 2, 2014.

Connors, S., and Sullivan, R. 2012. "It's that easy": Designing assignments that blend old and new literacies. *Clearing House*, 85(6), 221–225.

Cox, E. 2009. The collaborative mind: Tools for 21st-century learning. *MultiMedia & Internet@Schools*, 16(5), 10–14.

De La Paz, S., and Hernandez-Ramos, P. 2013. Technology-enhanced project-based learning: Effects on historical thinking. *Journal of Special Education Technology*, 28(4), 1–14.

Dewey, J. 1929. *The sources of a science of education.* New York: Horace Liveright.

Dikshit, J., Garg, S., and Panda, S. 2013. Pedagogic effectiveness of print, interactive multimedia, and online resources: A case study of IGNOU. *International Journal of Instruction*, 6(2), 193–210.

Dorfman, S.., and Rosenberg, R. 2013. Building a community that includes all learners. *Social Studies and the Young Learner*, 25(3), 5–8.

Douglas, O., Burton, K., and Reese-Durham, N. 2008. The effects of the multiple intelligence teaching strategy on the academic achievement of eighth grade math students. *Journal of Instructional Psychology*, 35(2), 182–187.

Eksi, G. 2009. Multiple short story activities for very young learners with multiple tastes. *Ekev Academic Review*, 13(40), 51–68.

Epstein, E. 2007. Blending individual and group assessment: A model for measuring student performance using mathematics as an example. *Dissertation Abstracts International Section A: Humanities and Social Sciences*, 68(4), 1373.

Esmonde, I. 2009. Ideas and identities: Supporting equity in cooperative mathematics learning. *Review of Educational Research*, 79, 1008–1043.

Fabio, R., and Antonietti, A. 2012. Effects of hypermedia instruction on declarative, conditional and procedural knowledge in ADHD students. *Research in Developmental Disabilities: A Multidisciplinary Journal*, 33(6), 2028–2039.

Gagnon, G. W., and Collay, M. 2001. *Designing for learning: Six elements in constructivist classrooms.* Thousand Oaks, CA: Corwin Press.

Gardner, Hillary. 2011a. Promoting learner engagement using multiple intelligences and choice-based instruction. *Adult Basic Education & Literacy Journal*, 5(2), 97–101.

Gardner, Howard. 1983. *Frames of mind: The theory of multiple intelligences.* New York: Basic Books.

Gardner, Howard. 1999. *Intelligence reframed: Multiple intelligences for the 21st century.* New York: Basic Books.

Gardner, Howard. 2006. *Multiple intelligences: New Horizons.* New York: Basic Books.

Gardner, Howard. 2011b. *Frames of mind: The theory of multiple intelligences* (3rd ed.). New York: Basic Books.

Gillies, R. 2008. The effects of cooperative learning on junior high school students' behaviours, discourse and learning during a science-based learning activity. *School Psychology International,* 29, 328–347.

Gillies, R., and Boyle, M. 2008. Teachers' discourse during cooperative learning and their perceptions of this pedagogical practice. *Teaching and Teacher Education: An International Journal of Research and Studies,* 24(5), 1333–1348.

Gray, J. H., and Viens, J. T. 1994. The theory of multiple intelligences: Understanding cognitive diversity in school. *National Forum: Phi Kappa Phi Journal,* 74(1), 22–25.

Hall, D., and Buzwell, S. 2013. The problem of free-riding in group projects: Looking beyond social loafing as reason for non-contribution. *Active Learning in Higher Education,* 14(1), 37–49.

Harris, R. 2010. Design on the go: How African American youth use mobile technologies for digital content creation. *Design and Technology Education,* 15(2), 9–17.

Herman, J. L., Aschbacher, P. R., and Winters, L. 1992. *A practical guide to alternative assessment.* Alexandria, VA: Association for Supervision and Curriculum Development.

Hersh, R. 2009. A well-rounded education for a flat world. *Educational Leadership,* 67(1), 51–53.

International Society for Technology in Educational. 2007. National educational technology standards for students [online]. Available at: https://www.iste.org/standards/standards-for-students. Retrieved on August 2, 2014.

International Society for Technology in Education. 2009. *Essential conditions: Necessary conditions to effectively leverage technology for learning* [online]. Available at: http://www.iste.org/docs/pdfs/netsessentialconditions.pdf?sfvrsn=2. Retrieved on August 2, 2014.

International Society for Technology in Education, Partnership for 21st Century Skills, and State Educational Technology Directors Association. 2007. *Maximizing the impact: The pivotal role of technology in a 21st century education system* [online]. Available at: http://www.p21.org/storage/documents/p21setdaistepaper.pdf . Retrieved on August 2, 2014.

Johnson, A., Ozogul, G., DiDonato, M., and Reisslein, M. 2013. Engineering perceptions of female and male K–12 students: Effects of a multimedia overview on elementary, middle-, and high-school students. *European Journal of Engineering Education,* 38(5), 519–531.

Johnson, D. W., and Johnson, R. T. 1999a. *Learning together and alone: Cooperative, competitive, and individualistic learning* (5th ed.). Needham Heights, MA: Allyn & Bacon.

Johnson, D. W., and Johnson R. T. 1999b. Making cooperative learning work. *Theory into Practice,* 38(2), 67–73.

Johnson, D., and Johnson, R. 2009. An educational psychology success story: Social interdependence theory and cooperative learning. *Educational Researcher,* 38, 365–379.

Jonassen, D. (Ed.). 2008. *Meaningful learning with technology.* Upper Saddle River, NJ: Pearson/Merrill Prentice Hall.

Jones, L. 2009. Supporting student differences in listening comprehension and vocabulary learning with multimedia annotations. *CALICO Journal*, 26(2), 267–289.

Kao, G. 2013. Enhancing the quality of peer review by reducing student "free riding": Peer assessment with positive interdependence. *British Journal of Educational Technology*, 44(1), 112–124.

Kay, R., and Knaack, L. 2009. Analysing the effectiveness of learning objects for secondary school science classrooms. *Journal of Educational Multimedia and Hypermedia*, 18(1), 113–135.

Ke, F. 2014. An implementation of designed-based learning through creating educational computer games: A case study on mathematics learning during design and computing. *Computers & Education*, 73, 26–39.

Kilpatrick, W. H. 1918. The project method: The use of the purposeful act in the educative process. *Teachers College Bulletin.* New York: Columbia University.

Kingsley, K., & Boone, R. 2008. Effects of multimedia software on achievement of middle school students in an American history class. *Journal of Research on Technology in Education*, 41(2), 203–221.

Korat, O. 2010. Reading electronic books as a support for vocabulary, story comprehension and word reading in kindergarten and first grade. *Computers & Education*, 55(1), 24–31.

Kosky, C., and Curtis, R. 2008. An action research exploration integrating student choice and arts activities in a sixth grade social studies classroom. *Journal of Social Studies Research*, 32(1), 22–27.

Kunkel, C. 2009. Schooling built on the multiple intelligences. *School Administrator*, 66(2), 24–25.

Lachs, V. 1998. Making the computer dance to your tune: Primary school pupils authoring hypermedia. *Journal of Computing in Childhood Education*, 9, 57–77.

Law, Y. 2008. Effects of cooperative learning on second graders' learning from text. *Educational Psychology*, 28(5), 567–582.

Lee, H., and Lim, C. 2012. Peer evaluation in blended team project-based learning: What do students find important? *Educational Technology & Society*, 15(4), 214–224.

Levin, H. M. 1994. Commentary: Multiple intelligence theory and everyday practices. *Teachers College Record*, 95(4), 570–575.

Linnenbrink-Garcia, L., Rogat, T., and Koskey, K. 2011. Affect and engagement during small group instruction. *Contemporary Educational Psychology*, 36(1), 13–24.

Liu, Y. 2013. A comparative study of integrating multimedia into the third grade math curriculum to improve math learning. *Journal of Computers in Mathematics and Science Teaching*, 32(3), 321–336.

Magana, A. 2014. Learning strategies and multimedia techniques for scaffolding size and scale cognition. *Computers & Education*, 72, 367–377.

Marlowe, B. A., and Page, M. L. 2005. *Creating and sustaining the constructivist classroom* (2nd ed.). Thousand Oaks, CA: Corwin Press.

Marr, P. M. 2000. Grouping students at the computer to enhance the study of British literature. *English Journal*, 90, 120–125.

Mastin, T., and Yoon, K. 2013. Benefits of group knowledge sharing for student teams. *College Teaching*, 61(4), 153–154.

Neo, M., and Neo, T. 2009. Engaging students in multimedia-mediated constructivist learning—students' perceptions. *Journal of Educational Technology & Society*, 12(2), 254–266.

Neo, M., and Neo, T. 2010. Students' perceptions in developing a multimedia project within a constructivist learning environment: A Malaysian experience. *Turkish Online Journal of Educational Technology—TOJET*, 9(1), 176–184.

Neo, M., Neo, K., and Tan, H. 2012. Applying authentic learning strategies in a multimedia and web learning environment (MWLE): Malaysian students' perspective. *Turkish Online Journal of Educational Technology—TOJET*, 11(3), 50–60.

Neo, T., Neo, M., Kwok, W., Tan, Y, Lai, C., and Zarina. 2012a. Mice 2.0: Designing multimedia content to foster active learning in a Malaysian classroom. *Australasian Journal of Educational Technology*, 28(5), 857–880.

Neo, T., Neo, M., Kwok, W., Tan, Y, Lai, C., and Zarina. 2012b. Promoting life-long learning in a multimedia-based learning environment: A Malaysian experience. *Journal of Educational Multimedia and Hypermedia*, 21(2), 143–164.

O'Hara, S., and Pritchard, R. 2008. Hypermedia authoring as a vehicle for vocabulary development in middle school English as a second language classrooms. *The Clearing House*, 82(2), 60–65.

Papastergiou, M. 2009. Digital game-based learning in high school computer science education: Impact on educational effectiveness and student motivation. *Computers & Education*, 52(1), 1–12.

Partnership for 21st Century Skills. 2011. P21 Common Core toolkit: A guide to aligning the Common Core State Standards with the Framework for 21st Century Skills [online]. Available at: http://www.p21.org/storage/documents/P21CommonCoreToolkit.pdf. Retrieved on August 2, 2014.

Partnership for 21st Century Skills. 2014. Our mission [online]. Available at: http://www.p21.org/about-us/our-mission. Retrieved on August 2, 2014.

Perez, L., and Beltran, J. 2008. A Spanish intervention programme for students with special education needs: Effects on intellectual capacity and academic achievement. European Journal of Special Needs Education, 23(2), 147–156.

Piliouras, P., Siakas, S., and Seroglou, F. 2011. Pupils produce their own narratives inspired by the history of science: Animation movies concerning the geocentric-heliocentric debate. Science & Education, 20(7), 761–795.

Poobrasert, O., and Cercone, N. 2009. Evaluation of educational multimedia support system for students with deafness. *Journal of Educational Multimedia and Hypermedia*, 18(1), 71–90.

Pope, C., Beal, C., Long, S., and McCammon, L. 2011. They teach us how to teach them: Teacher preparation for the 21st century. *Contemporary Issues in Technology and Teacher Education*, 11(4). Available at: http://www.citejournal.org/vol11/iss4/languagearts/article1.cfm. Retrieved on August 2, 2014.

Rouet, J., Levon, J. J., Dillion, A., and Spiro, R. J. 1996. An introduction to hypertext and cognition. In J. Rouet, J. J. Levon, A. Dillion, and R. J. Spiro (Eds.), *Hypertext and cognition* (pp. 3–8). Mahwah, NJ: Lawrence Erlbaum Associates.

Salmeron, L., and Garcia, V. 2012. Children's reading of printed text and hypertext with navigation overviews: The role of comprehension, sustained attention, and visuo-spatial abilities. *Journal of Educational Computing Research*, 47(1), 33–50.

Samples, B. 1992. Using learning modalities to celebrate intelligence. *Educational Leadership*, 50(2), 62–66.

Shamir, A., and Shlafer, I. 2011. E-books effectiveness in promoting phonological awareness and concept about print: A comparison between children at risk for learning disabilities and typically developing kindergarteners. *Computers & Education*, 57(3), 1989–1997.

Shapiro, A. 2003. The latest dope on research (about constructivism): Part II: On instruction and leadership. *International Journal of Educational Reform*, 12(1), 62–77.

Simons, P. R. J. 1993. Constructive learning: The role of the learner. In T. Duffy, J. Lowyck, and D. Jonassen (Eds.), *Designing environments for constructive learning* (pp. 291–313). Heidelberg, Germany: Springer-Verlag.

Slavin, R. E. 1994. *Cooperative learning: Theory, research, and practice* (2nd ed.). Needham Heights, MA: Allyn & Bacon.

Slavin, R. E. 1999. Comprehensive approaches to cooperative learning. *Theory into Practice*, 38(2), 74–79.

Slavin, R. E. 2011. *Educational psychology theory and practice* (10th ed.). Boston: Pearson Education.

Slavin, R. 2013. Effective programmes in reading and mathematics: Lessons from the best evidence encyclopaedia. *School Effectiveness & School Improvement*, 24(4), 383–391.

Spence, L. 2009. Developing multiple literacies in a website project. *Reading Teacher*, 62(7), 592–597.

Stelzer, T., Gladding, G., Mestre, J., and Brookes, D. 2009. Comparing the efficacy of multimedia modules with traditional textbooks for learning introductory physics content. *American Journal of Physics*, 77(2), 184–190.

Sternberg, R. J. 1994. Diversifying instruction and assessment. *Educational Forum*, 59(1), 47–52.

Su, K. 2008. An informative study of integrating multimedia technology into problem-solving for promoting students' abilities in general chemistry. *International Journal of Instructional Media*, 35(3), 339–353.

Tarhan, L., Ayyildiz, Y., Ogunc, A., and Sesen, B. 2013. A jigsaw cooperative learning application in elementary science and technology lessons: Physical and chemical changes. *Research in Science & Technological Education*, 31(2), 184–203.

Tuzun, H., Yilmaz-Soylu, M., Karakus, T., Inal, Y., and Kizilkaya, G. 2009. The effects of computer games on primary school students' achievement and motivation in geography learning. *Computers & Education*, 52(1), 68–77.

United Nations for Educational, Scientific and Cultural Organization. 2008. *ICT competency standards for teachers: Policy framework* [online]. Available at: http://unesdoc.unesco.org/images/0015/001562/156210E.pdf. Retrieved on August 2, 2014.

Urban-Woldron, H. 2009. Interactive simulations for the effective learning of physics. *Journal of Computers in Mathematics and Science Teaching*, 28(2), 163–176.

Vandendorpe, C. 2009. From *papyrus to hypertext: Toward the universal digital library*. Chicago: University of Illinois Press.

Vermette, P. J. 1998. *Making cooperative learning work: Student teams in K–12 classrooms*. Upper Saddle River, NJ: Prentice-Hall.

Vermonden, C., and Alcock, P. 2013. Using multiple intelligences to promote nature education. *Green Teacher*, 12–15.

Vygotsky, L. S. 1978. *Mind in society: The development of higher psychological processes*. Cambridge, MA: Harvard University Press.

Wieman, C., Perkins, K., and Adams, W. 2008. Oersted Medal Lecture 2007. Interactive simulations for teaching physics: What works, what doesn't, and why. *American Journal of Physics*, 76(4/5), 393–399.

Wilson, A. 2008. Moving beyond the page in content area literacy: Comprehension instruction for multi-modal texts in science. *Reading Teacher*, 62(2), 153–156.

Wolfe, P. 2010. *Brain matters: Translating research into classroom practice* (2nd ed.). Alexandria, VA: Association for Supervision and Curriculum Development.

Woolfolk, A. E. 1987. *Educational psychology* (3rd ed.). Englewood Cliffs, NJ: Prentice-Hall.

Ziden, A., and Rahman, M. 2013. The effectiveness of web-based multimedia applications simulation in teaching and learning. *International Journal of Instruction*, 6(2), 211–222.

A Model for the Design and Development of Digital Content Creation

A SCENARIO

After teaching fourth grade for 15 years, Martha was a bit skeptical when the district provided 30 iPads for student use in the classroom. Although the tablet computers looked robust enough in their sturdy cases, she wondered if the students would perceive them as learning tools.

She soon discovered that she had nothing to worry about—the students were obviously digital natives, having grown up in a world of WiFi, smartphones, and virtual reality. To them, technology encompassed shopping, gaming, learning, and living. It was second nature for the students to use word processors to write stories, spreadsheets to chart data, and web browsers to conduct research.

As Presidents' Day approached, Martha decided to implement an iBook project, wherein the students could research and share information about famous presidents. First, Martha downloaded a few examples of student-created iBooks that incorporated text, audio, animation, and video. As they reviewed the examples together, Martha pointed out the various design options, such as the background color, text position, navigation buttons, etc. Since the goal was to compile all of the individual "chapters" into a book that would be available on iTunes, the class worked together to formulate a style guide that would ensure that all of the chapters had a similar format.

Martha divided the students into groups of three and each group selected a U.S. president. The teacher also provided a checklist to each group that outlined the topics to be addressed for each president. Each chapter would begin with a short narration from the group about why they selected their specific president. Then, the remaining pages would include the information related to the following:

- Birthplace and youth activities
- Education/experience prior to being elected president
- Election process (opponents, platform, etc.)
- Important issues/accomplishments/criticisms while in office
- Family life (First Lady, children, etc.)

The students began the planning phase by filling in a KWL (What we Know; What we Want to find out; and What we Learned) chart. As the students conducted their research, they looked for original documents, images, and video of events that occurred during the president's tenure. As they collected their resources into their network folders, the groups used their planning sheets to outline the content (text, images, etc.) for each page in their chapter.

When all of the resources (including the audio narration) were ready, and their planning sheets were approved, each group used Book Creator to produce their chapter. As the students worked with their projects, Martha facilitated the activities by answering questions and providing guidance.

After all of the groups had completed their chapter, Martha combined the individual chapters in Book Creator and saved the book into iTunes. Because the students knew the book would be published on iTunes for their parents and others, they had been very motivated to do their best. As Martha reflected on the project, she was totally amazed at the students' level of engagement and commitment.

OVERVIEW

Every teacher understands that good instruction involves careful planning. Whether or not a teacher creates a detailed lesson plan to guide her instruction, she understands the importance of ensuring all students have equal access to the academic standards. In addition, experienced teachers always have a backup plan (or two) in case the lesson does not progress as expected.

Careful planning is especially critical when integrating digital projects into the classroom. Planning saves time, reduces frustration, eliminates fragmented learning experiences, and results in increased student achievement. Following a systematic plan is recommended for teachers who are using technology for instruction as well as for students who are creating digital content. This chapter outlines a model for projects and activities involving digital content. It is based on three Ds and an E: DECIDE, DESIGN, DEVELOP, and EVALUATE. The topics of this chapter include the following:

Overview of the DDD-E model

- DECIDE phase: Planning activities for teachers and students

- DESIGN phase: Outlining the project structure and implementation

- DEVELOP phase: Gathering and creating the media elements

- EVALUATE phase: Reflecting on the project and student achievement

OVERVIEW OF THE DDD-E MODEL

Implementing digital content in a classroom environment is a rewarding yet challenging undertaking. A multitude of issues will surface, such as the following: Which standards can be addressed? Should students work individually or in a group? Which digital components are appropriate? Should the activity result in a presentation, a digital movie, a web page, or another venue? Which software programs or apps are appropriate for the objectives? How many minutes/hours/days should the students work on the project? How should it be evaluated? The questions (and possible answers) are endless.

One way to address the numerous issues involved in designing and developing digital content in the classroom is to follow a process that outlines the analysis, design, development, and evaluation. The model we propose consists of DECIDE, DESIGN, DEVELOP, and EVALUATE (DDD-E). This model is intended to serve as a general outline for digital activities and projects, but it can be modified or expanded to meet specific needs. It provides a framework for the instructional phases of digital projects, but is also appropriate for constructivist approaches to instruction.

Creating digital content can be similar to cooking a gourmet meal. First, you must DECIDE exactly which dishes you plan to serve (which will be influenced by who is coming to dinner and which groceries you have in the cupboard). If more than one person is cooking the meal, you also must decide who is going to be responsible for preparing each dish.

Next, the DESIGN of the meal includes locating the recipes and organizing the ingredients. Recipes, like concept maps, flowcharts, and storyboards, provide the structure for the dishes, detailing the required amounts of each ingredient and the sequence of cooking events.

Next, you DEVELOP the meal by gathering all of the components, mixing everything in the correct sequence, and combining the ingredients. As each individual dish is prepared, the overall meal must be considered. For example, appetizers are usually prepared first and served before the main course.

You EVALUATE throughout the process of making the meal (e.g., licking the spoon and making sure a dish is not burning). Dinner guests provide the final assessment by providing feedback after the meal has been served.

The DDD-E model consists of three main phases (DECIDE, DESIGN, DEVELOP), surrounded by EVALUATE (see Figure 2.1, p. 28). This chapter provides a general outline of the model. Subsequent chapters provide in-depth treatments of each phase, with recommendations for classroom implementation and modification.

Each phase in the DDD-E model involves activities for both the teacher and the students. For teachers, the DECIDE phase focuses on determining the goals and objectives; the DESIGN phase specifies the program structure; the DEVELOP phase includes managing the production; and the EVALUATE phase facilitates ongoing assessments. During the DECIDE phase, students are involved in brainstorming and conducting research; during DESIGN, they outline the content via concept maps, storyboards, scripts, etc.; the DEVELOP phase focuses on producing and integrating the media elements; and the EVALUATE phase includes using rubrics and other assessment techniques. Table 2.1 (see p. 29) outlines teacher activities and student activities for each phase in the DDD-E model. These activities will be introduced in this chapter. Detailed descriptions are provided in Chapters 3–7.

DECIDE

The first phase in a technology-based activity is DECIDE. This phase sets the stage for the entire project. The DECIDE phase is influenced by many variables, including the content area, location and number of digital devices, available software, and students' experiences and expertise. The DECIDE phase includes the following activities for teachers and students:

Teachers

- Identify standards and set instructional objectives.

- Decide on a project and outline appropriate student outcomes.

- Assess prerequisite skills and knowledge.

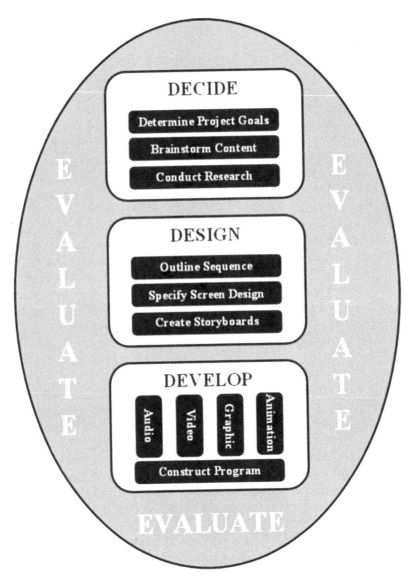

Figure 2.1. The DDD-E model.

- Determine assessment techniques.
- Create cooperative groups.
- Ensure necessary hardware and software.

Students

- Brainstorm and map content.
- Track required tasks.
- Conduct research.

Table 2.1. Teacher and Student Activities in the DDD-E Mode

Phase	Activities: Teacher	Activities: Student

DECIDE	PLANNING
	    Identify standards and instructional goals
	    Decide on project and outline outcomes
	    Assess prerequisite skills and knowledge
	    Determine assessment techniques
	ORGANIZING
	    Create cooperative groups
	    Ensure necessary hardware and software
		Brainstorm and map content
		Track required tasks
		Conduct research

DESIGN	Present design guidelines and templates Conduct formative assessment	Outline sequence/flowcharts Specify design, layout, scripts, etc.
DEVELOP	Manage media production Facilitate multimedia activities Conduct formative assessment	Create graphics Generate animations Produce audio Produce video Integrate digital elements
EVALUATE	Provide student assessment Reflect on activity and revise for future	Debug project Evaluate peers Conduct self-evaluations

Identify Standards and Set Instructional Goals and Objectives (Teacher)

The first step in the DECIDE phase is to identify the standards and goals that will be addressed with the activity or project. The Common Core State Standards focus on content areas, but also emphasize media, information, and technology literacy across subject areas. Technology can be used as a tool in the classroom to address a multitude of standards and 21st-century skills.

Decide on a Project and Outline Outcomes (Teacher)

Before embarking on an activity with digital content, educators need to consider whether it is the most effective way to achieve the desired learning outcomes; alternative approaches might be more effective or efficient.

When assigning a digital project, consider the following:

1. It should be relevant to the student. Projects are more meaningful if the students can see how the areas of study affect them. In other words, an activity about pollution can be introduced by focusing on how pollution has affected the beaches or air quality in the local area.

2. It should be relevant to the curriculum. Technology should be used as a tool, not as an end in itself. Therefore, each digital project should be closely aligned to instructional objectives. Keep in mind that digital projects are an excellent means to integrate content areas. For example, a project such as publishing an online magazine could involve social studies (researching current topics relevant to the community),

mathematics (managing the budget), and language arts (writing and editing the articles).

3. There should be sufficient resources. Some topics do not lend themselves to digital projects simply because there are not enough resources. For example, it may not be appropriate to ask students to create a digital project about authors and assign Mark Twain to one group and Catherine Gregory to another. Likewise, it can be frustrating to implement a project without sufficient hardware and software. Before starting a project, review the resources that will be available, such as cameras, scanners, probes, the Internet, tablets, and computers.

4. Allow sufficient time. Carefully evaluate the amount of time that can be devoted to project development. Short-term projects with well-defined scope could be completed in three to four hours or less. Long-term projects, involving research, synthesis of information, and complex production, could take several weeks to complete.

5. Encourage creativity. It is important to provide structure and guidelines for students' projects; however, be sure to allow sufficient opportunities for students to show their creativity and originality.

Assess Prerequisite Skills and Knowledge (Teacher)

It is crucial that students have the necessary prerequisite skills for using the software and digital devices. Teachers should ensure that students are familiar with basic technology skills (saving and copying files, navigating through folders and directories, etc.) and the skills necessary for creating the assigned project.

Determine Assessment Techniques (Teacher)

When the project begins, it is important to inform the students about the goals and assessment methods. Students should be aware whether products from the DESIGN phase, such as storyboards or content outlines, will be required, as well as which evaluation instruments and methods will be used. Be sure to state how much of the project grade will be based on knowledge, creativity, collaboration, technical aspects, etc.

Rubrics are common measurement tools for digital projects because they provide guidelines for assessment, while allowing room for creativity and subjectivity. In many cases, the teacher and students can work together to outline the requirements and establish the rubrics. Sample rubrics for digital projects are included in Chapter 7.

Create Cooperative Groups (Teacher)

Digital projects can be completed by groups of two or more students. It is important to establish the size and membership of the groups early in the process because the group members will need to work together to brainstorm and research their approach.

There are many alternatives for assigning students to a group, including student learning styles, multiple intelligences, student interests, random assignment, and areas of expertise. Chapter 3 provides detailed information on alternatives in group size, group composition, and group structure.

Teamwork and collaboration are important elements and outcomes of digital projects. Within each group, the members may take on a variety of roles, depending on the type of project. See example roles and projects listed in Table 2.2.

Table 2.2. Potential Team Members

Historical Movie	Public Service Announcement	Online Magazine	Instructional Program
Director	Researcher	Manager	Project manager
Costume designer	Communications manager	Editor	Instructional designer
Script writer	Production	Layout designer	Graphic artist
Production specialist	Editor	Marketing director	Production specialist
Video editor	Distribution	Production specialist	Program author

The team roles need not be independent of each other. In other words, one student may serve as both the costume designer and the script writer. Likewise, all students can take on all roles and work together for the final product. Chapter 3 provides more information about how to assign student roles.

Ensure Necessary Hardware and Software (Teacher)

It is not necessary to have a room full of equipment to implement digital technologies; however, one of the first steps is to take an inventory of the hardware and software options that are available at your school or district. Once you know what is available, you can begin to schedule access to digital devices and software (see Chapter 3).

A promising trend is the increased access to laptop and tablet computers, as well as other wireless devices in schools. As technology becomes more ubiquitous, digital projects can be developed with less and less concern about equitable access for all students (see Chapter 3). However, you cannot assume that all students have access to technology at home.

Brainstorm Content (Students)

After establishing the design teams, allow students time to explore the project by brainstorming with their group members. There are two aspects of the project that students can explore—content and approach. For example, if a group is creating a program about Florida history, the students may begin by generating ideas about topics. The project might include explorers, soldiers, transportation, or hurricanes, among other things. (Note: Brainstorming is effective only if the students are somewhat familiar with the content.)

After they have exhausted the ideas for content, they can explore possible media and approaches. Given the Florida history project, they might suggest making a video about a reenactment of an historical battle, collecting pictures of the explorers, or generating maps showing settlement patterns. Be sure to allow plenty of time for the students to explore the content and approaches thoroughly. See Chapter 3 for effective techniques for managing student brainstorming activities.

Concept mapping with programs such as Inspiration and Kidspiration can be very effective tools for brainstorming and organizing content. A concept map allows students to link concepts and ideas together with words, symbols, or pictures that explain the relationships.

Track Required Tasks (Students)

A project plan or checklist of tasks is very beneficial for projects—especially those that are long term (take place over several days or weeks). A task list helps students budget their time and sequence their actions. With access to intranets and the Internet in schools, students can track their progress in a central location, using software such as Google Docs, Moodle, Edmodo, Project Foundry, etc. It may be necessary to help students get started and to provide a checklist of required components for the project. For example, if the project is focusing on a country, you may require students to include information about the imports, exports, history, geography, politics, culture, and so on.

Conduct Research (Students)

Every project should include ample time for the students to research the content. For this step, students should have access to as many resources as possible, including the Internet, books, and journals. In addition to collecting the research, students should be encouraged to synthesize it and present it in a novel, concise manner. When groups are researching together, they can use online tools such as wikis or programs such as Evernote to store information in a manner that can be shared by all team members. See Chapter 3 for information about managing research activities.

DESIGN

The DECIDE phase outlines the goals and content of the project. In the DESIGN phase, the project often takes form through outlines, flowcharts, scripts, and storyboards. After teachers present design guidelines, demonstrate sequencing and flowchart techniques, and provide storyboard and scripting templates, students organize the sequence and specify the exact text, graphics, audio, and interactions of the project. It is crucial to emphasize the importance of the DESIGN phase to students. If they do not dedicate sufficient time and energy to this phase, they may end up wasting valuable time during the DEVELOP (production or build) phase.

Teachers

- Present design guidelines and templates.
- Conduct formative assessment.

Students

- Outline sequence/flowcharts.
- Specify design, layout, scripts, etc.

Present Design Guidelines and Templates (Teacher)

Digital projects can be simplistic or complex, depending on the age of the students, the length of the project, and the instructional goals. For example, second-grade students might write stories with a word processor or research a national monument and create a photo story; fifth graders could use probes to study ecology or create a podcast or eBook about recycling; eighth graders could build a city in SimCity or create movies that teach fractions and decimals. The opportunities to integrate technology in meaningful ways are limitless.

To help students understand the parameters of the project, it is often beneficial to show the students examples and nonexamples of finished projects. In this manner, teachers can introduce students to design guidelines for text, audio, color, transitions, and other elements. Soon, the students will be critiquing each other and providing insight into effective presentations and projects.

Templates are especially useful tools if several student projects are going to be integrated into one final project. For example, if six different groups of students each create a "chapter" for a digital book, they can easily be compiled into an online book if they all follow broad guidelines, such as the size of the text, placement of images, etc. Information about guidelines and templates is provided in Chapter 4.

Conduct Formative Assessment (Teacher)

As students begin to design their projects, through the use of content outlines, planning sheets, flowcharts, storyboards, and so on, it is important to provide feedback on their progress. At this point, teachers can help students determine whether they are staying within the project scope, addressing the project goals, and working well with their team members. Chapter 7 focuses on assessment techniques.

Outline Sequence/Flowcharts (Students)

After the brainstorming and research steps of the DECIDE phase, the students should synthesize, organize, and outline the content for the project. Many factors influence the content outline, including the intended audience and the time allotted to the project. These and other factors will be covered in detail in Chapter 4.

The flowcharting process illustrates a program's sequence and structure. It is important that students visualize how the various parts of a project fit together. Students should be encouraged to experiment with different ways of presenting content. To help them determine the best options, ask questions such as "Does one idea logically follow another throughout the program?" "Is there a central point from which all of the other ideas should be linked?" "Can you start with three or four choices and then subdivide the selections?" Be sure to demonstrate different projects with various structures to illustrate the alternatives. Additional information about flowcharts and sequencing project structure is provided in Chapter 4.

Specify the Design, Scripts, Layout, Etc. (Students)

Planning sheets, scripts, and storyboards for a project are essential tools to help students structure and design their project before starting the production aspects. Different projects will require different types of planning and design. For example, scripts are essential for podcasts; planning sheets (or notecards) work well for presentations; and storyboards are appropriate for interactive instruction. Sample templates for projects are provided in Chapters 4, 8, 9, 10, 11, and 12.

DEVELOP

After the scripts, storyboards, and other design components are complete, the development process can begin. Depending on the complexity of the project, the DEVELOP phase may involve producing audio elements, video segments, graphics, and/or text. Different members of the project team can develop these components simultaneously, or they can be developed in sequence by all of the members working together. The DEVELOP phase also includes the integration of all of the media elements of the program.

As the class approaches the DEVELOP phase, teachers should ensure that they have the knowledge and skills necessary to work with the development tools (such as graphics programs and video editors). They should also emphasize the restrictions or constraints that may apply. For example, if the projects are being created for web delivery, the file size will be an important factor. Activities in the DEVELOP phase include the following:

Teachers

- Manage media production.
- Facilitate multimedia activities.
- Conduct formative assessment.

Students

- Create graphics.
- Generate animations.
- Produce audio.
- Produce video.
- Integrate digital elements.

Manage Media Production (Teacher)

The configuration and management of a multimedia activity will vary, based on the number of available devices, the grouping strategy, and other factors. Chapter 5 addresses various configurations for computer access and outlines the Jigsaw cooperative learning approach, wherein students assume various roles and interact with peer groups.

Facilitate Multimedia Activities (Teacher)

As the students engage in the technology-based activity, the teacher's role becomes that of a facilitator. This includes the following activities:

- Ensuring that all of the necessary equipment (batteries, software, etc.) is available
- Reviewing necessary prerequisite skills related to the technology or concepts related to the content
- Circulating the room, assisting students
- Monitoring the progress of each group or student
- Ensuring that students stay on task
- Troubleshooting hardware and software issues
- Conducting formative evaluation and providing ongoing feedback on students' progress

- Being aware of the time allotted for the activity in relation to the progress

- Having a backup plan (or two) in case the technology crashes

- Emphasizing the lesson's goals

Conduct Formative Assessment (Teacher)

Continuous feedback for students is important throughout the DEVELOP phase. As students create their media elements, teachers should ensure that the elements are appropriate for the content, follow design guidelines, and are stored in the correct file formats. Chapter 7 focuses on assessment techniques.

Create Graphics (Students)

Graphics—pictures, charts, diagrams, and drawings—can play a major role in conveying the content of a digital project. After the requirements are specified in the planning sheets or storyboards, students work to create the appropriate graphics. The procedures for creating graphics with software programs, scanners, and digital cameras are outlined in Chapter 5.

Generate Animations (Students)

In some cases, the project may also include animations—graphics that move in rapid sequence to create the illusion of motion. Animations can convey many complex abstractions, such as water moving in a pipe, or they can be used to attract attention to a particular screen or project. Details on animation techniques are provided in Chapter 5.

Produce Audio (Students)

All the sound elements of a program (narration, music, and sound effects) are referred to as *audio*. Students can record the audio elements of a project themselves, or they can incorporate sounds from the Internet or other sources. The procedures and alternatives for audio production are outlined in Chapter 5.

Produce Video (Students)

Video is an integral part of our students' world, available 24/7 on televisions, smartphones, tablets, and so. In addition to making it easy for students to become consumers of video, today's technologies make it easy for students to be producers of video. Students can readily capture video segments through smartphones, tablet and laptop computers, digital cameras and camcorders, and so on. The video clips can then be integrated into an application program or used to create a stand-alone video. Many factors must be considered when producing, editing, and implementing video segments; these factors are discussed in Chapter 5.

Integrate Digital Elements (Students)

One of the last steps in the DEVELOP phase is to incorporate all the text, graphics, and other media components into a finished program. Many tools can be used to create a digital project, including application software (such as word processors, spreadsheets, or image programs), hypermedia programs, presentation programs (such as PowerPoint), web-based editors (such as

DreamWeaver), video editors (such as iMovie and Movie Maker), and eBooks. All of these options are inexpensive; relatively easy to use; and can include text, graphics, audio, and video. Chapter 6 outlines popular development tools for school-based projects. Chapters 8, 9, 10, 11, and 12 focus on sample presentation, hypermedia, web-based, video, and eBook projects.

EVALUATE

The evaluation of digital projects is both formative and summative. Formative assessment is done throughout project development by both the teacher and the students. For example, the teacher should assess research and brainstorming during the DECIDE phase. She or he should also provide feedback for the students on their flowcharts and storyboards before they begin the development process. Summative evaluation takes place at the end of the project. The steps in the EVALUATE phase include the following:

Teachers

- Provide student assessment.
- Reflect on activity and revise for future.

Students

- Debug project.
- Evaluate peers.
- Conduct self-evaluations.

Provide Student Assessment (Teacher)

Digital projects are a great way to provide alternate assessments for students, reinforce 21st-century learning skills, and support the Common Core Approach of having students explain their thinking to others. Rather than judging their knowledge based on a multiple-choice test, teachers can assess students' abilities to construct knowledge and communicate it through a variety of media. The exact method for determining a project's overall grade will vary. Most important is to provide a meaningful way to communicate the progress to students and their parents. See Chapter 7 for more information on student assessment and evaluation techniques.

Reflect on Activity and Revise for Future (Teacher)

Reflection is an important aspect of all digital content creation activities—for both students and teachers. Teachers who systematically reflect and modify their lessons will be better prepared to offer a similar, perhaps even more effective, lesson in the future.

Debug Project (Students)

Throughout the project development, students should test and debug the project. This process includes testing the media elements on various devices, correcting grammar and punctuation errors, and ensuring that all elements are integrated appropriately. When students complete their projects, student groups should review each other's programs for possible bugs before the projects are submitted for final evaluation.

Evaluate Peers (Students)

Group dynamics are an important part of most classroom projects. Besides the teacher's assessment, students should be encouraged (or required) to evaluate their peers' projects. Instruments for peer evaluation are included in Chapter 7.

Conduct Self-Evaluations (Students)

It is also important for students to conduct self-evaluations and to report on their progress through checklists, journal entries, or other assessment tools. For more information on self-evaluations, see Chapter 7.

DDD-E BENEFITS

There are many learning benefits for students who use technology as tools, information vehicles, and context to support knowledge construction, communication, and representation of ideas. Participating in the design and development of digital projects can improve students' creativity and attitudes and promote a deeper and more sophisticated understanding of the content. Table 2.3 outlines

Table 2.3. Cognitive Skills for Students

Phase	Student Activities	Cognitive Skills
DECIDE	Brainstorm and map content Track required tasks Conduct research	• Formulate questions • Design search strategies • Select and interpret information • Analyze and synthesize information
DESIGN	Outline sequence/flowcharts Specify design, layout, scripts, etc.	• Organize and structure content • Chunk information into logical patterns • Sequence tasks into a timeline • Write meaningful scripts • Convey information through appropriate media • Demonstrate creativity
DEVELOP	Create graphics Generate animations Produce audio Produce video Integrate digital elements	• Translate storyboard information into media elements • Select appropriate media formats • Construct media elements
EVALUATE	Debug project Evaluate peers Conduct self-evaluations	• Produce and verify program • Analyze program effectiveness • Engage in self-reflection

student activities and correlates them to some of the cognitive skills and activities that are involved in each phase of the DDD-E process.

SUMMARY

Careful planning is critical when developing digital projects. Models such as DDD-E can help teachers and students structure the development of digital projects while encouraging student creativity. The DDD-E model provides a framework for students to work collaboratively in designing and developing their projects, and allows opportunities for ongoing evaluation throughout each phase of the DDD-E process. Chapters 3 through 7 focus on each phase of the DDD-E model; Chapters 8 through 12 provide project ideas based on the DDD-E model.

RESOURCES

Book Creator: http://www.redjumper.net/bookcreator/

DreamWeaver: http://www.adobe.com/products/dreamweaver.html

Edmodo: http://www.edmodo.com/

Evernote: http://evernote.com/

Google Docs: http://docs.google.com/

iMovie: https://www.apple.com/mac/imovie/

Inspiration: http://www.inspiration.com/

iTunes: https://www.apple.com/itunes/

Kidspiration: http://www.inspiration.com/Kidspiration/

Moodle: https://moodle.org/

Movie Maker: http:// windows.microsoft.com/en-us/windows-live/movie-maker #t1=overview

Project Foundry: http://www.projectfoundry.org/

SimCity: http://www.simcity.com/

Chapter 3

DECIDE

A SCENARIO

Ms. Corral was thrilled to have a student teacher this semester. Connie had experience using an iPad in her method courses and in her first student teaching assignment. Ms. Corral's school recently became a one-to-one iPad school, so Connie's assistance was much appreciated. Ms. Corral had taken several training classes for the iPad, but she looked forward to co-teaching with Connie to share each other's expertise. Ms. Corral brought pedagogical expertise to their lessons; Connie shared her technology savvy. While planning their first lesson, addressing the Common Core State Standard *ELA-Literacy. L.4.5.b: Recognize and explain the meaning of common idioms, adages, and proverbs*, Connie suggested that students create multimedia presentations or stories on their iPads to demonstrate meanings of different idioms. Ms. Corral liked the idea because it provided students with the opportunity to explain their thinking to others, supported multimodal composition, and reinforced 21st-century learning skills. Ms. Corral stated she had several books they could use to introduce idioms to her students, including *In a Pickle: And Other Funny Idioms* by Marvin Terban and *Raining Cats and Dogs* by Will Moses. Connie shared that the students could also look up idioms on the Internet and recommended a couple of websites to Ms. Corral: Idiom Site (http://www.idiomsite.com/) and The Idiom Connection (http://www.idiomconnection.com/). "Let's put them in cooperative groups," said Ms. Corral, "and assign each group a set of idioms. We'll make sure each student within the group has a designated role so everyone contributes to their project. Just because everyone has their own iPad doesn't mean they have to work independently. It is important students learn to work together and develop real-world learning skills."

"Like us!" Connie beamed. "I'll show you a couple of different apps and websites that the students could use to create their stories or presentations. Let me know which ones you think would be most appropriate for the students."

"Wonderful!" replied Ms. Corral. "We'll also want to discuss how we want to assess their work."

"I know some great websites that have ideas and tools for creating our own rubrics," shared Connie.

"This is going to be a great semester," thought Ms. Corral, as they continued to plan their lesson.

OVERVIEW

Planning is a key component to a successful lesson. After deciding on the standards to be addressed, teachers must determine which instructional strategies and assessments should be used in order to best meet the needs of their students and the learning goals. When choosing to focus on digital content creation, teachers also need to consider if the necessary resources are available, if a digital project is appropriate for the task or time period allowed, and if students have the necessary prerequisite skills. These considerations and others are addressed in the first stage of the DDD-E process—the DECIDE stage. The DECIDE stage sets the foundation for the remaining stages of the DDD-E process; hence, the planning and organization of the DECIDE phase contribute to the overall success of the students' learning through digital content creation. The DECIDE stage includes determining the project's goals (deciding on relevant standards and benchmarks), establishing whether a digital project is appropriate, assessing students' prerequisite skills and background knowledge, deciding on assessment techniques, and planning grouping strategies and roles. Much of the teacher's time will be spent planning and organizing the projects. Students' time will be spent brainstorming and conducting research. Topics in this chapter include the following:

Planning digital content creation projects

- Identifying standards and student learning goals

- Deciding on a project

- Assessing prerequisite skills

- Determining assessment techniques

Organizing digital content creation projects

- Examining grouping alternatives

- Creating cooperative groups

- Working in a one-to-one mobile device classroom

- Managing one-to-one technology classrooms

Managing brainstorming and research activities.

PLANNING DIGITAL CONTENT CREATION PROJECTS

DECIDE is the first phase of the DDD-E process and, as mentioned, involves a significant amount of planning and organization. This section discusses identifying standards and student learning goals, deciding on a project, assessing and developing prerequisite skills, and deciding how the projects will be assessed.

Identifying Standards and Student Learning Goals

Educators are responsible for ensuring students meet specific content standards across a variety of subject areas. District, state, and other tests are used to measure students' progress. For states that have adopted the Common Core State Standards (see http://www.corestandards.org/

in-the-states), a computer-based, shared assessment system is used to provide benchmark, formative, and summative assessments. States have the choice of using the system designed by the Smarter Balanced Assessment Consortium or the Partnership for Assessment of Readiness of College and Careers. No matter which system or other assessments are used to measure students' progress, teachers are held accountable for their students' success. Teachers are expected to identify the appropriate content standards and learning goals (objectives and outcomes) in their lessons. Using a Common Core Approach, teachers are being challenged to not rely strictly on textbooks and drill sheets, but rather to provide constructivist and meaningful learning environments for their students to support collaboration, communication, creativity, and critical thinking. As discussed in Chapter 1, students are more likely to retain what they have learned when constructing knowledge.

Digital content creation provides students with the opportunity to be multimodal composers, and it can be used across all subject areas. When deciding to use digital projects to address a specific content standard or set of standards, consider the time needed to complete the project, how the standard(s) will be addressed through the project, and the students' ability levels, including special needs. Consider whether a digital project is the most effective way to achieve the desired learning outcomes. Textbooks, worksheets, independent research, field trips, or other hands-on activities may address an instructional goal more effectively. For example, students may more effectively classify objects (e.g., rocks, plants, leaves) in accordance with appropriate criteria by actually touching, handling, examining, testing, and manipulating the objects rather than researching and creating a digital project about the information they have gathered. This is not to say that creating a digital project could not assist with students' learning; digital projects can be used to elevate hands-on learning experiences by helping students create, collaborate, and share what they have learned with others. Today's tools make it easy, affordable, and quick to capture students' learning experiences.

When identifying student learning goals for a digital project, it is critical that the goals reflect the identified content standard(s) and that there is a clear way to assess the students' learning. It is important that students learn something beyond technology skills and that the appearance of the final presentation does not overshadow the project's content. It is easy to become overly involved and influenced by multimedia special effects (such as sound, animation, video, transitions, and so on) and to forget about the purpose of the project. Assessing a digital project solely on its looks is comparable to rating a car based on its exterior instead of its engine or judging a cake's taste by its looks. Student learning goals and assessment criteria need to be introduced at the beginning of a digital project to ensure learning outcomes are addressed and students know what is expected of them.

In addition to addressing specific content standards, student learning goals should be designed to:

- Accommodate multiple learning styles and interests.

- Encourage cooperative learning and social skills.

- Foster active learning by promoting interdisciplinary investigations.

- Develop critical-thinking, reasoning, problem-solving, and metacognitive processes.

- Enhance presentation and speaking skills.

- Address necessary adaptations for students with special needs (e.g., language, learning, or physical limitations).

Student learning goals will vary depending on the ability level of the learner, available resources, and the learner's experience.

Deciding on a Project

After identifying the appropriate content standards and defining student learning goals, the teacher can select and design a project to meet the desired goals. The teacher will need to decide if the goals can best be achieved through a digital project. Teachers will want to choose multimedia programs and tools based on the ability level and experiences of their students. For example, teachers may opt to use tablet computers or other mobile devices to make it easy for younger or low-ability students to capture video, incorporate text, take pictures, and record sound. Numerous apps—many free—target younger or lower-ability students as well, making digital content creation possible for almost anyone. For more able students, programs such as PowerPoint, Keynote, HyperStudio, Captivate, iMovie, MovieMaker, Scratch, Prezi, and many others can be used to create digital projects. Ideas for projects are endless. Table 3.1 presents a variety of projects by subject area.

In addition to student learning goals, time is another consideration when deciding on a digital project. Students need to be given projects that can be completed within a prescribed time period. For example, if the project is part of a three-week unit on the California Gold Rush, teachers should limit the size and complexity of the project to what their students are capable of completing in the time allotted.

Table 3.1. Sample Project Ideas

Subject	Project Ideas
Language arts	Book reports; interactive and multiple-ending stories; poetry collections; news reports; phonemic awareness activities for younger students; famous authors; parodies; mythology; reports on stories from multiple cultures or time periods; word origins; grammar, spelling, or vocabulary activities; rhyming games; story starters; prompted writing; creative writing
Mathematics	Problem-solving adventures; famous mathematicians; number recognition activities for younger students; number systems; geometry concepts; math puzzles and solutions; addition, subtraction, multiplication, or division concepts; history of mathematics; units of measure; currency exchange; stock market; inflation; finance; retailing; advertising; proofs
Science and health	Space exploration; pollution; animals; plant growth; weather; insects; nutrition; inventions and inventors; body systems; dissection; simple machines; chemical properties; ocean life; diseases; light and colors; science magic tricks; drugs, alcohol, or smoking; home remedies; exercise; senses; technology; volcanoes; plate tectonics; natural disasters; diet
Social studies	State or country reports; famous people in history; World Wars; Industrial Revolution; Civil War; Holocaust; Gold Rush; geography; Westward Movement; community events and history; family tree; explorers; hobbies and interests; government; careers; cultural holidays, foods, or celebrations; ancient civilizations; American Revolution; national symbols; current issues
Fine arts	Famous artists or musicians; film history; cinematography; music history; musical instruments; film or music genre; history of dance; music, movie, or play reviews; opera; music notation; song writing; animation; special effects; music and culture; famous paintings; art styles; famous entertainers

Available resources affect the amount of time that may be needed to create a digital project. Educators need to assess the availability of the technology needed for the project (e.g., laptops, tablets, software, apps, and so on) and what additional resources may be needed. This will help teachers schedule computer or device time if one-to-one technology is not available, arrange groups, and ensure that the necessary resources are available. For example, in situations where one-to-one technology is not available, teachers may need to plan additional time in a computer lab, borrow resources from other classrooms, have students bring in their own laptops or tablets, request Digital Video Disc Rewritables (DVD-RWs) media or flash (or keychain, thumb) drives or other storage (e.g., Cloud) for their students, or ensure that the necessary software/apps are installed or available for all of the computers. After a teacher has ensured the availability of all necessary components, she or he is ready to introduce the project to the class.

Assessing Prerequisite Skills

Once the learning goals and project have been defined, teachers must ensure that their students have the skills needed to complete the project successfully (see Chapter 2 for recommended technology profiles that have been outlined by ISTE). These include basic computer or tablet operations (e.g., properly turning on and off the system, saving and printing files, opening and closing programs); the use of the assigned tools and peripherals; searching, evaluating, and citing Internet (and other) resources; understanding and following fair use and copyright laws; or other background knowledge teachers deem necessary for a particular project. Teachers can assess students' skills and background knowledge from past projects (if available), observations, skills tests and activities, and so on. Necessary skills may be taught as a whole class, in small groups, or by student experts (e.g., peer teaching).

It is important that the use of technology does not obstruct the students' learning. Students should be made to feel comfortable with the technology prior to their use of the tool for content learning. Fortunately, most students have been exposed to and already use interactive technology tools in their everyday lives. For example, Madden, Lenhart, Duggan, Cortesi, and Gasser (2013) report that 93 percent of teens (ages 12 to 17) have a computer or access to one at home, and about 74 percent access the Internet on cell phones, smartphones, and tablets. Rideout (2013) notes that "seventy-two percent of children age 8 and under have used a mobile device for some type of media activity such as playing games, watching videos, or using apps" (p. 9). Rideout also reports that 38 percent of children under two years of age have accessed media through a mobile device. While today's students may be very tech-savvy, it is still important for educators to provide learning opportunities for more complex programs. For example, educators may use a Jigsaw approach to teach certain elements of a complex program, ensuring each group has a member who is an "expert" in a particular part of the program. Additional or more advanced skills can be taught as the students design and prepare their projects. Another technique is to have mentors from an older class. For example, students in a fifth-grade class may assist in a video production project at the third-grade level.

Determining Assessment Techniques

Educators also need to consider how they will monitor and assess students' work in the classroom projects. The method of assessment will vary according to the type of the project, although a daily log or journal of the students' progress is something that may be applied across many projects. Chapter 7 discusses multiple strategies for assessing projects throughout each stage (DECIDE, DESIGN, and DEVELOP) to ensure instructional goals and standards are being met. Rubrics for formative and summative assessments are included, as are strategies for evaluating individual and group work. Educators may design their own assessment activities, borrow from others, use the examples in this book, or access websites such as RubiStar (http://rubistar.4teach ers.org) for more ideas and resources for creating rubrics. Deciding on methods of assessment before students start their projects helps to ensure students know what is expected of them, that they are on the right track, and that objectives are being met.

ORGANIZING DIGITAL CONTENT CREATION PROJECTS

In addition to planning, the DECIDE phase of the DDD-E process involves organizing the students' learning environment. This includes examining grouping alternatives, creating cooperative groups, and designing computer schedules.

Examining Grouping Alternatives

Depending on the project, students may work individually, collaboratively or cooperatively. Students in collaborative groups work toward the same goal, but they are not necessarily accountable for each other's learning. Students in cooperative groups work toward a common goal and are accountable for each other's learning, providing both academic and personal support. Cooperative group members are taught social skills to help them coordinate their efforts, and teamwork is emphasized.

There are many types of cooperative group methods. These include Student Teams Achievement Divisions (STAD), Teams Games Tournament (TGT), Team-Assisted Individualization (TAI), Jigsaw, Group Investigation, and Learning Together. Groups may be heterogeneous or homogeneous. Most research supports heterogeneous groups (Johnson and Johnson 1999, 2009). Heterogeneous groups are usually formed with a mixture of ability, gender, or ethnicity; homogeneous groups consist of students with similar abilities or interests. Johnson, Johnson, and Holubec (1994, 26) state that "heterogeneous groups tend to promote more elaborate thinking, more frequent giving and receiving of explanations, and greater perspective-taking during discussions about material, all of which increase students' understanding, reasoning, and long-term retention." Although heterogeneous groups are recommended, there are some instances when homogeneous groups are advantageous. For example, educators may find homogeneous groups best for specific class topics, students with specific needs, the creation of interest groups, or competition within groups (Han, Hu, Liu, Jia, and Adey 2013; Johnson and Johnson 1999; Schullery and Schullery 2006).

Grouping Variables

Both grouping styles (heterogeneous and homogeneous) have advantages and disadvantages, depending on the grouping variable. Grouping variables include (but are not limited to) ability, learning style, intelligence, cognitive preference, gender, and background. Ability grouping is based on high, middle, and low achievement. Learning styles may include textual, visual, tactile, and auditory. Intelligences include linguistic, logical-mathematical, spatial, bodily-kinesthetic, musical, interpersonal, intrapersonal, and naturalist. Cognitive preference defines learners according to how they place themselves on a continuum between "global processing" and "analytical processing." Global individuals tend to be more sensitive to others, better communicators, and more socially oriented. Analytical individuals tend to be more introverted but are better at organizing and analyzing content. The next variable, gender, is self-explanatory. Background may include ethnicity, experiences, age, and likes and dislikes. Table 3.2 presents the advantages and disadvantages of these grouping variables.

In addition to heterogeneous and homogeneous grouping, groups may be established by interest or random assignment. For example, students whose favorite pet is a cat may work together to produce a project about cats, or students may be randomly assigned to groups by picking topics out of a hat. These grouping methods also have advantages and disadvantages. Interest groups may enhance communication among members and identify common interests and similarities among students. The disadvantage of interest groups is that they are self-selected, which may generate more off-task behavior, result in undesired homogeneous grouping (ability, ethnicity, or gender), and eliminate possibilities for students to expand their circles (Johnson, Johnson, and Holubec 1994).

Random assignment can provide variety and is perceived as one of the best ways to assign students to groups (Johnson and Johnson 1999). However, general random assignment may pair incompatible students. As an alternative, teachers may want to use stratified random assignment. This is the process of categorizing select groups (e.g., low-, average-, and high-ability students) and randomly selecting a member from each group to form a mixed team. For example, a teacher may randomly select a low-ability student, an average-ability student, and a high-ability student from predefined groups to serve as a three-member team rather than randomly select three students from one large group. Stratified random assignment may be used to ensure that certain students do not get placed together or that each group has students with one or two characteristics (e.g., reading level, math ability, or computer skills).

Stratified random assignment can be used to create groups of students with preferred intelligence. For example, by using stratified random assignment, the teacher can ensure that each group has one member with high linguistic intelligence, another member with high logical-mathematical intelligence, another member with high spatial intelligence, and another member with high interpersonal intelligence.

Groups can be teacher-selected or self-selected. Teacher-selected groups allow teachers to decide which students will work together, ensuring balance and the potential for positive relationships. At-risk students can be assigned to a group with supportive students in the class. Teachers can also ensure that students with non-achievement-oriented and disruptive behavior are not grouped together. Self-selected groups are the least recommended (Johnson and Johnson 1999). Typically, self-selected groups are homogeneous, spawning isolated groups of high achievers, males, minorities, socialites, females, and nonachievers. This leads to more off-task behavior and limited social experiences.

Group Numbers

In addition to grouping variables, the number of students placed in each group can make a difference in the group's success. Group numbers may depend on the students' abilities, number of computers (including laptops and tablets) in the classroom, time constraints, project requirements, cooperative group method, and other variables. Most studies on cooperative learning support group sizes ranging from two to six students. Johnson, Johnson, and Holubec (1994) provide the following points about group size:

1. As the size of the group increases, the range of abilities and viewpoints increases. Additional resources (members) may help the group succeed, and varying

Table 3.2. Advantages and Disadvantages of Various Grouping Variables

Grouping Variable	Type	Advantages	Disadvantages
Ability	Heterogeneous	Best opportunity for peer support and tutoring	Free-rider effect
Ability	Homogeneous	Students tend to bond and communicate more effectively	Low-ability students are often at a significant learning disadvantage
Learning style, intelligence, or cognitive preference	Heterogeneous	Students are exposed to multiple perspectives and problem-solving methods, stimulating students' learning and cognitive development	May be hard to group if students display a preference for one dominant learning style, intelligence, or cognitive preference; communication skills may be more difficult to develop because of different interests
Learning style, intelligence, or cognitive preference	Homogeneous	Students tend to bond and communicate more effectively	Students' focus and exposure to different perspectives are limited
Gender or background	Heterogeneous	Reduces stereotypes, promotes equality among perceived ability and leadership roles	Teachers may need to ensure that social skills are in place to eliminate preconceived biases
Gender or background	Homogeneous	May benefit specific special interest groups or class topics	May cause unnecessary tension between groups; not representative of the real world

viewpoints will challenge the students to evaluate their own perspectives and opinions more critically.

2. The larger the group, the more skillful the members must be at ensuring that everyone remains on task, has a chance to speak, reaches a consensus, understands the material being learned, and maintains good working relationships. Interactions increase as the group size increases, requiring additional interpersonal skills.

3. As group size increases, there is less face-to-face interaction among members and a reduced sense of intimacy. Lower individual responsibility may result, as well as a less cohesive group.

4. If a short period of time is available, smaller groups should be used. Smaller groups can take less time to get organized, and they may operate more quickly.

5. The smaller the group, the more difficult it is for students to avoid their share of the work. Small groups make students more accountable by increasing the visibility of their work.

6. The smaller the group, the easier it is to identify group difficulties, including leadership struggles, unresolved conflicts, and learning difficulties. Problems are more visible and more easily addressed in small groups.

Advantages and disadvantages of various group sizes for multimedia design teams are listed in Table 3.3.

Design teams generally consist of several people, depending on the size of the project and the number of available computers and other devices. With large groups, individuals or pairs of students can be assigned specific tasks. For example, following the group's research efforts, one person may be responsible for the graphics and video, one person may be responsible for the music and narration in the project, two more people may be responsible for completing the storyboards (based on a group-approved template), and two students may be responsible for entering information into the computer. Group members will have additional responsibilities as well; hence, it may not be possible for one member to complete his or her main responsibility until other members of the group complete their parts of the project. Students will need to ensure that everyone stays on task and assists other members.

Creating Cooperative Groups

The success of cooperative groups depends on positive interdependence, a group goal, and individual and group accountability. Teamwork and social skills must be taught just as purposefully and precisely as academic skills. Several models have been designed to assist teachers promote a sense of community, cooperation, and social acceptance in their classrooms. For example, Tribes (see http://tribes.com/) focuses on four basic agreements: attentive listening, appreciation, mutual respect, and the right to pass or participate. Students learn to help each other work on tasks, set goals and solve problems, monitor and assess progress, and celebrate achievements. Active learning strategies are used to engage students in meaningful learning and peer leadership. Kagan Structures (see http://www.kaganonline.com/) provide teachers with a variety of strategies for creating cooperative learning opportunities. For example, in Numbered Heads Together, students are placed in heterogeneous groups of four (one high, two middle, and one low) and each given a number, 1 through 4. The teacher asks a question and groups work together to ensure each team member knows the answer. The teacher chooses a number (1 through 4) and team members with the assigned numbers

Table 3.3. Advantages and Disadvantages of Various Group Sizes in Multimedia Design Teams

Group Size	Advantages	Disadvantages
One	• Work at own pace • Not dependent on others • May provide more hands-on computer time • Increases accountability	• Requires more classroom computer access time • Does not promote learning from different perspectives • Does not encourage cooperative problem solving • May take longer to complete a project • Individual may not be capable of handling all of the project's requirements
Two or three	• Learn from each other • Share project responsibilities • Supports real-world learning, learning from different perspectives, and cooperative problem solving • Classroom computer access time is cut in half because students can work together at the computer	• Need to ensure that everyone contributes and has a chance to speak
Four	• Learn from each other • Share project responsibilities • Supports real-world learning, learning from different perspectives, and cooperative problem solving • Increases classroom computer access time • More talent and resources are available to create the project • Projects may be completed in less time	• Need to ensure that everyone contributes and has a chance to speak • May be difficult to share computers • Requires greater interpersonal skills
Five or six	• Same as four	• Same as four • Easier for a member not to contribute • More chance of group disputes, leadership difficulties, and off-task behavior, which may delay project • Group dynamics may be more appropriate for older, more mature students

respond. Kagan Cooperative Learning is based on PIES: Positive Interdependence, Individual Accountability, Equal Participation, and Simultaneous Interaction (Kagan and Kagan 2009).

For most classroom multimedia projects, teamwork is essential. The following sections focus on the importance of introducing social skills, placing students into cooperative groups, and assigning roles.

Introducing Social Skills

Before placing students into cooperative groups, it is important to determine the goal of the project and what types of student interactions are desired. In most cases, students will need to be taught or reminded how to work cooperatively. Vermette (1998, 158) suggests the following working relationship skills:

- Acknowledging contributions
- Checking for agreement
- Disagreeing in an agreeable way
- Encouraging others
- Expressing support
- Inviting others to talk
- Keeping things calm and reducing tension
- Mediating
- Responding to ideas
- Sharing feelings
- Showing appreciation

The teacher may want to have groups model or practice these skills, as well as discuss the importance of listening, politeness, and other appropriate communication habits. Teachers may want to create social skill objectives. These may be defined by monitoring student groups and diagnosing the specific problems students are having working together or by asking students which social skill would improve their teamwork. Based on the teacher's observation and students' input, a social skill can be taught to help solve the problem.

Placing Students into Cooperative Groups

After social skills have been introduced, decide on the cooperative group method (e.g., STAD, TGT, TAI, Jigsaw, Group Investigation, or Learning Together) that will be most beneficial for the students and their assigned project. Depending on the project, desired interactions, and cooperative group method, assess students' strengths and weaknesses, their interests, who they like to work with, and so on. Consider group dynamics and create heterogeneous conditions. Along with the survey found at the end of this chapter (see the Self Survey blackline master), a teacher's own observation and background with his or her students can help facilitate student placement. Teachers may want to create their own surveys using an online program such as Survey Monkey, Polldaddy, or SurveyGizmo.

Students can be placed on design teams before or after introducing the project. Teachers may poll student interests before introducing the project or may wait to assess student interest until after the project has been introduced. For example, an informal survey might be created to assess students' interest in certain animals. On the basis of the survey results, the teacher can heterogeneously group students according to their interests before introducing a project about animals. Alternatively, the teacher could introduce a project about animals and let students group themselves according to their interests. Precautions must be taken, however, because of the disadvantages associated with self-selected groups. Hence, some students may choose groups based on the animal's popularity (not their true interest) and friends' choices. In addition, some animals may not draw enough students or they may attract too many students, creating bad feelings and a sense of unfairness if students are assigned to a different animal. Polling students' interests and assigning teams before introducing a project is recommended.

Assigning Roles

Another important aspect of cooperative group learning is role assignment. Assigning roles helps to ensure that all students participate and that no one person dominates a group. Roles may be based on group behaviors, computer and other digital tasks, or project assignments. For example, in a group of four students, one person may ensure that everyone gets a chance to speak (turn-taking monitor), one person may record the group's activities (record keeper), one person may ensure that the group's noise level is kept to a minimum (noise monitor), and one person may be responsible for keeping the group on task (task master). These group-behavior roles may be rotated on a daily basis. Computer tasks may include keyboarder (enters information into the computer), editor (oversees computer input), and record keeper (keeps track of the group's progress). Project assignment roles may include a graphic artist, instructional designer, production specialist, program author, etc.

Assignment roles may also become the basis for forming the groups. For example, a survey can be used to form the groups according to Gardner's theory of multiple intelligences (see the Self Survey blackline master). Students are placed into teams based on their interests and observed strengths. Each design team might contain one student who ranked high in linguistics (I like to read books, write, and tell stories), one student who ranked high in logic-mathematics (I like math, strategy games, and working with puzzles), and two students who ranked high in spatial skills (I like to draw and I understand things better by looking at a picture). Student "linguistic experts" may take on the responsibilities of the subject matter experts, "spatial experts" may be considered the teams' graphic artists and storyboard designers, and "logical-mathematical experts" may be responsible for the project's flowchart and programming needs. Additional project roles may be assigned according to the students' self-rankings in the remaining areas of the survey: bodily-kinesthetic (I have a hard time sitting still), musical (I am a good singer and I know when music is off key), interpersonal (I get along well with others and I am a good listener), intrapersonal (I am dependable and self-confident), and naturalist (I enjoy the outdoors and can easily identify and classify the things around me).

Optimizing Project Creation Time

In classrooms without one-to-one laptop, tablet, or other mobile devices, the most challenging aspect of designing and developing digital projects may be computer access. Various situations are possible. Computer labs are typically available for one 30- or 40-minute time slot a week. A computer assistant may or may not be available, and stations may range from 10 to 30 or more computers. Classrooms may have one or more computers, with or without a projection system. Some schools have mobile computer carts with laptops available for checkout, increasing the number of computers possible in a classroom. Mobile computer carts may not always be available if other teachers request them, however. There are several advantages and disadvantages for each situation when creating digital projects (see Table 3.4).

Table 3.4. Advantages and Disadvantages of Computer Situations

Computer Setting	Advantages	Disadvantages
Lab (10 to 15 computers)	• Working in groups, all students have access to the computers at the same time; teacher can facilitate whole-class instruction • Computer coordinator may be available to assist students • Students can take turns working individually on computers with computer coordinator while other students work on noncomputer assignments with teacher • Less cost to secure and network computers	• Usually limited to 30 or 40 minutes a week • Fire drills, assemblies, and holidays, may cause lab time to be missed • Computer use is more likely to be an isolated activity than an integral part of the curriculum • Whole school uses the same computers and printers, causing more wear and tear on the systems, more variable problems, and additional software costs to meet everyone's needs • Instructional time is lost going to and from computer lab
Lab (20 or more computers)	• Same as other lab situation • Individual students have access to the computers at the same time; teacher can facilitate whole-class instruction • Additional computers may be available for multimedia purposes (e.g., editing videos)	• Same as other lab situation
One or two computers in the classroom	• Computer available every day for "teachable moments" • If a projector device or large monitor is available, can be used to facilitate whole-class/small-group instruction • Some software is specifically designed for whole-class/small-group instruction (e.g., Tom Snyder Productions Inc.) • Software funds can be used to purchase a variety of software that meets students' and teachers' individual needs vs. lab sets that may not be used by all teachers or students • Students may take better care of their "own" classroom computers	• Individual computer time is difficult to manage • Some group computer projects may take an undesirable length of time to complete due to limited access • More cost involved with purchasing computers and printers for every classroom, networking, and securing every room (alarm system)
Three or more computers in the classroom	• Same as other classroom situation • Student groups can have daily access • Computers are more likely to be used as an integral part of instruction and tool for learning	• Requires more classroom space than one or two computers • More cost involved with purchasing computers and printers for every classroom, networking, and securing every room (alarm system)

(continued)

Table 3.4. (Continued)

Computer Setting	Advantages	Disadvantages
Mobile computer carts	• Can provide additional access for group projects • Can be removed from classroom and stored in secure location • Provides more flexibility (e.g., can be taken outdoors or on field trips)	• May not always be available • Time needed to move computer cart in and out of the classroom • Computers may be damaged in transit • May have batteries that need to be recharged

In most cases, a minimum of three computers in the classroom is necessary to ensure that every student gets some time at the computer during a single classroom period. This requires that students work in groups of three or four. While students are waiting for their group's turn at the computer, they work on a related, noncomputer task. For example, students may be engaged in a silent reading activity, follow-up materials about the computer lesson, or another related activity. Teachers should resist teaching a directed lesson when students are actively engaged on classroom computers for several reasons:

1. Students on the computers are missing the lesson.

2. Students near the computers will more likely be watching their computer classmates rather than the teacher.

3. Some computer programs require sound (interrupting the teacher's directed lesson), and headphones are not always available.

4. The teacher cannot immediately assist students on the computers if he or she is involved in a directed lesson.

5. Students not on the computers may be more concerned about the clock and their turn at the computer than what the teacher has to say.

6. Scheduling may require students to take their computer turn during the middle of the directed lesson, as well as returning students to the directed lesson without having participated in the beginning of the lesson.

For some teachers, the thought of three or more computers in the classroom may seem unrealistic; however, one-to-one programs are becoming more and more common as technology becomes more affordable. The National Center for Educational Statistics (2012) reports that about one in every three students has access to an instructional computer connected to the Internet. More schools are investing in one-to-one programs, including the use of tablets. Wireless networks and lower costs have helped make one-to-one access a reality in many school districts. The trend is here, but how soon all teachers will have ample and updated technology in their classrooms is uncertain. Change occurs slowly. In the meantime, teachers can place more computers in their classroom to facilitate the creation of digital projects by borrowing other classrooms' computers or arranging to borrow an additional computer from a computer lab. Parents and businesses may also lend support. Teachers may research organizations such as ClassWish or DonorsChoose to request computer, tablet, and other donations or Computers for Learning to learn how to receive excess federal computer equipment.

To help teachers address the various computer situations possible, computer schedules have been developed to assist teachers in managing digital projects in their classroom (see Figures 3.1 through 3.5).

Time	Computer Time	Project Assignments	Four-Computer Classroom Daily Computer Use (Version 1)
9:00 a.m. to 9:30 a.m.	A B C D	E F G H	• 24 to 36 students • 2 to 3 students per group • 20-minute rotation schedule • When students are not at computers, they work on related project assignments. For example, Groups A, B, C, and D have computer time between 9:00 a.m. and 9:20 a.m. Groups E, F, G, and H and groups I, J, K, and L work on related, non-computer assignments.
9:30 a.m. to 10:00 a.m.	E F G H	A B C D	

Figure 3.1. Computer schedule for a four-computer classroom (version 1).

Time	Computer Time	Project Assignments		Four-Computer Classroom Daily Computer Use (Version 2)
		1	2	
9:00 a.m. to 9:20 a.m.	A B C D	I J K L	E F G H	• 24 to 32 students • 3 to 4 students per group • 30-minute rotation schedule • When students are not at computers, they work on related project assignments. For example, Groups A, B, C, and D have computer time between 9:00 a.m. and 9:30 a.m. Groups E, F, G, and H work on related assignments.
9:20 a.m. to 9:40 a.m.	E F G H	A B C D	I J K L	
9:40 a.m. to 10:00 a.m.	I J K L	E F G H	A B C D	

Figure 3.2. Computer schedule for a four-computer classroom (version 2).

Time	Computer Time	Project Assignments		Four-Computer Classroom Daily Computer Use (Version 2)
		I	2	
9:00 a.m. to 9:20 a.m.	A B C	G H I	D E F	• 27 to 36 students • 3 to 4 students per group • 20-minute rotation schedule • When students are not at computers, they work on related project assignments. For example, Groups A, B, and C have computer time between 9:00 a.m. and 9:20 a.m. Groups D, E, F, G, H, and I work on related, non-computer assignments (projects I and 2).
9:20 a.m. to 9:40 a.m.	D E F	A B C	G H I	
9:40 a.m. to 10:00 a.m.	G H I	D E F	A B C	

Figure 3.3. Computer schedule for a three-computer classroom.

Time	Computer Time	Project Assignments			Four-Computer Classroom Daily Computer Use (Version 2)
		I	2	3	
9:00 a.m. to 9:15 a.m.	A B	C D	E F	G H	• 24 to 32 students • 3 to 4 students per group • 15-minute rotation schedule • When students are not at computers, they work on related project assignments. For example, Groups A and B have computer time between 9:00 a.m. and 9:15 a.m. Groups C, D, E, F, G and H work on related, non-computer assignments (projects I, 2, and 3).
9:15 a.m. to 9:30 a.m.	C D	E F	G H	A B	
9:30 a.m. to 9:45 a.m.	E F	G H	A B	C D	
9:45 a.m. to 10:00 a.m.	G H	A B	C D	E F	

Figure 3.4. Computer schedule for a two-computer classroom.

Note that four computers in the classroom can provide students with 30 minutes of daily access to computers versus the 30 minutes of weekly access provided by computer labs. Two or three computers in the classroom can provide student groups with 75 to 110 minutes of computer time a week, respectively. One-computer classrooms provide limited group access, but they can be used to facilitate whole-class projects. For example, the class may decide to create a project about African American inventors to present to the community during Black History Month. Students may be placed in groups of three to research a specific inventor and to design a one-card or one-page presentation about their inventor. A template can be designed to assist students with their presentation. Student groups can take turns at the classroom computer (see Figure 3.5), inputting

Time	Computer Time		Project Assignments				Four-Computer Classroom MW/TTH Computer Use
	MW	TTH	MW 1	TTH 2	MW 3	TTH 4	• 24 to 32 students • 3 to 4 students per group • 15-minute rotation schedule • When students are not at computers, they work on related project assignments. For example, Groups A and B have computer time between 9:00 a.m. and 9:15 a.m. Groups C, D, E, F, G and H work on related, non-computer assignments (projects 1, 2, and 3).
9:00 a.m. to 9:15 a.m.	A	E	B F G H	B F G H	C D E	A C D	
9:15 a.m. to 9:30 a.m.	B	F	F G H	B G H	A C D E	A C D E	
9:30 a.m. to 9:45 a.m.	C	G	A D E	A C D E	B F G H	B F H	

Figure 3.5. Computer schedule for a one-computer classroom.

their data while others are finishing their research or working on a related small-group activity. A blackline master for scheduling computer time can be found at the end of this chapter. Teachers who are lucky enough to have one-to-one access in their classroom should not encounter problems scheduling computer time. Schedules may still be needed to share specific peripherals (still and video cameras, scanners, etc.) if these resources are limited or printers and Internet connections if the classroom is not wireless.

Working in a One-to-One Mobile Device Classroom

One-to-one mobile device (e.g., laptops, tablets, iPods, and so on) environments should not be equated to isolated learning environments. Students should still be encouraged to work in groups. As described earlier, each student can take on a different responsibility and work as a team. Each student can use his or her own mobile device to contribute to the team's progress. Tips for working in a one-to-one mobile device classroom include the following:

Make sure the mobile devices are charged. Establish a routine or procedure for ensuring batteries are charged.

Have a backup plan. Have outlets and cables available if mobile devices need to be recharged. Backup batteries are possible, too. Have a backup device or a "sharing" plan if a device is not working. Remember, it is not always necessary for students to be working on their device at once. Some projects may require students to be conducting a different task on and off the mobile device.

Set rules and expectations and be consistent. Let students know up front what you expect and the rules for using mobile devices in the classroom. Discuss consequences. You may want to have your students help to create these. Follow through and be consistent.

Make sure students are focused on you. When students are working on their mobile devices and you need their attention, make sure you wait until all eyes are on you and not on their screens. One way to accomplish this is to ask students to place their device under a folder or, with laptops or tablets with covers, asks students to close the cover.

One-to-one mobile device environments make it easier to integrate technology in the classroom if the teacher is ready to plan instruction to take advantage of the devices' resources and potential. Professional development opportunities can help teachers in one-to-one mobile device environments increase student engagement and students' use of technology as a learning tool. Although one-to-one mobile device classrooms are not a requirement for digital content creation, they ensure that every student has the opportunity to engage in 21st-century learning environments. One-to-one mobile device classrooms support cooperative and collaborative learning, project learning, the teacher acting as coach or facilitator, independent research and inquiry, and highly focused academic class time (Dawson, Cavanaugh, and Ritzhaupt 2008; Inserra and Short 2013; Rosen and Beck-Hill 2012). See the No Strings Attached website (http://etc.usf.edu/plans) and the Technology Integration Matrix Grade Level Index (http://fcit.usf.edu/matrix/gradelevel.php) to review exemplary models of technology integration in classrooms. The lesson plans include video examples across numerous content areas for all grade levels.

MANAGING BRAINSTORMING AND RESEARCH ACTIVITIES

After the preliminary management issues of the DECIDE phase have been addressed, the teacher can provide students with time to brainstorm and research the topic of their project. This step should be prefaced with the purpose of the students' projects, and each group should be provided with guidelines and rubrics for their project (see Chapter 7). To solidify the groups, let teams develop their own name or "company" logo.

Brainstorming Activities

After student groups have established their project roles (e.g., graphic artist, instructional designer, production specialist, and program author), behavior roles (e.g., turn-taking monitor, noise monitor, record keeper, task master), and team name, provide students with time to brainstorm. Depending on the ability level and experience of the students, brainstorming may be conducted as a whole class or by individual groups. Teachers may wish to provide students with the BrainStorm or KWL Knowledge Chart blackline masters at the end of this chapter, or rely on brainstorming software such as Inspiration or Kidspiration (see http://www.inspiration.com). These tools are also available for the iPad (see Inspiration Maps, Kidspiration Maps, and Popplet at the App Store). Additional tools can be used on the web (e.g., Bubble.us, Coggle, and Popplet) or downloaded for free (e.g., Freemind and Xmind). For high-ability and experienced groups, provide a rubric of questions or guidelines that covers the assigned instructional content. For example, if students are creating a digital project on Egypt, provide them with specific content questions and related pictures to research and include in their presentations. If students are creating a digital project about family history, provide them with guidelines as to the type of information that should be included. These guidelines can help focus the students' thoughts as they brainstorm ideas.

For younger and lower-ability students, make sure they have previous background knowledge in the assigned topics. Guide them through a KWL Knowledge Chart—What we Know, what we Want to find out, and what we Learned (see the KWL Knowledge Chart blackline master at the end of this chapter). Each student can participate in the chart activity at his or her desk as the teacher directs the whole class using an interactive whiteboard or a transparency of the chart on an overhead projector. Student groups can exchange their thoughts and share their ideas with the class. Following the introduction of the KWL Knowledge Chart, student groups can be assigned a particular outcome on the chart. For example, if the chart is about the solar system, student groups might be assigned to find out what the class wants to know about a particular planet. Group 1 might answer class questions about Jupiter, Group 2 might answer class questions about Mercury, and so on. The chart would be completed after the students presented their final projects.

Additional brainstorming techniques include recording students' sensory experiences. For example, many teachers pop popcorn in class to facilitate the students' creative writing skills. Students experience and discuss the sound, smell, taste, texture, and sight of popcorn before they write about it. A similar approach may be taken toward a particular multimedia project. For example, if the goal of the project is to develop and present a persuasive advertisement, such as why a group's hamburger is the best, educators may bring in different hamburgers for the students to sample, as well as let the students view videos of hamburger commercials, examine newspaper and magazine advertisements for hamburgers, inspect the packaging, and so on. As a class, the students can brainstorm and discuss how the hamburgers and their advertisements are the same or different and what issues (price, taste, nutrition, popularity, or convenience) may affect consumer choice. Following this whole-class experience, students can return to their groups and brainstorm strategies for their projects based on their new background knowledge. Final projects might include a persuasive presentation and samples of the group's hamburger creations.

Research Activities

After students have brainstormed about their topic, the teacher reviews the group's brainstorming chart and asks clarifying questions to ensure that the group is on track. After the group's work is approved, the students can begin researching the different areas of their topic. Students may want to assign each group member a specific task.

Research activities may take place on or off the computer. Computer schedules can be designed that allow student access to the Internet and other digital media to further their research (see Figures 3.1 through 3.5). Students not assigned to computers can conduct research at the school library or in the classroom, using newspapers, textbooks, literature books, magazines, and other resources. High-ability students will need time to organize and synthesize gathered information and assign further research responsibilities. Younger and lower-ability students will need to work together to find the answers to their assigned questions from the KWL Knowledge Chart. Field trips, guest speakers, experiments, and other opportunities may be arranged to assist students with their research. Students can use a bibliography information sheet (see the Bibliography Information blackline master at the end of this chapter) to record and track their sources throughout the DDD-E process.

Students may also have the opportunity to conduct research outside the classroom. Groups can assign members to conduct research via the Internet, locate or create graphics, or develop narration or audio clips on their home computers or in the media center. Students can also create portions of their group's project at home, provided they have the appropriate software. Many web tools and noncommercial programs (e.g., freeware) are free, allowing students to work on their projects at home. Never assume, though, that students have access to home computers, the Internet, or other research materials. It is inappropriate to assign homework if all of the students do not have the skills or resources to complete it. In situations where skills and access to technology are not an issue, teachers may incorporate the use of wikis, blogs, Google Docs, learning management systems (e.g., Blackboard, Moodle, etc.), and other online tools for group collaboration, journal entries, sharing of information, formative assessment, and so on (e.g., Edmodo and Project Foundry).

Each group's record keeper should keep a journal (see the Journal Entry # blackline master at the end of this chapter) of his or her group's progress, including the time spent brainstorming. Journal entries can help students reflect on their work, social experiences, and how they are achieving their goals. Journals may be kept online as a wiki or other format. Teachers should review journal entries on a daily basis to help students keep focused and to address problems before they get out of hand. Groups can keep their journal entries in a binder and submit it with their final project. Groups may spend two to five class periods conducting the initial research for their projects.

SUMMARY

There are many variables to consider when assigning students to create a digital project: standards and benchmarks, computer access, student experience, grouping variables, group size, student roles, time needed to complete the project, and so on. The DECIDE phase of the DDD-E process encourages teachers to address these variables before assigning a digital project.

After determining the project goals, appropriate background knowledge, guidelines, and rubrics are provided to assist student groups with the brainstorming and research activities. These activities provide the foundation for the next step of the DDD-E process: DESIGN. Journal entries continue throughout the DDD-E process, helping students to reflect on their progress and project goals.

There are multiple stages to digital content creation, but the DECIDE phase is the most critical to their success. The stages that follow (discussed in Chapters 4–7) depend on the planning, organization, and research activities conducted in the DECIDE phase; each stage depends on its predecessor. The time needed to complete each stage will depend on the size and complexity of the project, as well as the level and number of students in each group. Well-managed classrooms and organized projects will add to the success of students' digital content creation endeavors and learning.

RESOURCES

Bubble.us: https://bubbl.us/

Coggle: http://coggle.it/

Common Core State Standards: http://www.corestandards.org/

Computers for Learning: http://computersforlearning.gov/

ClassWish: http://classwish.org

DonorsChoose: http://www.donorschoose.org

Edmodo: https://www.edmodo.com

Freemind: http://freemind.sourceforge.net/wiki/index.php/Main_Page

Inspiration: http://www.inspiration.com/

Kagan Structures: http://www.kaganonline.com/

Kidspiration: http://www.kidspiration.com/Kidspiration

No Strings Attached: http://etc.usf.edu/plans/

Partnership for Assessment of Readiness of College and Careers: https://www.parcconline.org/

Polldaddy: http://polldaddy.com/

Popplet: http://popplet.com/

Project Foundry: http://www.projectfoundry.org/

RubiStar: http://rubistar.4teachers.org

Smarter Balanced Assessment Consortium: http://www.smarterbalanced.org/

Survey Monkey: http://www.surveymonkey.com/

SurveyGizmo: http://www.surveygizmo.com/

Technology Integration Matrix Grade Level Index: http://fcit.usf.edu/matrix/gradelevel.php

Tribes: http://tribes.com/

XMind: http://www.xmind.net/

BLACKLINE MASTERS

Several blackline masters are presented in this chapter to assist teachers with the DECIDE phase. These include:

- Self Survey: one method of organizing students into groups based on Howard Gardner's theory of multiple intelligences

- Computer Schedule: a template for organizing classroom computer time

- BrainStorm: a webbing activity designed to help students link their ideas

- KWL Knowledge Chart: a chart to help students organize what they know and what they want to find out about a topic

- Bibliography Information: one way to record and identify sources used throughout the DDD-E process

- Journal Entry #: a method of recording and tracking a group's progress

Blackline masters may be copied for educational purposes. They may also be used to help educators create their own DECIDE activity and organization sheets, such as a modified survey, computer schedule, or bibliography information sheet.

REFERENCES

Dawson, K., Cavanaugh, C., and Ritzhaupt, A. 2008. Florida's EETT leveraging laptops initiative and its impact on teaching practices. *Journal of Research on Technology in Education*, 41(2), 143–159.

Han, Q., Hu, W., Liu, J., Jia, X., and Adey, P. 2013. The influence of peer interaction on students' creative problem-finding ability. *Creativity Research Journal*, 25(3), 248–258.

Inserra, A., and Short, T. 2013. An analysis of high school math, science, social studies, English, and foreign language teachers' implementation of one-to-one computing and their pedagogical practices. *Journal of Educational Technology Systems*, 41(2), 145–169.

Johnson, D. W., and Johnson, R. T. 1999. *Learning together and alone: Cooperative, competitive, and individualistic learning* (5th ed.). Needham Heights, MA: Allyn & Bacon.

Johnson, D., & Johnson, R. 2009. An educational psychology success story: Social interdependence theory and cooperative learning. *Educational Researcher*, 38, 365–379.

Johnson, D. W., Johnson, R. T., and Holubec, E. J. 1994. *Cooperative learning in the classroom*. Alexandria, VA: Association for Supervision and Curriculum Development.

Kagan, S., and Kagan, M. 2009. *Kagan cooperative learning*. San Clemente, CA: Kagan Cooperative Learning.

Madden, M., Lenhart, A., Duggan, M., Cortesi, S., and Gasser, U. (2013). *Teens and technology 2013*. PewResearchCenter: The Berkman Center for Internet & Society at Harvard University. Available at: http://www.pewinternet.org/files/old-media//Files/Reports/2013/PIP_TeensandTechnology2013.pdf. Retrieved on August 2, 2014.

National Center for Educational Statistics. 2012. *Digest of education statistics: 2012*. U.S. Department of Education, Institute of Education Sciences, National Center for Education Statistics. Available at: http://nces.ed.gov/programs/digest/d12/index.asp. Retrieved on August 2, 2014.

Rideout, V. (2013). *Zero to eight: Children's media use in America 2013*. Common Sense Media. Available at: http://cdn2-d7.ec.commonsensemedia.org/sites/default/files/uploads/about_us/zero-to-eight-20131.pdf. Retrieved on August 2, 2014.

Rosen, Y., and Beck-Hill, D. 2012. Intertwining digital content and a one-to-one laptop environment in teaching and learning: Lessons from the Time To Know program. *Journal of Research on Technology in Education*, 44(3), 225–241.

Schullery, N., and Schullery, S. (2006). Are heterogeneous or homogeneous groups more beneficial to students? *Journal of Management Education*, 30, 542–556.

Vermette, P. J. 1998. *Making cooperative learning work: Student teams in K–12 classrooms*. Upper Saddle River, NJ: Prentice-Hall.

Self Survey

Rank the following statements according to how well they describe you. Give the statement that describes you the best a "1," the second best a "2," and so on.

Name _____

- [ ] I like to read books, write, and tell stories.
  (linguistics)

- [ ] I like math, strategy games, and working with puzzles.
  (logic-mathematics)

- [ ] I like to draw and I understand things better by looking at a picture.
  (spatial)

- [ ] I have a hard time sitting still.
  (bodily-kinesthetic)

- [ ] I am a good singer and I know when music is off key.
  (musical)

- [ ] I get along well with others and I am a good listener.
  (interpersonal)

- [ ] I am dependable and self-confident.
  (intrapersonal)

- [ ] I enjoy the outdoors and can easily identify and classify things around me.
  (naturalist)

From *Digital Content Creation in Schools: A Common Core Approach* by Karen S. Ivers and Ann E. Barron. Santa Barbara, CA: Libraries Unlimited. Copyright © 2015.

Computer Schedule

		Mon.	Tues.	Wed.	Thur.	Fri.	Sat.
Team Name: _____ **Team Members:** _____ _____ _____	Comp.						
	Time						
	Role						
	Role						
	Role						
	Role						

		Mon.	Tues.	Wed.	Thur.	Fri.	Sat.
Team Name: _____ **Team Members:** _____ _____ _____	Comp.						
	Time						
	Role						
	Role						
	Role						
	Role						

		Mon.	Tues.	Wed.	Thur.	Fri.	Sat.
Team Name: _____ **Team Members:** _____ _____ _____	Comp.						
	Time						
	Role						
	Role						
	Role						
	Role						

BrainStorm

Create a web or "brainstorm" of your related ideas. Add additional thoughts as necessary.

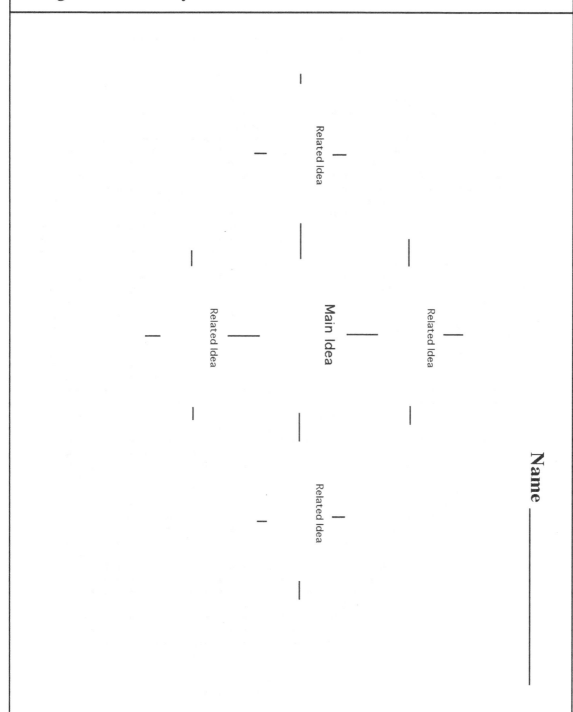

Related Idea

Related Idea

Main Idea

Related Idea

Related Idea

Name _____

KWL Knowledge Chart

What we know	What we want to find out	What we learned

Bibliography Information

Team Name _____

Description	Media Type	Story-board#	Source

Journal Entry # [ ]

Date _____   Team Name _____

Today's accomplishments: _____

_____

_____

_____

_____

Today's problems: _____

_____

_____

_____

Goals for tomorrow: _____

_____

_____

_____

Group dynamics:	1	2	3	Recorder's	[ ]
	poor	okay	great	initials:	

Comments: _____

_____

_____

Chapter 4

DESIGN

A SCENARIO

Ms. Stone was outlining the requirements for a public service project that integrated science, social studies, and language arts in her sixth-grade class. Each team was tasked with creating a persuasive presentation to increase awareness of "Going Green" through "Reduce, Reuse, or Recycle" strategies. Since the students were proficient with several technology tools, they could elect to include audio and video in their presentations. When complete, the projects would be shown to the rest of the elementary school to encourage students to be more ecologically friendly in their daily lives.

Andy's team decided to focus "Reuse"—how children could help the economy by reusing some everyday items. After brainstorming several ideas, they began by mapping the content and sequence with Inspiration. Next, they filled in the information required on storyboards (for the presentation program); agreed on a style guide for fonts, colors, etc.; wrote the scripts for the narrations; and filled in the shot lists for the video segments. They felt confident that when they entered the DEVELOP phase, they would be able to work divide the tasks in the production process (with two students producing the videos), one recording the narrations, and two constructing the presentation. Because their planning documents were complete, they felt confident that all of the components would come together nicely by the deadline.

Adam's group selected "Recycle" for their focus. Instead of "wasting" time on the storyboards, flowcharts, style guide, and other design documents, they decided it would be more fun and efficient to immediately start the production of the video, audio, and presentation. Two students in the group found a smartphone and started shooting video, another student searched the Internet for images, and two students began the PowerPoint presentation. They enjoyed working with the technology; however, since they did not have a shot list, the video group had to shoot the same scenes several times, and since they had not written a script, the editing process was extremely frustrating. Meanwhile, the students creating the PowerPoint slides had no idea where or how the video, images, and narration would fit into the program. When the deadline loomed, and they had to compile the components, they discovered they did not have a cohesive program. In fact, it looked like the project was thrown together by several students who had used completely different content and approaches. They soon realized that the time and energy invested in the DESIGN phase could pay many dividends later in the project.

OVERVIEW

The DESIGN phase is extremely important because it produces the blueprint for the entire project in the form of content outlines, scripts, flowcharts, and storyboards. At the beginning of the DESIGN phase, teachers may want to show examples of well-designed projects as well as poorly designed projects. They should also set the parameters for the project, such as delineating the content, detailing the research requirements, and outlining the media components (audio, animation, video, images, text, etc.). Student teams should be provided with a list of other requirements or expectations, such as due dates, supporting documentation, etc. (See the Project Checklist blackline master at the end of this chapter.)

To assist teachers with aspects of the DESIGN phase, this chapter provides techniques for introducing topics that are important to design; it also presents design guidelines and recommendations for structuring and formatting projects with multimedia digital content. Keep in mind that the scope and complexity of projects will vary, as will the components of the design. The chapter concludes with several blackline masters that are correlated to the activities in the DESIGN phase. Topics that the teacher should present to the students include:

Outlining the content

- Creating flowcharts
  - Linear structures
  - Tree structures
  - Cluster structures
  - Star structures
  - Flowchart symbols
- Specifying screen design
  - Screen design for web pages
  - Screen design for hypermedia programs
  - Screen design for presentation programs
- Creating scripts and storyboards
  - General planning sheet
  - Style guides
  - Detailed storyboards and scripts
- General design guidelines
  - Design guidelines for text
  - Design guidelines for menus

- Design guidelines for links and navigation

- Design guidelines for color

OUTLINING THE CONTENT

In the DECIDE phase, the broad instructional goals are stated for the project, and a brainstorming session may help to determine the possible topics. In addition, research can be conducted to further delineate the topics that will be included in the project.

As the students enter the DESIGN phase, the content can be solidified with outlines, flowcharts, scripts, and storyboards. Several factors will influence the content, including the timeline, age of students, subject area, and the venue for the project.

When a project is assigned, it is often wise for the teacher to specify the project requirements in terms of content and components. For example, teachers may assign a topic, such as a famous author, and require that the students provide background information on the author's childhood, a synopsis of his or her publications, and the author's impact on society. An Intention Outline or similar template can be used to help students specify the goals and outcomes of the project, its target audience, and an outline of the content (see blackline masters at the end of this chapter).

When the Intention Outlines are complete, the teacher should review them to ensure that the students' goals are clearly stated and aligned with the assignment's instructional objectives, that the content outline contains the depth required for the project, and that the topics are organized logically.

The teacher should also determine the primary venue for the project and how the audience might influence the content. Venues might include presentations for classroom peers, school assemblies, community groups, or external audiences via the Internet. If a project is designed for third graders, the content, presentation, and elements will be noticeably different from the content, presentation, and elements of a project designed for adults.

CREATING FLOWCHARTS

After the Intention Outline is complete, students should be encouraged to think through the flow of the project. A flowchart can be used to visually depict the sequence and structure of a program. This is especially pertinent if the project (such as a website or hypermedia program) involves interactivity and branching. To introduce the logic of flowcharts, teachers can use exercises such as "The Bunny Hop" or "Medusa's Market" (see blackline masters at the end of this chapter). Such exercises encourage students to think through decision points and represent their paths in a logical manner.

There are several common flowchart structures, including linear, tree, star, and cluster. Teachers should demonstrate various projects that use different structures and point out the advantages and disadvantages of each. The Project Structures blackline master at the end of this chapter can be used to help students differentiate among the various options for project flow and choose the appropriate structure for their projects. Students should be encouraged to experiment with different ways of presenting content. Content-mapping programs, such as Inspiration and Kidspiration, are excellent tools for creating concept maps and developing flowcharts. The symbols and drawing tools in programs such as PowerPoint, KeyNote, Google Docs, and Word are also effective options for creating flowcharts.

Figure 4.1. Linear structure.

Linear Structures

Linear structures are appropriate for podcasts and videos and when there is a specific sequence or a step-by-step procedure (see Figure 4.1). For example, a student may create a linear project that details the process required to dissect a frog. Projects designed as presentations (such as those created with PowerPoint, Keynote, and Photo Story) are usually linear in design.

Movement options in a linear structure may branch forward or backward. Most linear programs also include a method for starting over at the beginning.

Tree Structures

A tree structure is appropriate when the main idea branches into a few other topics, which in turn are subdivided further. Tree structures are common in both web and hypermedia projects. For example, Figure 4.2 illustrates a tree-shaped project in which the user can select any of three states from a Main Menu. When he or she clicks on a state, a submenu appears with state politics and state history.

Movement options in a tree structure usually allow users to branch forward and backward, return to the previous menu, or return to the Main Menu.

Cluster Structures

The cluster approach combines tree and linear structures. For example, Figure 4.3 illustrates a Main Menu where the user can select an option, then proceed to a linear presentation about adding or multiplying fractions.

Movement options in a cluster structure allow users to branch forward and backward within the linear segments or return to the Main Menu. In most cases, the linear segments should not contain more than five or six screens.

Star Structures

Star structures are used when one idea or screen branches to several other, single ideas. Many web pages and hypermedia programs are designed with a star format. For example, a web page may provide information about a school (see Figure 4.4). From the main page, hyperlinks allow access to other pages with the sports schedule, school address, student activities, and so on. Each of the linked pages branches directly back to the introduction/menu page.

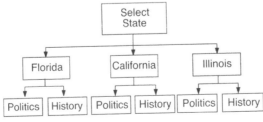

Figure 4.2. Tree structure.

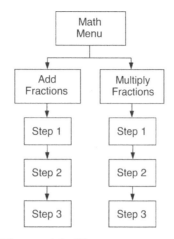

Figure 4.3. Cluster structure.

A star structure allows the user to branch out in any direction from the Main Menu. At that point, you can return to the Main Menu or explore the current topic/area.

Flowchart Symbols

Students should be encouraged to flowchart their lessons after the content outline is complete. Several standard symbols are used in flowcharts. For example, a diamond generally represents a decision point, and a small circle serves as a connector from one part of the flowchart to another. These symbols can be created by hand, with rulers, with drawing templates, or with computer programs (such as Inspiration, PowerPoint, etc.).

When creating flowcharts, ask the students to label each element. With proper labeling, they will be able to easily match the flowchart components with the details of the program. Figure 4.5 is a flowchart of a program about Florida that was created with Inspiration. Each symbol in the figure has a short title, and connectors are used to return to the menu.

Young students can also create flowcharts using the symbol libraries in Kidspiration. For example, the flowchart in Figure 4.6 was created for a third-grade presentation about farm animals.

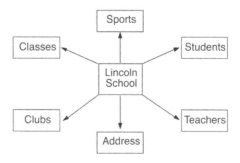

Figure 4.4. Star structure.

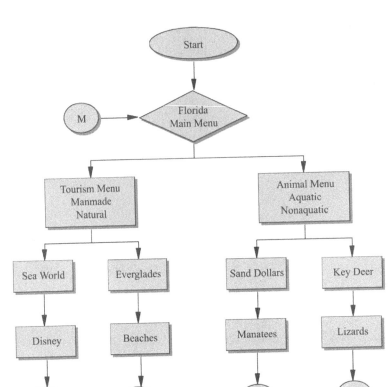

Figure 4.5. Flowchart for project about Florida (created in Inspiration).

SPECIFYING SCREEN DESIGN

After the sequencing and general flow of the project is diagrammed, the students should determine the "look and feel" of the screens that will be used in the project. Screen design is especially important for web pages, hypermedia programs, and presentations. Specifying the functional areas of the screen generally includes defining the location and size of titles/banners, main content area, navigation, and other items.

Depending on the project type and method of delivery, the navigation within a project may vary considerably. For example, if the project is a podcast or video, the navigation options are generally preset and limited to Stop, Play, or Rewind. However, if the project is designed as a website or interactive program, there must be sufficient prompts, menus, or links to help users navigate through the project.

Screen Design for Web Pages

For consistency, pages on a website should contain defined functional areas. For example, web pages are generally divided into the following major areas:

- *Banner or Header.* The title of each screen is usually located at the top of the page. It may be a graphical banner or a logo with large text.

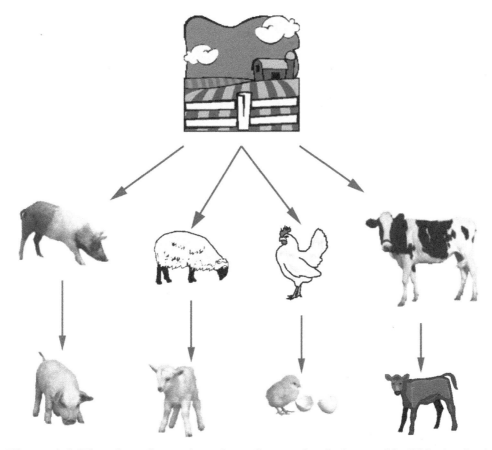

Figure 4.6. Flowchart for project about farm animals (created in Kidspiration).

- *Navigation.* The navigation menu (tabs or buttons) are most often located directly under the header, or on the left side of the screen (see Figure 4.7).

- *Content Area.* The content is generally the largest area. It generally contains text and images. In some cases, it may be divided into two or three columns (see Figure 4.7).

- *Footer.* The footer runs across the bottom of the page. If the page is long and involves lots of scrolling, the footer may contain a secondary, textual menu.

A wide variety of screen templates are appropriate for web pages, including two or three columns of content, sidebars with links, galleries of photos, etc. If your students are using Weebly to

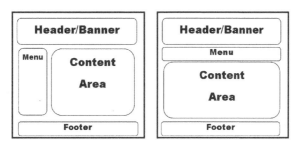

Figure 4.7. Common screen designs for websites.

create a website, they will have a wide variety of structures from which to choose. Templates and examples of web-based pages and projects are provided in Chapter 10.

Screen Design for Hypermedia Programs

Hypermedia programs usually contain three major screen types: instructional screens, menu screens, and question screens. The functional areas will vary based on the purpose of each screen and on the programming tool used. The primary functional areas for a presentation or instructional screen may include:

- *Title.* The title of each screen is usually located at the top or on the left side.

- *Informational/instructional text.* The text should be located in a consistent area of the screen.

- *Graphics.* The graphics can be placed on the side of the text, above it, or below it.

- *Directions or student prompt.* If user input is required, a prompt area should be included.

- *Navigation options.* The navigational options (buttons) are usually located along one of the edges of the screen.

Note that in Figure 4.8, the text in the first image is on the left, the graphic is on the right, and the navigation options are on the bottom. This is only one example of the numerous possibilities for instructional templates. For example, the text could be above the graphic; or it might be a text-only screen.

Menu screens and question screens will have slightly different functional areas. For example, the second image in Figure 4.8 contains the following areas:

- *Title.* The title of each screen is usually located at the top or on the left side.

- *Directions and Question.* The question should be located in a consistent area of the screen.

- *Answer Choices.* The answers choices might consist of textual options or graphical areas.

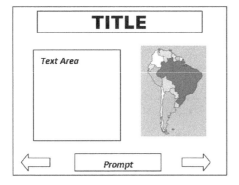 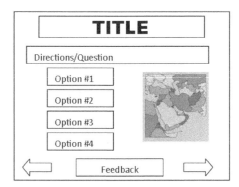

Figure 4.8. Common screen designs for hypermedia.

- *Graphics.* Graphics may be used as part of the question or as answer options.

- *Feedback.* Feedback may appear in a pop-up dialog box or in a consistent location on the screen.

- *Navigation options.* Because of their branching ability, questions and other types of interactions are common in hypermedia programs. The feedback for correct and incorrect responses may be provided by branching to a different screen, or a pop-up dialog box might provide the feedback. The navigational options (buttons) are usually located along one of the edges of the screen.

Screen Design for Presentation Programs

Presentation programs, such as PowerPoint and Keynote, are not designed to provide as much interactivity as hypermedia programs (although action buttons can be inserted to provide branching capabilities). Presentation programs generally include design templates and backgrounds that have been professionally developed. Figure 4.9 illustrates some of the basic layouts that are provided with PowerPoint. Most of these layouts and templates are designed for projecting to a large audience. In most cases, the font is large and the text is presented in bulleted lists. See Chapter 8 for project ideas using presentation programs.

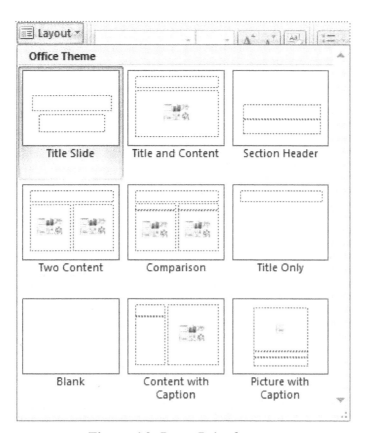

Figure 4.9. PowerPoint layouts.

CREATING SCRIPTS AND STORYBOARDS

After the content has been outlined and the screen designs have been determined, the storyboards can be created. Storyboards contain all the information that will be placed on the screens as well as information that will help the programmer and production specialists develop the media components. Storyboards can be thought of as "blueprints" for the program or project. They provide the visual representation of the screen, as well as scripts for the audio, details for the video, and branching information.

General Planning Sheet

Before beginning the storyboards, it may be helpful to have the students fill out a general planning sheet. This sheet provides an opportunity for the students to allocate, or chunk, the information into separate screens without specifying all the details. Figure 4.10 illustrates the manner in which a title screen and instructional screen can be completed. (A Planning Sheet blackline master is provided at the end of this chapter as a tool for students.)

An alternative to using a planning sheet is to have the students outline their screens on 3- × 5-inch or 5- × 8-inch index cards. Each card can be used to represent one computer screen or page. The students can divide each card into functional areas and place the content (text and graphics) on the screen in the appropriate places. The backs of the cards can be used to provide information for navigation and media elements. An advantage of using this method is that the students can arrange (and rearrange) the cards on a desk in the sequence appropriate for the program, before finalizing the storyboards.

Style Guides

In some cases, students should have full rein to select any color, text style, images, etc., that they think are appropriate for their projects. Sometimes, however, it is a good idea to discuss options and create a style guide as a class, prior to individuals or groups beginning their projects. For example, if each group is creating a chapter that will be compiled into an eBook, it is important not only to use the same screen design but also to have consistent text, colors, and buttons from chapter to chapter. Likewise if *different groups are* producing pages on a single website or portions of a presentation, they need to have the same navigation and a consistent look.

An example style guide might include items such as:

- Titles: 18-point font; navy, bold, all caps; Arial

- Content: 12-point font; black, Arial

- Backgrounds: Light blue

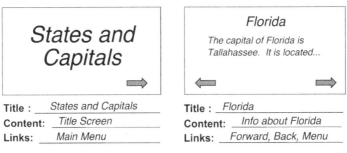

Figure 4.10. General planning sheet.

- Images: No more than two per page

- Navigation: Forward and Back icons are arrows in the lower corners of the screen (see network file and template)

Detailed Storyboards and Scripts

After the general plan is outlined, encourage the students to write detailed storyboards and scripts for the project, especially if it is complex. Storyboards are more detailed than planning sheets because they contain all the descriptive information required to produce the text, graphics, animations, audio, and video for the project. Each storyboard should contain a display area, branching information for the programmer (if appropriate), details about the font size and color, script for narration, sketches of images, etc.

Storyboarding is not an easy task for many students. One way to encourage good techniques is to review and "sign off" on the storyboards before the students begin producing the projects (see the Storyboard Review blackline master at the end of this chapter). If the students have thoroughly outlined their content and approach via storyboards, their time spent on the computer or with the video camera will be much more efficient. Keep in mind, however, that the level of detail required in storyboards may vary based on the age of the students, the complexity of the project, the time allotted to the project, and other factors.

There are many different ways to structure a storyboard—they can be single pages for each screen, or several screens can be depicted on one page. For example, Figure 4.11 represents a storyboard for a digital video program. Note that the first column of the video storyboard is used to specify the different screen shots (such as close-up, wide shot, over the shoulder, etc.), action, costumes, etc. The middle column can be used to draw a rough sketch of the scene; and the last column outlines the narration audio components.

On the other hand, a storyboard for hypermedia contains information about buttons, links, and colors, as well as a display area for sketches and text (see Figure 4.12).

Blackline masters are provided at the end of this chapter for creating storyboards for hypermedia, presentation, web-based, podcast, and video projects. These storyboards can be copied and distributed to the students. Advanced students may want to create their own storyboards in PowerPoint, word processors, databases, or other applications. Storyboard tools and templates are also available on the web (see the Resources section at the end of this chapter).

GENERAL DESIGN GUIDELINES

As students add details to their storyboards for presentations, hypermedia, or web pages, they will have to make numerous decisions. The following design guidelines can help students specify information related to text, menus, icons, and buttons. Guidelines for media elements, such as graphics, animations, audio, and video, are provided in Chapter 5. Information about development programs, such as HyperStudio, PowerPoint, HTML, etc., is included in Chapter 6.

Guidelines for Text

- Left-justify the text (not centered).

- Use mixed case (not all caps).

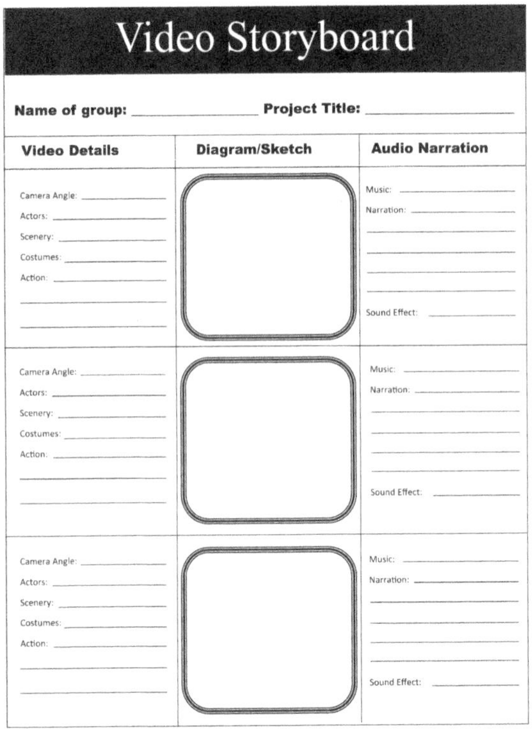

Video Storyboard

Name of group: ______ Project Title: ______

Video Details	Diagram/Sketch	Audio Narration
Camera Angle: ______ Actors: ______ Scenery: ______ Costumes: ______ Action: ______		Music: ______ Narration: ______ Sound Effect: ______
Camera Angle: ______ Actors: ______ Scenery: ______ Costumes: ______ Action: ______		Music: ______ Narration: ______ Sound Effect: ______
Camera Angle: ______ Actors: ______ Scenery: ______ Costumes: ______ Action: ______		Music: ______ Narration: ______ Sound Effect: ______

Figure 4.11. Video storyboard (see full-size blackline master at end of chapter).

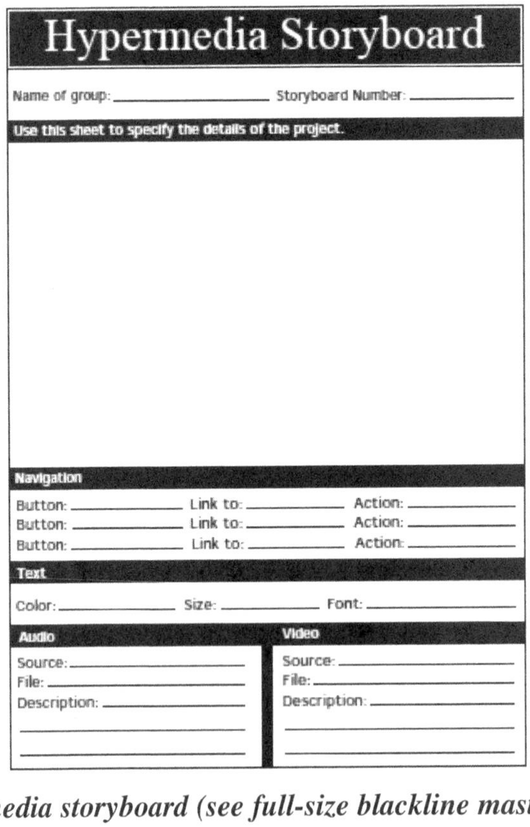

Hypermedia Storyboard

Name of group: ______ Storyboard Number: ______

Use this sheet to specify the details of the project.

Navigation

Button: ______ Link to: ______ Action: ______
Button: ______ Link to: ______ Action: ______
Button: ______ Link to: ______ Action: ______

Text

Color: ______ Size: ______ Font: ______

Audio

Source: ______
File: ______
Description: ______

Video

Source: ______
File: ______
Description: ______

Figure 4.12. Hypermedia storyboard (see full-size blackline master at end of chapter).

- Avoid long lines of text.

- Double-space text if possible.

- Keep sentences short and sweet.

- Use active tense.

- Chunk information into short paragraphs.

- Do not blink text unnecessarily.

- Use at least 12-point font size for hypermedia and web pages.

- Use at least 24-point font size for presentation projects.

- Use generic fonts that are available on all computers.

- Do not place text on a background that has a pattern or graphic.

Guidelines for Menus

- Provide between three and six options on a menu.

- Include an exit option on all menus.

- Clearly state the directions for selecting menu options.

- Include titles on all menus.

- Place menu options in logical sequence.

Guidelines for Links and Navigational Buttons

- Place links in consistent locations throughout the program.

- Use common icons (such as arrows) for navigation.

- If a link is inactive, remove it or make it dim.

- Make links big enough for users to click.

- Provide instructions to help users navigate.

- Place permanent links along the edge of the screen.

- Include options for users to back up and exit.

Guidelines for Color

- Use fewer than seven colors per screen.

- Use consistent background colors.

- Use consistent text colors.

- On dark backgrounds, use light text.

- On light backgrounds, use dark text.

- Highlight key words in a contrasting color.

- Do not use red backgrounds.

SUMMARY

The DESIGN phase is crucial to developing a successful digital project. Teachers should emphasize the importance of outlining the content of the project and present design guidelines through the use of examples and nonexamples. In addition, teachers can demonstrate the use of storyboards and scripts to help students plan and structure their projects prior to the production of graphics, video, and other media. The blackline masters at the end of this chapter, as well as Internet resources, can assist teachers and students in the design aspects of digital projects.

RESOURCES

How to Create Storyboards: http://digitalstorytelling.coe.uh.edu/page.cfm?id=23&cid=23&sublinkid=37

Inspiration: http://www.inspiration.com/

Kidspiration: http://www.kidspiration.com/Kidspiration

Multimedia in the Classroom: http://fcit.usf.edu/multimedia/

Photo Story: http://www.microsoft.com/en-us/download/details.aspx?id=11132

Storyboard Depot: http://theelearningcoach.com/resources/storyboard-depot/

Storyboard Pro (Atomic Learning): http://www.atomiclearning.com/storyboardpro

BLACKLINE MASTERS

A variety of blackline masters are presented in this chapter to help teachers and students design digital projects. Practice activities are included to help students with flowcharting. The following blackline masters conclude this chapter:

- Project Checklist: a general checklist of expectations for multimedia projects

- Intention Outline: an outline of intent that specifies the goals and content of a project

- Project Structures: illustrations of different flowcharts

- The Bunny Hop: a flowchart sequencing activity

- Medusa's Market: a flowchart sequencing activity
- Planning Sheet: a tool to assist students in planning their storyboards
- Presentation Storyboard: a sample presentation storyboard template
- Hypermedia Storyboard: a sample hypermedia storyboard template
- Web Storyboard: a sample storyboard template for Web projects
- Video Storyboard: a sample storyboard for digital video projects
- Storyboard Review: a preliminary evaluation sheet to help students produce and revise their storyboards.

Project Checklist

Team Name _____

Before developing your project at the computer, complete the following:

☐ Intention Outline   ☐ Flowchart
☐ Planning Sheet   ☐ Storyboards

Make sure your project has:

☐ a minimum of _____ pages (or cards).

☐ a maximum of _____ pages (or cards).

☐ a Title page (or card).

☐ credits (designers and bibliography information).

☐ a Main Menu.

☐ appropriate navigation options.

☐ text that is easy to read and is accurate.

☐ complete sentences with correct punctuation, grammar, and spelling.

☐ the assigned media requirements.

_____ Clip Art   _____ Animation   _____ Video

_____ Scanned Image   _____ Digitized Camera Photo

_____ Original Audio   _____ Clip Sound (digitized)

_____ MIDI File   _____ Original Graphic

☐ Other: _____

_____

Intention Outline

Project Title: _____

General Goal: _____

Specific Outcomes: _____

_____

Audience

Who will use this project (e.g., students, teachers, parents)?

Content Outline

I. _____

    A. _____

    B. _____

    C. _____

II. _____

    A. _____

    B. _____

    C. _____

III. _____

    A. _____

    B. _____

    C. _____

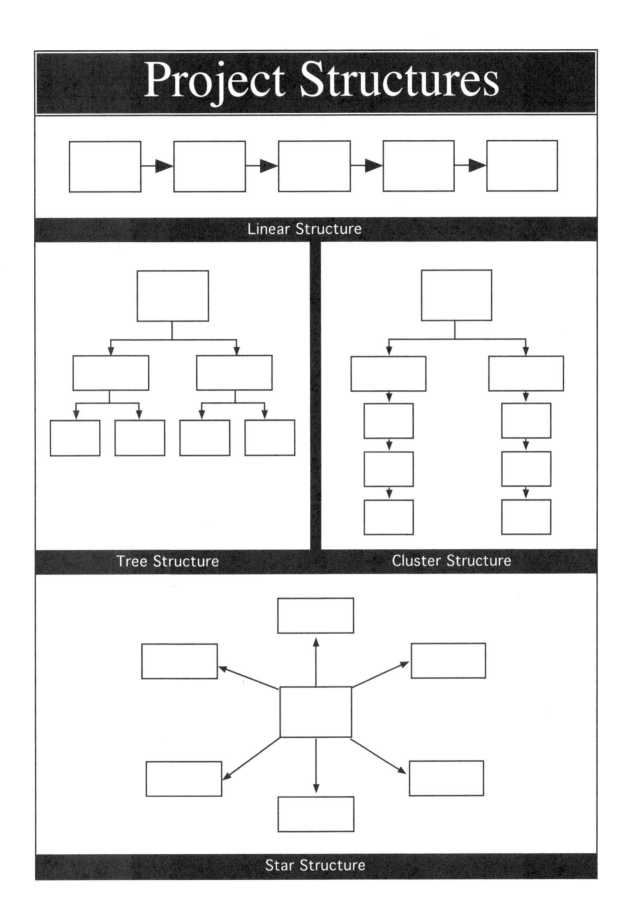

Project Structures

Linear Structure

Tree Structure

Cluster Structure

Star Structure

The Bunny Hop

Benjamin Bunny is helping his friend hide eggs. Help Benjamin figure out what to do by placing a letter in the correct section of the flowchart. Remember that diamond shapes are for asking questions and box shapes are for decisions. Two are already done for you.

_____ A. Wait ten minutes.

_____ B. Hide egg.

_____ C. Is anyone peeking?

_____ D. Continue to hop down the bunny trail.

_____ E. Place colored eggs into basket.

_____ F. Are there eggs in the basket?

_____ G. Hop down the bunny trail.

_____ H. Look for a place to hide egg.

_____ I. Go home.

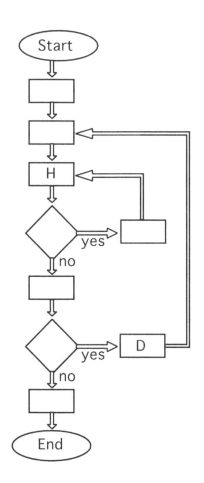

Extension ideas: Create a flowchart for getting ready for school in the morning, cooking your favorite meal, or packing for a vacation.

Answer: E, G, H, C (yes is A), B, F (yes is D), I

Medusa's Market

Medusa needs to go to the grocery store. Help her get into her car and drive to the grocery store's parking lot by placing a letter in the correct section of the flowchart. Remember that diamond shapes are for asking questions and box shapes are for decisions. Three are already done for you.

_____ A. Insert ignition key.

_____ B. Shut door.

_____ C. Is the light green?

_____ D. Put on safety belt.

_____ E. Open door.

_____ F. Wait.

_____ G. Is there a parking space?

_____ H. Get into car.

_____ I. Pull into parking space.

_____ J. Drive to stop light.

_____ K. Drive into parking lot.

_____ L. Look for parking space.

_____ M. Turn off ignition.

_____ N. Exit parking lot.

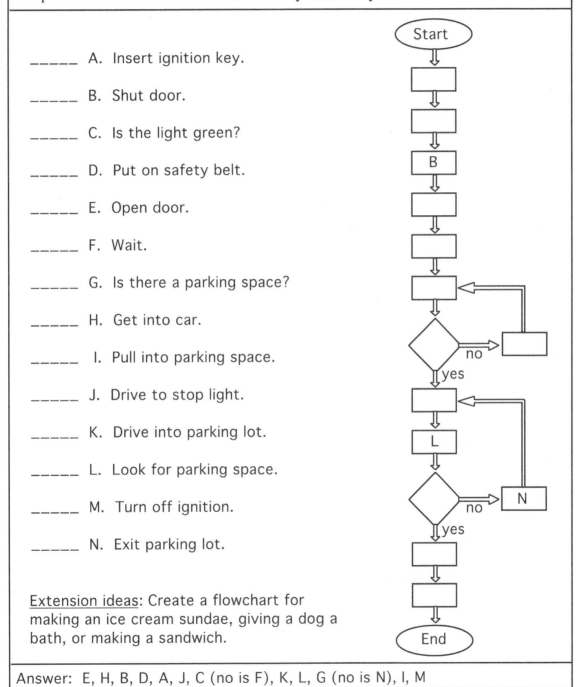

Extension ideas: Create a flowchart for making an ice cream sundae, giving a dog a bath, or making a sandwich.

Answer: E, H, B, D, A, J, C (no is F), K, L, G (no is N), I, M

Planning Sheet

Name of group: _____

Use this sheet to plan the general content of your pages.

```
┌─────────────────────────┐        ┌─────────────────────────┐
│                         │        │                         │
│                         │        │                         │
│                         │        │                         │
│                         │        │                         │
│                         │        │                         │
│                         │        │                         │
└─────────────────────────┘        └─────────────────────────┘
```

Title: _____   Title: _____
Content: _____   Content: _____
Links: _____   Links: _____

```
┌─────────────────────────┐        ┌─────────────────────────┐
│                         │        │                         │
│                         │        │                         │
│                         │        │                         │
│                         │        │                         │
│                         │        │                         │
│                         │        │                         │
└─────────────────────────┘        └─────────────────────────┘
```

Title: _____   Title: _____
Content: _____   Content: _____
Links: _____   Links: _____

```
┌─────────────────────────┐        ┌─────────────────────────┐
│                         │        │                         │
│                         │        │                         │
│                         │        │                         │
│                         │        │                         │
│                         │        │                         │
│                         │        │                         │
└─────────────────────────┘        └─────────────────────────┘
```

Title: _____   Title: _____
Content: _____   Content: _____
Links: _____   Links: _____

Presentation Storyboard

Name of group: _____ Storyboard Number: _____

Use this sheet to specify the details of the project.

Template

Name: _____ Color: _____ Layout: _____

Text

Color: _____ Size: _____ Font: _____

Transition: _____ Build: _____

Audio

Source: _____

File: _____

Description: _____

_____

_____

Video

Source: _____

File: _____

Description: _____

_____

_____

Hypermedia Storyboard

Name of group: _____ Storyboard Number: _____

Use this sheet to specify the details of the project.

Navigation

Button: _____ Link to: _____ Action: _____
Button: _____ Link to: _____ Action: _____
Button: _____ Link to: _____ Action: _____

Text

Color: _____ Size: _____ Font: _____

Audio

Source: _____
File: _____
Description: _____
_____
_____

Video

Source: _____
File: _____
Description: _____
_____
_____

Web Storyboard

Name of group: _____ Storyboard Number: _____

Use this sheet to specify the details of the project.

Navigation

Hyperlink: _____ Link to: _____

Hyperlink: _____ Link to: _____

Hyperlink: _____ Link to: _____

Text and Background

Text Color: _____ Size: _____ Font: _____

Background Color: _____ Background Graphic: _____

Audio

Source: _____

File: _____

Description: _____

_____

Graphic

Source: _____

File: _____

Description: _____

_____

Video Storyboard

Name of group: _____ **Project Title:** _____

Video Details	Diagram/Sketch	Audio Narration
Camera Angle: _____ Actors: _____ Scenery: _____ Costumes: _____ Action: _____ _____ _____		Music: _____ Narration: _____ _____ _____ _____ _____ Sound Effect: _____
Camera Angle: _____ Actors: _____ Scenery: _____ Costumes: _____ Action: _____ _____ _____		Music: _____ Narration: _____ _____ _____ _____ _____ Sound Effect: _____
Camera Angle: _____ Actors: _____ Scenery: _____ Costumes: _____ Action: _____ _____ _____		Music: _____ Narration: _____ _____ _____ _____ _____ Sound Effect: _____

Storyboard Review

Students included:	Yes	No	N/A
a title screen	–––	–––	–––
a credit screen	–––	–––	–––
directions/information for the user	–––	–––	–––
a main menu	–––	–––	–––
forward and back links	–––	–––	–––
factual and interesting information	–––	–––	–––
consistent and clear layout designs	–––	–––	–––
required media elements	–––	–––	–––
font information for text boxes	–––	–––	–––
font information for titles	–––	–––	–––
background information	–––	–––	–––
––––––––––––––––––––––	–––	–––	–––
––––––––––––––––––––––	–––	–––	–––
––––––––––––––––––––––	–––	–––	–––

Comments:

_____

_____

_____

_____

Chapter 5

DEVELOP: Media Elements

A SCENARIO

Joey, Paula, Rudy, and Olivia decided to create a public awareness message about childhood cancer for the research project in social studies. Olivia's two-year-old cousin had recently been diagnosed with neuroblastoma, and Olivia was all too aware of the frustrations and stress the family was facing with his treatment.

Their first step was to conduct web searches and learn more about pediatric cancer. The students were amazed to learn that seven children die each day from cancer in the United States and that only 4 percent of the dollars allocated to cancer research is targeted toward children's cancers. There were plenty of facts for their project, but they also wanted a personal perspective so they wrote questions and set up interviews with the Olivia's aunt and uncle.

As a team, they worked together to design the program by sketching storyboards with the text for each screen and writing scripts for the narration. They decided to use PowerPoint as their authoring tool, where all of the slides, images, narration, and interviews could be compiled. When the project was complete and approved by their teacher, they planned to save the presentation as a movie file and upload their message to YouTube.

Rudy suggested that they use his tablet computer to record the interviews. It worked great. Olivia and Rudy conducted the interviews, saved the files, and edited them in Audacity, an audio editor. Then, Rudy cropped parts of the audio they did not need and adjusted the volume levels to make everything consistent. Meanwhile, Joey and Paula created the slides in PowerPoint, adding the images and narration they had specified. When all of the components were compiled and tested, they added the transitions and saved the file as a movie.

After their teacher reviewed the project, the digital movie was uploaded to YouTube. The students were very hopeful that their message would encourage others to become more aware of the need to focus more research in this critical area.

OVERVIEW

The third phase of the DDD-E model is DEVELOP, which includes producing the media components, such as text, graphics, animations, audio, and video. It also covers the authoring or construction of the program. This chapter focuses on designing and producing the media; Chapter 6 outlines the tools available for authoring and delivery.

Media elements (graphics, animation, audio, and video) are key components of digital projects. They can help bring a presentation to life by providing realism, color, motion, and sound. Used effectively, media elements add many instructional benefits, enhance visual literacy, and address multiple intelligences and learning styles. This chapter outlines the procedures for creating and editing graphics, animations, audio, and video elements. Guidelines for implementing media elements and an appendix of media resources are also provided. Topics include:

Graphics

- Creating a graphic
- Importing an existing graphic file
- Scanning graphics
- Capturing digital images with a camera
- Guidelines for graphics

Animations

- Frame animations
- Stop motion animations
- Path animations
- Guidelines for animations

Audio

- Digital audio
- Recording audio with computers
- Synthesized speech
- Music

Composition software

- Digital audio file formats
- Using existing audio files
- Podcasting audio
- Guidelines for audio

Digital video

- Digitizing and editing video
- Digital video file formats
- Guidelines for video

GRAPHICS

The term *graphics* refers to images or any information that is presented via pictures, drawings, or paintings. There are many ways to obtain graphics for a project: they can be created from scratch with a software program, they can be imported from an existing file, they can be scanned from a hard copy, or they can be digitized with a camera. Each method has advantages and disadvantages.

Creating a Graphic

Many image programs are available, including Adobe Photoshop, CorelDraw, Microsoft Paint, iPhoto, Pixlr, and GIMP. These programs vary in price, sophistication, and many other attributes, but they can all be used to manipulate digital graphics and then save them in various file formats. Digital graphics (and image programs) can be roughly divided into two types: paint (bitmapped) or draw (vector).

Paint (Bitmapped) Graphics

To visualize bitmaps, think of a piece of graph paper. Each of the individual small squares represents a *pixel* (which means *pic*ture *el*ement). When you are "painting" a bitmapped image, all you are doing is filling in each individual pixel or group of pixels with a solid color. The small pixels can be arranged to form a graphic, similar to a Lite-Brite toy. In this type of program, the pixels retain their independence. In other words, even if the pixels are positioned to form the appearance of a square, when you zoom in, you can see that the square is made up of tiny, individual pixels (see Figure 5.1). If students want to move a graphic (such as a square) after it has been created or edited, they must use a selection tool (such as the lasso) to select all of the pixels that are to be moved.

If the pixels are small, the picture will look sharper. The number of pixels you have for your image is called the image resolution. The resolution of a computer screen or graphic is expressed as the number of pixels wide by the number of pixels tall. For example, a resolution of 1,024 × 768 means it is 1,024 pixels wide by 768 pixels tall.

There are numerous software programs that can be used to create or manipulate bitmapped graphics; they are often referred to as *paint programs*. Popular examples include Adobe Photoshop,

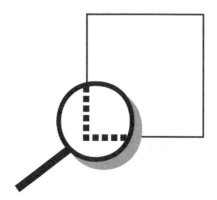

Figure 5.1. A bitmapped graphic is made up of individual pixels.

Microsoft Paint, and Pixlr (to create or edit images) and iPhoto and Picasa (to edit images). With these programs, you can easily add effects such as distortions, textures, or gradients.

Draw (Vector) Graphics

A vector (object-oriented) graphic might look similar to a bitmapped image when it appears on the computer screen, but it is stored in a very different manner. Object-oriented drawings consist of geometric shapes instead of individual pixels, and they work more like a collage (made up of shapes). When you draw an object (for example, a square), the computer knows it as a square and will always treat it as a square. If you were to zoom in to the graphic, you would not see individual pixels (see Figure 5.2).

Object-oriented images are ideal for geometric drawings such as blueprints, charts, or line drawings. Because the images consist of geometric figures, they can be layered on top of each other and still retain their identity. When an object is "selected," tiny handlebars appear to allow you to change the size of the image. It is possible to select an object and bring it on top, push it back, or move it around, without affecting anything else on the screen. Any object can be selected at any time, and you can change its attributes, such as line thickness, line color, line style, and so forth. If the object is a closed figure, you can also determine the color and pattern that fill the enclosed region.

Popular software programs for vector graphics include CorelDraw and Adobe Illustrator. Software applications, such as PowerPoint and Word, also contain drawing features that can be used to create vector graphics.

One of the main differences between bitmaps and vector drawings is that bitmaps are resolution dependent whereas vector drawings are resolution independent. That means that if you create a bitmapped image at a certain size, it should be viewed at that size. Enlarging it would make it look awful—all of the pixels would be stretched, and the image would look very pixilated (blocky). Vector drawings, however, can be enlarged to any size, even stretched to different aspect ratios, and they will always look smooth, because they will adjust to the resolution of the screen or printer. For example, the first image in Figure 5.3 was created as a bitmap and then stretched; the second figure was created as a vector graphic and then stretched. Note that the lines on the second image are smooth.

Importing an Existing Graphic File

In some cases, students may not have the time or software programs required to create their own graphics, and they may find it more expedient to use existing images. Many programs provide

Figure 5.2. Vector graphics do not contain individual pixels.

Figure 5.3. Stretching bitmaps and vector images.

a collection of clip art that can be easily imported. For example, PowerPoint and Keynote both have options to "*Insert Clip Art.*" In addition, there are numerous clip art sites available on the Internet such ClipArt and ClipPix ETC (see Graphic Resources at the end of this chapter). You can also go to Google and click on "Images" to search the web for images.

Some clip art is *public domain* (meaning it is free for anyone to use), and some may be *royalty free* (meaning that someone owns the copyright but allows you to use it with certain restrictions). Many people incorrectly believe that everything posted on the Internet is public domain; the truth is the exact opposite. All images and documents are protected by copyright laws, whether they are on the Internet or not. If you or your students see a graphic on a web page that you would like to use, you must read the copyright notice and, if necessary, request permission from the artist who created it—especially if it will be used beyond the classroom.

The key to importing existing graphics files into a program is to make sure that the files are in a compatible format. For example, PowerPoint will open and display graphics files that have the extension BMP, PICT, TIFF, GIF, JPG, and others, whereas graphic files on websites are almost always stored in GIF, JPEG, and PNG format. See Table 5.1 for a list of common graphics formats.

If you have a graphic that is not in the appropriate format, you can use an image program or a graphic converter to change the format. For example, if you had a PICT graphic and you wanted to place it on a web page, you could open it in Adobe PhotoShop and save it as a GIF file. It is important to note that the file extension (such as image.gif) indicates only the type of file format; it is not the file format itself. Merely changing the extension on a file does not change the file's contents any more than changing the label on a can of peas will turn it into applesauce. To change a file from one format to another, you must use an image editor or an image conversion program.

Scanning Graphics

There are many times when students may want to use an image for a project that currently exists only as a hard copy, such as a photograph or a drawing in a book. *Scanners* are computer peripherals used to convert print materials (hard copies) and other objects into images on

Table 5.1. Common Graphic Formats

Extension	Description	Platform	Application
BMP	Microsoft Bitmap	Windows	Windows applications
WMF	Windows Metafile	Windows	Windows applications
PICT	Macintosh Picture Format	Macintosh	Macintosh applications
TIFF	Tagged Image File Format	Windows, Macintosh	Common format for exchanging files between platforms
EPS	Encapsulated PostScript	Windows, Macintosh	Common for printed documents
GIF	Graphics Interchange Format	Windows, Macintosh	Common on the web
JPEG (JPG)	Joint Photographic Experts Group	Windows, Macintosh	Common on the web
PNG	Portable Network Graphic	Windows, Macintosh	Common on the web

a computer. Capturing images with a scanner makes it possible to incorporate a wide variety of photographs and other images into digital projects.

The typical scanning process is similar to copying a piece of paper on a photocopy machine. The paper copy is placed on a scanner, a light passes under it, and a bitmapped image is created. The difference is that instead of producing a copy on paper, the image is transferred to the computer.

Scanners come with software that offers several settings. These settings can have an impact on the quality of the scanned image and the size of the file. When students scan graphics, caution them to scan only the portion of the picture that they need. Also, they should select a resolution of about 72 dots per inch (dpi) or pixels per inch (ppi). Scanning at a higher resolution for display on a computer screen will result in a very large file, with little or no difference in quality on the display. After the image is scanned, it should be saved, or exported, in a format that is compatible with the presentation—in other words, if it is going to be used on a web page, it should be saved as a GIF or JPG file.

Capturing Digital Images with a Camera

Images can also be captured with a digital camera, smartphone, tablet, etc. Current cameras are capable of taking very high resolution images. For example, a single image can easily be more than $3,264 \times 2,448$ pixels and more than three megabytes in file size. Images of this size are far too large to display efficiently on a computer, will quickly fill a digital storage device, and are slow to transfer over the Internet. There are two ways the file size can be constrained. First, you could caution students to capture images at a lower resolution, and, second, teach them how to resample and compress the images after they are captured. For example, pictures inserted in Microsoft Word can be compressed using the "Compress Picture" option in the Picture Tools.

Guideline for Graphics

The following guidelines can help you and your students determine the appropriate use of graphics in digital projects.

- Use graphics to enhance the project and illustrate important concepts.
- Do not include graphics that distract from the project.
- If possible, use several simple graphics rather than one complex graphic.
- If complex graphics are required, add arrows or highlight boxes to help focus attention on the relevant areas.
- If graphic icons are used for buttons or other similar elements, be consistent—always use the same icon for the same function.
- Be consistent when placing graphics—designate one part of the screen for graphics and another part for text, title, and so on.
- Keep file sizes as small as possible (by using compression, etc.).
- Graphics should be scanned at 72–100 dpi (if they are going to be displayed on a computer screen).
- Check copyright restrictions on all graphics that will be used outside the classroom.
- Graphics that are incorporated into web pages should be less than 50K to minimize transfer time.
- Before editing, cropping, or compressing images, save a copy of the original file.

ANIMATIONS

Animations are graphics that imitate movement. All animations consist of a series of images (with minor changes from one to the next) that are shown in rapid succession and "fool" the eye into seeing motion. Animations help convey and reinforce complex concepts. For example, an animation may be used to depict the flow of electricity, cell division, or a volcano eruption. Although animations can add a wealth of information and excitement to multimedia projects, they can also be time-consuming to develop. This section outlines three types of animations (frame, stop motion, and path), presents resources for locating animations, and provides guidelines for the use of animations.

Frame Animations

Frame animations were popularized by movie and cartoon animators who use them to create the illusion of motion. The first Mickey Mouse cartoon was created by drawing many images with very slight differences between the images. When the images are played in rapid sequence

Figure 5.4. Graphics for a frame animation.

(usually 5–15 frames per second), they blend together, and we see Mickey walking and dancing. Likewise, to create frame animations on a computer, you must draw several frames and play them in rapid succession (see Figure 5.4).

GIF animations (which are made up of a series of GIF images) are common on the web. GIF animations are popular because they are small (in file size) and easy to create. For example, if you watch an animation of a small mailbox that opens and closes, you will note that it is made up of three or four images that cycle over and over again. You can locate thousands of GIF animations in clip art galleries on the web.

You can also create your own GIF animations by producing a series of still images that have slight alterations from one image to the next. Then, using image editors or software tools such as GIMP or PhotoShop, you can set the play time so that each image will display a split second before the next one appears.

Stop Motion Animations

Stop motion animation is similar to frame animation, except it uses real objects instead of two-dimensional images. The object (which could be a clay figure, a doll with movable joints, a ball, a person, etc.) is photographed as it is repositioned or changed in small increments between frames. Then, when the frames are played in a continuous sequence, the illusion of motion appears.

There are several software programs that can be used to create stop motion animation (including iMovie and Windows Movie Maker). Two popular programs include Stop Motion Animator and Monkey Jam. Both are free. The general procedure for creating stop motion animation involves:

1. Plan your animation (with planning sheets, scripts, storyboards, etc.).

2. Make or obtain objects/figures for your animation. This could be clay figures, pipe cleaners, play-doh, action figures, etc.

3. Find or create a set (a cardboard box would work).

4. Place a camera (or webcam) in front of your set—be sure it is on a tripod or something so it will be very steady.

5. Set up adequate lighting (the final animations are generally a bit darker than the original images).

6. Take a single photo of the figure(s) in the initial position. If you are using a software program, such as Stop Motion Animator, with a camera attached to the computer, you can simply click "Grab."

7. Move the object(s) in small increments, taking a photo after each movement/change (see Figure 5.5).

Figure 5.5. Single photos for stop motion animation.

8. Save the photos. Then record the images with a very short duration for each (<3 seconds each).

9. Add audio, sound effects, etc.

10. Save the completed file in an appropriate format.

Path Animations

A *path animation* involves moving an object on a screen that has a constant background. For example, a title may "fly in" from the left side, an airplane may fly across the page, or a ball may bounce through a scene. Creating a path animation is much easier then creating a frame animation; you create the object you want to animate, then you move it along a path.

Some programs include features that can easily create path animations. For example, Power-Point provides numerous predesigned animation schemes (such as "fade in and dim" or "boomerang and exit") for titles and bullets on the slides. The timing, sequence, speed, and direction of these schemes can be easily modified.

PowerPoint also has a path (called motion) animation option that allows you to specify the path an object (text or graphic) will follow. For example, if you wanted to animate a plane flying across the screen, you would follow these steps:

1. Create a slide and insert a small picture of an airplane.

2. Select "Add Animation" from the Animations menu.

3. Highlight (click) the object (airplane) that you want to animate.

4. Scroll down and select "Custom Path" from the "Motion Paths" category on the Effects menu.

5. Click the mouse and hold it down as you drag the airplane across the screen to define the path (see Figure 5.6).

6. Double-click the mouse when you reach the end of the path.

7. Select "Play" to see the complete animation.

Flash by Adobe is another popular program for creating animations. Flash is popular for creating web animations because it uses vector graphics, which are often much smaller than the bit-mapped graphics. Flash also offers many sophisticated options, such as key frames and in-betweens. With these features, you can draw a character on frame 1, go to frame 10, grab its left

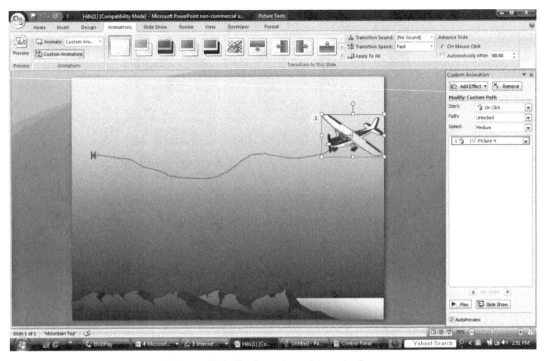

Figure 5.6. Path animation window.

arm, and raise it. The software will then calculate the arm's motion for frames 2 through 9 and create the individual images.

Guidelines for Animations

The following guidelines can help you and your students determine how to use animations appropriately:

- Use frame animation for two-dimensional sequences involving multiple changes.

- Use frame animation for three-dimensional sequences involving incremental differences.

- Use path animations to move one or two objects on a screen.

- Make sure the animation has a purpose.

- Do not include animations that distract from the content.

- Keep the animation sequences short, or allow the user an option to interrupt and proceed with the program.

- Avoid animations that loop infinitely—they can be distracting when the viewer is attempting to read the text on the page. If it must loop, limit it to two or three times.

- Test the animations on various computers and different browsers to ensure they display correctly.

- If the animation is designed for the web, keep the file size small.

AUDIO

Audio refers to sound elements in a program. These elements can include recorded narration, music, and sound effects (such as a bird singing or a telephone dial tone). Audio can assist students' learning, as well as add realism, excitement, and motivation to projects. For example, students can record oral histories, compose music, narrate a presentation, or add sound effects to a project.

There are many ways your students can add audio components to their projects. They can record the audio with a microphone (digital audio), use synthesized speech, create music, post podcasts, or import clip audio (elements that are available for free or for sale).

Digital Audio

Audio can be recorded with a computer and stored in a digital format on computer, smartphone, networks, and other storage devices. A major advantage of this technology is that teachers and students can record their own voices or sounds.

Bringing sound into the digital domain of computer bits and bytes requires a sampling process. At small but discrete time intervals, the computer takes a "snapshot" of the sound. This process is called sampling, and the number of samples taken each second is referred to as the sampling rate. The more samples, the better the sound quality. For example, audio sampled 44,000 times per second (44 kilohertz or kHz) will provide better quality than audio sampled 22,000 times per second (22 kHz). The most common sample rate is 44 kHz and most devices will default to this sampling rate, although a lower rate (such as 11kHz or 22kHz) is sufficient for voice narration.

Recording Audio with Computers

The recording process for digital audio is not difficult. Most digital devices have the necessary components built in for recording audio. To digitize audio, follow this procedure:

1. Plug a microphone into the audio input (or activate the internal microphone).

2. Open an audio recording program (for example, in PowerPoint, select "Insert . . . Audio . . . Record Audio").

3. Select a sampling rate and other parameters if they are available.

4. Click "Record."

5. Speak into the microphone.

6. Select "Stop" when you have recorded the segment you want.

7. Test the recording with the "Play" command. If it is acceptable, name the file and save.

Digitized sounds can be viewed and edited like text (see Figure 5.7). With the appropriate software program (such as Audacity, GarageBand, or GoldWave), sounds can be selected, cut, copied, pasted, and mixed with other sounds. Audio editing is a powerful tool that allows you to rearrange sounds or cut out parts you do not need.

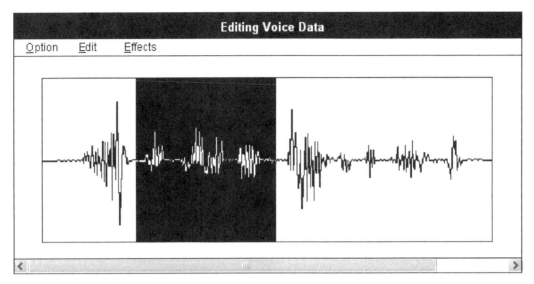

Figure 5.7. Editing an audio wave.

Synthesized Speech

Synthesized speech uses a computer program to translate text into spoken output without any recording process. It simply applies its phonetic rules to pronounce all of the words. The disadvantage of the text-to-speech synthesis method is that it may have an unnatural and mechanical sound. For instance, problems arise with words such as *live* that do not follow consistent rules of pronunciation. Most computer synthesizers cannot accurately differentiate between the use of *live* in these two sentences: "I live in Florida" and "We are using live bait."

Another problem with synthesized speech is that synthesizers do not have the natural inflections of a human voice; they may not "drop off" to indicate the end of a sentence as we do in natural speech. Most digital devices have built-in synthesized speech options in their Accessibility menu. For example, Narrator on a PC and VoiceOver on the Mac can read text on a screen. Other accessibility programs, such as Jaws and Thunder Screen Reader, can also be installed to provide narration for people who are sight impaired. Because the only component that the computer has to store is the text, the file size is very small for this type of audio. You can also convert text to an MP3 file with free programs such as the one found at SpokenText.net.

Music

There are several options for students who want to compose or play music on a computer. They can record MIDI files from an electronic keyboard or compose original music using a composition software program such as GarageBand.

Musical Instrument Digital Interface (MIDI)

One of the most compact and flexible formats used to store, transfer, and play music is *MIDI* (Musical Instrument Digital Interface). MIDI does not record the actual sounds; instead, it stores the instructions needed to tell the computer (and any connected MIDI devices) which instrument sound to use, which note to play, how loud it should be played, and so on. Similar to sheet music, MIDI files provide the instructions on how to reproduce the music. The computer then interprets the MIDI instructions and produces the music using the sounds that are embedded in the sound card or sound module.

The configuration for the MIDI includes MIDI software, a MIDI-equipped audio card or interface box, cables, speakers, and one or more MIDI instruments. Piano keyboards and other electronic instruments that contain synthesizers can be used to input the musical information to the computer software and to output the recorded songs.

A major advantage of MIDI technology is that it can store complex music in very small files. The MIDI files are a fraction of the size of digital audio files (up to 100 times smaller). This small file size results from the fact that MIDI music is *not* sampled and digitized like digital audio files. Instead, MIDI contains information *about* the sound, not the sounds themselves. Many computer games store music in MIDI files to conserve disk space.

There are many ways to find or generate MIDI files. If you are a musician, you can use sequencing software (such as Cakewalk), which captures everything that you play on a synthesized instrument. The *sequencing* software can record and play back several parts or instruments in perfect synchronization—sort of like an old-fashioned player-piano roll. After the musical information is loaded into the computer, it can be edited or revised in relation to its rhythm, meter, tone, and many other parameters. With MIDI sequencing software, you can experiment with harmonies, record different parts, and play them back as a complete arrangement.

If you are not musically talented, you can still create MIDI files by scanning sheet music. Programs, such as Musiteck SmartScore, can scan the sheet music and translate the print notation into MIDI commands. Other music recognition software (such as AKoff Music Composer) will allow you to hum, sing, or play music to record a MIDI song. Internet sites also offer access to thousands of MIDI songs that can be purchased and downloaded.

Composition Software

Composition software offers a wide variety of options for novice and expert musicians, and the compositions can be saved in a variety of formats, including MP3 and MIDI. For example, Apple's GarageBand is a mini-music studio that provides prerecorded rhythm sections (called loops), solo instruments, and instrumental performances that can be used as backgrounds or can be combined to create "original" compositions. Students can also record music with GarageBand, via a microphone or MIDI synthesizer (such as a keyboard or electric guitar). Final compositions can be saved as individual files or added to playlists to play on iPods, computers, or other devices.

Digital Audio File Formats

Many file formats are used for digital audio, and some may be recognized by one program and not another. For example, .AIFF formats are common on Macintosh computers, and .WAV is the most common format for Windows computers. Some programs (on either platform) may be able to recognize and play files, such as MIDI; others may not. The following formats are common for audio:

- WAV. The WAV format is the default standard for most Windows-based computers.

- AIFF. The AIFF format is widely used on Apple's operating systems.

- MP3. Common MP3 format for transmitting audio over the Internet.

- WMA (Windows Media Audio). An audio format produced by Microsoft.

- QT or MOV. Although QuickTime was originally designed for digital video, it can also be used for a combination of audio and video or for audio-only files.

- AAC (Advanced Audio Coding). ACC is a compressed audio format is used on iTunes, iPhones, etc. It competes with MP3.

- SWA. Shockwave Audio is a file format used by Adobe for audio on the Internet.

- MID or MIDI (Musical Instrument Digital Interface). A standard for communicating musical information among computers and musical devices.

If you have an audio file that is not in the correct format, there are programs that will convert files from one format to another. For example, Audacity will convert to and from .WAV, .MP3, and .AIFF, etc.

Using Existing Audio Files

Audio files in various formats are available from clip media sites and other archives on the Internet (e.g., see FindSound). These files can be downloaded, edited, and imported into projects.

The fair use portion of the copyright law is generally interpreted as allowing students to use copyrighted music in a classroom situation to fulfill an instructional objective (such as an assignment to create a multimedia project). If students want to use music on their website, however, they must have the rights to record and play the music files. Recording a song from the radio and adding a link to it from a website would definitely violate copyright laws. Before incorporating audio files into a digital project that will be distributed beyond the classroom, you should carefully read the permission statements. If a permission statement is not associated with the file, send an e-mail message to the site administrator to request permission.

Podcasting Audio

Podcasting is a technique that was originally popularized by the iPod. Currently, in broad terms, podcasts can refer to audio files saved as MP3 and posted on a web server. In a strict definition, podcasting refers to audio files that allow users to "subscribe" to a series of audio files on the web and download updates when they are posted. For example, some schools are broadcasting their daily (or weekly) news as podcasts. To do so, they record an audio file of the news each week, save it as an MP3 file, and post it on a web server (or post it through iTunes or an online blog). Another file, called RSS for Really Simple Syndication, is included to allow users to "subscribe" to the show.

Several websites (such as Podbean) provide free hosting of podcasts, along with the recording tools needed to create them. The list of podcasts shown in Figure 5.8 provides an example of podcasts that are available in the K–12 area of iTunes. For example, the children in Room 33 at South Elementary recorded bedtime stories for their parents and the community.

After you subscribe to a podcast, you can set the parameters, telling your computer or device to check for new files at a particular site on an hourly, daily, weekly, or other basis. Imagine the possibilities of having students listen to the stories and news on their mobile devices on the bus ride home!

Figure 5.8. K–12 podcasts in iTunes.

Guidelines for Audio

There are many situations when audio is appropriate in a digital project. For example, if the project is designed for nonreaders or students with sight impairments, then audio is definitely required. In addition, audio is a great way to teach someone a different language or to include sound effects (such as heartbeats) and music. However, audio files can be quite large, and students should be cautioned to use them only when appropriate. The following guidelines should be considered for audio.

- Use audio only when it is appropriate to the content.

- If possible, use MIDI or MP3 for music—the files are much smaller than digital audio stored in WAV and other formats.

- Do not add audio that will distract from the screen display.

- Check copyright restrictions if the audio will be played outside the classroom environment.

- If your software program does not recognize the audio file format, locate an audio converter program to change the file format.

DIGITAL VIDEO

Digitized video refers to motion sequences that are stored in a digital format; usually it is recorded with a digital video camera (which may be in a smartphone or tablet). Digital video has the potential to add realism to multimedia projects. Students can record school assemblies, document field trips, add video to websites, or create commercials—the possibilities are endless!

Digitizing video, however, is one of the most demanding operations that we ask of a digital device. At high resolution, a single digitized image of video requires roughly 1 million bytes or 1 megabyte (MB) for storage and transfer. With 30 images required for each second of full-motion video, a digitized stream of motion video requires the flow of 30 megabytes of information per second. A minute of video would then consist of 1,800 megabytes, or 1.8 gigabytes of data, and a 30-minute video would require 54 gigabytes!

Mass storage devices are improving rapidly, but there are still few economical methods for storing 54 gigabytes of data for each half hour of video. An equally challenging issue involves how to move that much data through a computer at a steady 30 megabytes per second to produce the 30 frames per second required to present smooth motion. Even for the most powerful modern desktop computers, this is an astonishing amount of data to process.

Because of the tremendous amount of data, trade-offs are necessary. For example, note that most videos on the Internet are presented in a small window, rather than full screen. In addition, they might appear a bit jerky because they are displayed at less than 30 frames per second, or there may be pauses as the next segment is downloaded over the Internet.

Digitizing and Editing Video

After digital video is recorded, video software allows students to sequence video clips, add audio, overlay titles, and experiment with transitions (see Figure 5.9). Through these programs (such as iMovie, Windows Media Player, etc.), students can manipulate the video files and other

Figure 5.9. Import video controls in Movie Maker.

media to tell a story or teach a concept. When the project is complete, they can save it as a stand-alone file, record a DVD, create a podcast, upload to YouTube, or integrate the video into another application, such as PowerPoint.

Although the features and interfaces vary, all of the editing software provides basic functions for editing video. The process consists of these general steps:

1. Edit the video clips to the desired length by cropping the unwanted portions.

2. Import other media elements, such as photographs, animations, and audio tracks, into the editing software.

3. Place the video clips and still images on a timeline in the desired sequence.

4. Add transitions, such as dissolves and cuts, between clips (if desired).

5. Add title slides or textual overlays (if desired).

6. Work with the audio track by adjusting the volume and importing sound effects, music, and so on.

7. Combine the elements into one movie file.

8. Save the movie file in the desired format.

9. Export the movie file to videotape, web server, DVD, mobile media, or other device.

10. Test the video, and make adjustments as necessary.

Digital Video File Formats

"RAW" digital video is generally recorded in the DV (digital video) format, and the files are very large. Several common file formats are used to compress and play digital video, including QuickTime, AVI, and MPEG:

- QuickTime (.MOV and .QT). QuickTime provides both editing and playback interfaces for synchronized video and audio. It works well on both Macs and PCs, and it provides good compression, resulting in smaller file sizes.

- Windows (.AVI, .WMF, .WMV). Microsoft introduced a similar but incompatible product called Video for Windows, which uses an .AVI file extension. Since then, Microsoft has introduced other file formats, including .ASF (Advanced Streaming Format), .WMF (Windows Media Format), and .WMV (Windows Media Video).

- MPEG (.MPG, MP3, and MP4). MPEG stands for Motion Pictures Expert Group. It is used as a file format as well as compression technique, and it is popular for high-end video applications.

- FLV (Flash Video Format). Flash video is playable within Flash movies files.

If you do not have the inclination, equipment, or time to produce your own digital video movies, you may be able to obtain appropriate files through the web or on a DVD. Be sure you check the copyright restrictions, especially for applications that will be used or accessed outside the classroom.

Guidelines for Video

Digital video files are generally very large; therefore, you must carefully assess whether you want to use video in a digital project—especially one for the web. The following guidelines should be considered for video:

- Use digital video only when appropriate.

- Keep the window size as small as possible (about one-quarter screen) to help improve performance.

- Check the size of the video files after they are recorded, especially if you are going to transfer them via the Internet.

- Make sure there is adequate lighting when recording digital movies.

- Use a tripod for shooting video to minimize extra motion and achieve better compression.

- Shoot close-ups because the video will be viewed in a small window on the computer.

- Experiment with different compression options to obtain the best quality at the smallest file size.

- Check copyright restrictions on video segments, especially for material that will be used outside the classroom.

SUMMARY

Graphics, animations, audio, and video can add life and interest to digital projects. They can also be used to illustrate and convey abstract concepts, and they can enhance students' visual literacy and their ability to think, learn, and communicate through visuals and other media. Designing and developing media files allow students to be creative and to investigate the presentation of information from several perspectives. Most students are very enthusiastic about working with sound, graphics, and video.

Creating media files also presents some challenges for educators and students. The media files can be stored in many formats, and problems may arise when students have media files ready to incorporate into a project, but the program will not "see" or open the files. In addition, recording and editing usually require additional software and hardware, which may be in limited supply in classrooms.

This chapter presented a wide array of options for incorporating graphics, animations, audio, and video files. Although each software program will incorporate the media elements in a slightly different manner, almost all software programs (including basic word processors) now have the ability to add graphics, sound, and video. The potential is limited only by the imagination (and hardware) available to the students.

RESOURCES

Graphics and Animation Resources

Adobe (DreamWeaver, Flash, PhotoShop, Acrobat, Illustrator, Premier, etc.):
http://www.adobe.com

Apple iPhoto: http://www.apple.com/mac/iphoto/

Apple iMovie: http://www.apple.com/mac/imovie/

Corel (CorelDraw and Paint Shop Pro, etc.): http://www.corel.com

ClipArt ETC: http://etc.usf.edu/clipart/

ClipPix ETC: http://etc.usf.edu/clippix/

Clip Media (Art): http://etc.usf.edu/clip/

Clip Media (Photos): http://etc.usf.edu/clip/photos.htm

GIMP: http://www.gimp.org

How to Create a Stop Motion Animation: http://www.wikihow.com/Create-a-Stop-Motion-Animation

LView Pro: http://lview.com

Monkey Jam: http://monkeyjam.org/

NASA Images: http://www.nasa.gov/multimedia/imagegallery/

Picasa: http://picasa.google.com

PIXLR: http://pixlr.com/

Scanning Tips: http://www.scantips.com/basics01.html

Stop Motion Animator: http://www.clayanimator.com/english/stop_motion_animator.html

Tux Paint: http://www.tuxpaint.org

Audio Resources

Akoff Music Composer: http://www.akoff.com

Audacity: http://audacity.sourceforge.net

Cakewalk: http://www.cakewalk.com

Classical MIDI Archives: http://www.classicalarchives.com

Find Sounds: http://www.findsounds.com/

GarageBand: http://www.apple.com/mac/garageband/

GoldWave: http://www.goldwave.com

Jaws: http://www.freedomscientific.com/jaws-hq.asp

PodBean: http://www.podbean.com

SmartScore: http://www.smartscore.com

Spoken Text: http://www.spokentext.net/

Thunder Screenreader: http://www.screenreader.net/

Video Resources

Adobe (Premier): http://www.adobe.com

Apple iMovie: http://www.apple.com/mac/imovie/

Library of Congress Motion Pictures: http://lcweb2.loc.gov/ammem/browse/ListSome.php?format=Motion+Picture

NASA Video Gallery: http://www.nasa.gov/multimedia/videogallery/

Windows Movie Maker: http://www.soft76.org/windows-movie-maker.html

Chapter 6

DEVELOP: Digital Content Creation Tools

A SCENARIO

As part of their service learning project, Mrs. Thompson's students had to create a marketing campaign that included the creation of a website and YouTube video. Emily, Nora, Kia, and Caprice had already worked through the planning and design stages of their project and were ready to gather the necessary media elements. They decided to use Weebly, a free online web tool, to create their website and Movie Maker to create their video. Emily and Nora were tasked with getting the necessary digital photos, and Kia and Caprice worked on capturing the required video. The team made sure they were familiar with the development tools and any special requirements or limitations they needed to be aware of before they gathered their media elements. As they discussed the content of their project, they realized how much time they had saved by thoroughly planning their project and knowing what they needed to successfully complete their project. It seemed time-consuming in the beginning, but now that they were in the development phase of their project, they realized they saved time by making time—something their teacher, Mrs. Thompson, had told them over and over again, "Save time by making time." They realized the value of organization and structure, especially when creating elaborate projects. "Sure," thought Kia, "I can take a video and share it with my friends, but this is a lot more complex—much more like I see my mom doing in the real world. She has to work with others and persuade clients to see her point. She's always putting together a presentation of some sort. She develops training material, too."

"Kia!" cried Caprice. "We need to go! Come back to the real world! Stop daydreaming!"

"Ha!" thought Kia. "I am in the real world and how lucky we are to have a teacher who makes sure our learning is, too. I am career and college ready!"

"Coming!" Kia said with a smile.

OVERVIEW

After the media elements are created, they are brought together into a final project with a software program. These tools are also available as website and mobile apps. There are many affordable (and free) software programs and apps that can be used to create and present multimedia digital content.

This chapter provides an overview of programs that are commonly available in school environments, on the web, or as mobile apps. These include word processors, spreadsheets, presentation programs, and hypermedia software. It also presents information on developing multimedia web pages with HTML, web editors, and various app tools, along with image programs and digital video editors, such as iMovie, Movie Maker, and Animoto, as well as eBooks. All of these options are inexpensive, relatively easy to use, and can include text, graphics, audio, and video. Whether the final project will be burned to a DVD, published on the web, or stored in the cloud, there are many options for developing multimedia digital content.

This chapter includes:

Multimedia documents and apps

- Word processors

- Spreadsheet programs

- Google Apps

Presentation programs and image programs

- Presentation programs

- Image programs

Hypermedia programs

- Hyperstudio

- Scratch

- Adobe Captivate

Web page production

- Text editors

- Web editors

- Web apps

- Application programs

Digital video programs and editors

- iMovie

- Microsoft Movie Maker

- Animoto

eBooks

Selecting a development tool

Facilitating multimedia projects in the classroom

WordArt WordArt WordArt

Figure 6.1. WordArt in Microsoft Word.

MULTIMEDIA DOCUMENTS AND APPS

Almost all application programs (such as word processors and spreadsheets) can incorporate multimedia components. Most of these programs are inexpensive (or free) and available in school environments, on the web, or as a mobile app. The mobile apps mentioned in this chapter are available for the iPad; some are available for the iPhone and Android operating system as well. In many cases, these tools can be used to create media elements that are later incorporated into a multimedia project. However, students and teachers can also use these applications to combine video, audio, text, and graphics to create multimedia digital content.

Word Processors

Word processors, such as Microsoft Word and Apple's Pages (both available as apps, also), are important tools for all classrooms. In addition to enhancing students' writing abilities, word processors can be used to create multimedia documents and web pages. For example, in Microsoft Word, several media types can be inserted, including clip art, photographs, animations, and sounds. In addition, it is easy to insert and edit WordArt (see Figure 6.1), graphs, charts, tables, organizational charts, and shapes.

Word processors can also play an important role in digital content creation by serving as storyboard and flowchart tools. By using the styles and forms features, teachers can create storyboard templates for students to populate with scripts, links, images, and other details. Flowcharts are also easy to create in word processors by using the shape and line drawing features. Alignment and grouping tools can assist in formatting the layouts and locking the elements (see Figure 6.2).

Flowcharts can be created using mobile apps such as Inspiration Maps, Kidspiration Maps, and Popplet, too (see Chapter 3).

Numerous productivity apps are available for mobile devices. CloudOn is a free app that allows users to create and edit fully compatible Microsoft Office documents. Other apps that can be used to create and edit Microsoft Office documents include Word Offline, Textilus, Office^2 HD, and Microsoft Office 365. Microsoft Office 365 features OneDrive, allowing users to collaborate on shared documents.

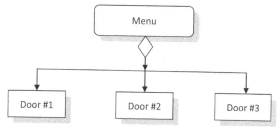

Figure 6.2. Creating a flowchart in Word with shapes and lines.

Spreadsheet Programs

Spreadsheet programs, such as Microsoft Excel or Apple's Numbers, can be great tools for short- or long-term multimedia projects. For example, imagine a project that involves students using a spreadsheet to record the number of calories and the nutritional value of three brands of hot dogs, hot dog buns, and potato chips. For younger students, the teacher could set up a template for the values and formulas; older students could set up the spreadsheet in groups. In addition to entering data, students can add images of the picnic items; generate graphs and charts comparing the different brands; experiment with formulas; and save the worksheet in various formats (including a web page).

Spreadsheets can also be implemented as a supplement to other tools. For example, charts can be generated in a spreadsheet and then cut and pasted into another program, such as HyperStudio. Charts from spreadsheets can also be embedded directly into a word processor or presentation program. Several spreadsheet programs are available for mobile devices. These include Numbers (Apple), iSpreadsheet, Excel (Microsoft Office 365), and Permanent 2.

Google Apps

Google Apps are multifaceted web applications that allow users to create and collaborate on documents, presentations, and other creations virtually. Google Apps includes many free tools, including a word processor (Docs), spreadsheet (Sheets), presentation (Slides), and drawing (Drawing) program. Users can share their work with designated users. Google Apps also includes tools for creating a survey (Forms), and website (Sites), as well as translation tools, media searchers, and other helpful applications for digital content creation.

PRESENTATION AND IMAGE PROGRAMS

Presentation and image programs provide students with an easy way to share their multimedia digital content in a linear, slide show format. Most programs are easy to learn, allow users to create or import their own digital content, and provide students with opportunities to share their work via the web. Some programs allow virtual collaboration as well.

Presentation Programs

Presentation programs, such as PowerPoint by Microsoft and Keynote by Apple, are popular because they are inexpensive, easy to learn, easy to use, and can incorporate multimedia elements such as graphics, digital video, and digital audio. Google Slides, Prezi, and Glogster are popular presentation tools on the web, allowing students and teachers to collaborate and create virtually. Prezi is cloud based and can be accessed from multiple devices (e.g., desktop, browser, iPad, and iPhone). Glogster offers Glogster EDU, a secure environment for teachers and students.

Presentation programs generally include a variety of predesigned templates with colorful backgrounds and preformatted fonts to make the presentations look professional. These templates are useful for novices who are developing their first presentations. Some templates have a particular theme (such as a beach or party); others are more generic. Remind students to select a design template that offers high contrast between background and text so the words will be easy to read. Presentation software also includes a wide array of clip art and media elements to incorporate into projects.

As the term *presentation* implies, presentation programs are often used for projects that will be presented to a large group, rather than projects designed for individual use. Linear projects, such as lectures and multimedia reports, where one screen automatically follows another, are easy for teachers and students to develop with presentation software. The current version of PowerPoint also includes "action buttons," where hotspots can be created on a screen to branch to a specified slide, web address, or file. By incorporating action buttons, students can add interactivity, such as menu options and questions.

A nice feature of most presentation programs is that by simply clicking "Insert audio," students can record and test narration directly on the slides. They can also easily control the audio. For example, the sound can be programmed to play automatically when the slide opens or after the mouse is clicked.

Multiple presentation apps are available for mobile devices. These include Keynote (Apple), PowerPoint (Microsoft Office 365), ShowMe, Bitsboard, SlideShark, Prezi, and Haiku Deck. These can be used for large-group presentations, while others (ShowMe and Bitsboard) are appropriate for individual interactivity as well.

Image Programs

Image programs, such as KidPix 3D, Tux Paint, iPhoto, and Picasa, are excellent tools for creating multimedia digital content. KidPix 3D is an easy-to-use image program that is designed for students ages 4 to 12. It provides tools for creating and editing images, and it can be used to inspire creativity in young children. With KidPix 3D, students can create a slideshow with the built-in tools, and they have the option to save the slideshow as a QuickTime video. A free 15-day trial is available.

Tux Paint is another image program that is designed for children (ages 3 to 12). It is also available as a mobile app. Tux Paint is free and combines an easy-to-use interface, fun sound effects, and an encouraging cartoon mascot who guides children as they use the program (see Figure 6.3, p. 120).

Two popular programs for editing, managing, and organizing images include iPhoto (by Apple and also available as a mobile app) and Picasa (from Google). iPhoto allows students to import, organize, edit, and share photographs and other graphics. In addition, students can add titles, transitions, and sounds. The images can be displayed in a slideshow, shared on the web, or made into photo books, cards, or calendars (see Figure 6.4, p. 120).

Picasa helps students organize, edit, and share their photos, too. They can even add geotags to the photos and link them to places on Google Earth (see Figure 6.5, p. 121).

Many mobile apps are available for helping students edit and add special effects to their photos. Photo Reflection Editor is a free app that allows users to crop and rotate photos, add numerous visual effects, add animation and text, and share via the Internet. Photo Editor by Aviary is also free and is a highly acclaimed app incorporating professionally designed filters, touch-up tools, stickers and frames, text and drawing options, and more. Additional free photo-editing apps include Photo Editor by Fotoir, Split Pic Photo Editor, and PicShop Lite.

HYPERMEDIA PROGRAMS AND APPS

Hypermedia programs are designed so that information stored as text, graphics, audio, video, or animations can be accessed in associative, nonlinear ways. For example, the opening screen of a hypermedia application might contain a menu with four options. Buttons (areas) on the menu can be activated, allowing students to select one of the options and branch to the

Figure 6.3. Interface for Tux Paint.

Figure 6.4. Creating a photo book in iPhoto.

Figure 6.5. Adding geotags to photos in Picasa. Google and the Google logo are registered trademarks of Google Inc., used with permission.

corresponding screen, audio file, video file, or animation. Hypermedia applications are often used for stand-alone projects (as opposed to class presentations) because they enable users to make their own choices and follow their own paths. Many incorporate authoring or scripting features not available in presentation programs, also.

HyperStudio

Although the concept of hypermedia has existed for many years, it has become much more popular because of inexpensive, cross-platform programs such as HyperStudio. The basic structure of HyperStudio consists of stacks and cards (a file is referred to as a *stack*, and a computer screen is called a *card*). Each card can contain text items, buttons, graphics, and other multimedia elements (see Figure 6.6).

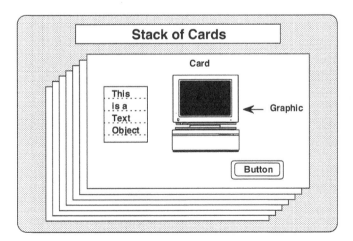

Figure 6.6. Structure of HyperStudio.

Text objects are similar to miniature word processing blocks and are designed to contain text of various styles and sizes. *Buttons* are designated areas of the screens that can initiate an action, such as moving (branching) to another card or playing an audio, video, or animation. Graphics can be created with paint tools within HyperStudio, or they can be imported from clipart or other graphics programs.

With HyperStudio, a series of pull-down menus and dialog windows are used to develop the applications. HyperStudio is an impressive package that provides built-in links to digital movies and audio, recording options, live video, and more. Paint tools, animation tools, web tools, and testing functions that can track correct and incorrect answers are also available. In more recent editions, presentations can be exported to iPod video format, QuickTime, HTML5, and PNG. Users can import YouTube videos, open web pages, and link to other programs. A free 30-day trial is available.

Scratch

Scratch is a free program, developed by the Lifelong Kindergarten Group at the MIT Media Lab. See http://scratch.mit.edu. It is designed to help students work collaboratively, think creatively, and reason systematically. It is a block-based programming language, enabling users to "snap together" preexisting programming blocks or commands to control objects called "sprites." Students can add sprites from a preexisting library, draw their own sprite, upload an image, or take a picture using a webcam. The programming blocks are organized into 10 different categories: Motion, Looks, Sound, Pen, Data, Events, Control, Sensing, Operators, and More Blocks. Students create projects by adding sprites to the Stage area and dragging programming blocks to the Script area (See Figure 6.7).

Different backdrops can be added to the stage, creating the ability to move from one backdrop to another, similar to the idea of moving from one card to another in HyperStudio. In addition to different backdrops, students can add sounds, animation, hyperlinks, text, and other media

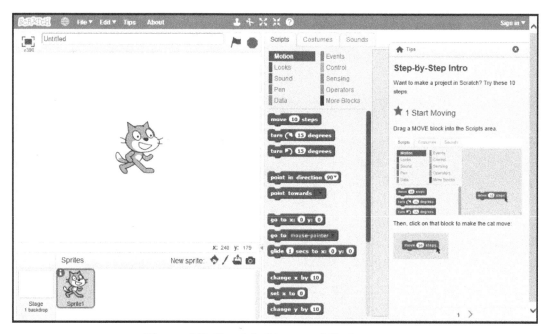

Figure 6.7. Scratch Stage and Script areas.

elements to their projects and share their work with others around the world. Students can create interactive stories, games, tutorials, animations, and much more. The Scratch website provides numerous project examples. In addition, there is a ScratchEd online community for educators.

Adobe Captivate

Adobe Captivate is an authoring program that provides users the ability to create interactive and HTML5-based content without programming. Captivate makes it easy to create simulations, drag-and-drop modules, quizzes, and more. Published work can be delivered through the web, desktops, Learning Management Systems, and mobile devices.

Several new features have been integrated into the later versions of Adobe Captivate. These include the drag-and-drop interactivity, the ability to convert PowerPoint presentations to HTML5, and new and updated Smart Learning Interactions—modules that can be inserted to enhance user interactivity. These include notes, games, videos, glossaries, and more.

Adobe Captivate provides users with a Stage to create their slides for the project. Multiple slides can be viewed as a Filmstrip (to the left of the stage), a Timeline of events is below the Stage, and various support features are provided as Tabs to the right of the Stage. Figure 6.8 shows the creation of an interactive slide using the Drag and Drop interaction option.

Adobe Captivate is available for a 30-day trial and provides special pricing for students and educators. Multiple tutorials are available (see http://blogs.adobe.com/captivate/adobe-captivate-tutorials).

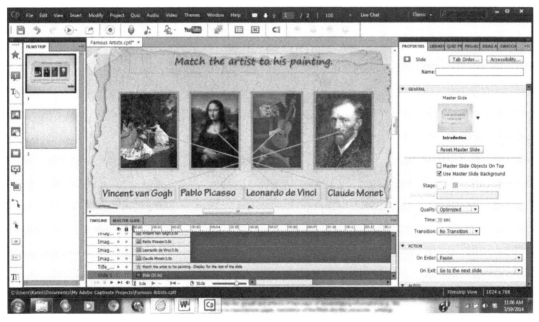

Figure 6.8. Creating an interactive slide in Adobe Captivate. Adobe product screen shot reprinted with permission from Adobe Systems Incorporated.

WEB PAGE PRODUCTION

Access to the Internet provides a great environment for publishing multimedia digital content in school. With a simple word processor, students can easily create web pages that can be viewed by people around the world. Even if a school is not connected to the Internet, it is possible for students to use web technology to publish documents that are available on school networks or stand-alone computers.

All web pages are derived from text files that are interpreted and displayed by web browsers (such as Firefox, Safari, Chrome, or Internet Explorer). For example, when the text file shown in Figure 6.9 is displayed through a browser, the student will see the web page illustrated in Figure 6.10.

The text files used in web documents adhere to a specific format called the *HyperText Markup Language* or HTML. HTML files use *tags* (words embedded between the < and > characters) to define how information is formatted on the screen. For example, in the line <B>This is bold.</B>, the first tag turns the bold attribute on, and the second one (the one with the /B) turns the bold attribute off. A few common style tags are illustrated in Table 6.1.

```
<html>
<head>
<title>Geography Home Page</title></head>
<body>
<img src ="geo.gif">
<br>
<h2>This page provides links relevant to Freshman Geography</h2>
<p>
Click to see a <a href="CA.mov">movie about Central America.</a>.
<br>
<hr>
<ul>
<li><a href="http://www.geo.gov/">Geography sites</a>
<li><a href="http://www.chs.edu/assign/">Assignments</a>
<li><a href="http://www.chs.edu/reports/">Student reports</a>
</ul>
<hr>
</body>
</html>
```

Figure 6.9. Text file (HTML) for a web page.

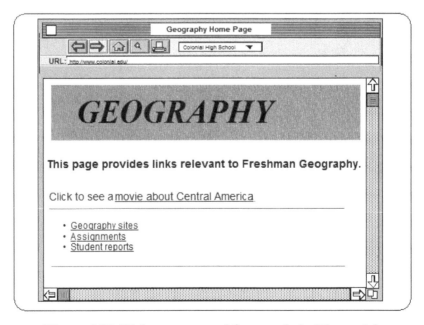

Figure 6.10. Web page created from code in Figure 6.9.

Table 6.1. HTML Quick Reference Guide

	Tag	Definition
<b>Essential Parts</b>	<html> <head> <title>...</title> </head> <body>...</body> </html>	These tags represent the template or "skeleton" of an HTML document. HTML tags identify the beginning and ending of the document; HEAD tags contain the TITLE tags, which identify the page's bookmark name; and BODY tags contain the text, pictures, headings, etc., of the document
Formatting Text: Headings	<h1>...</h1> <h2>...</h2> <h3>...</h3> <h4>...</h4> <h5>...</h5> <h6>...</h6>	HTML has six levels of headings that are displayed in bolder and separate type than the regular body text. Level 1 is the largest heading; Level 6 is the smallest heading.
Formatting Text: Physical Styles	<em>...</em> <i>...</i> <u>...</u>	Physical style tags tell browsers how to display text. For example, text within the tags <em>...</em> will be **emphasized;** text within the tags <I>...</I> will be *italicized;* <U> will be /U> will be <u>underlined.</u>
Formatting Text: Paragraphs	<p>...</p>
	<P>...</P> identifies a paragraph; and <BR> inserts a carriage return (break).
 does not have an ending tag.
Making Lists	<ul> <li>first item <li>second item <li>third item </ul>	<UL>...</UL> creates an unordered (bulleted) list. <LI> tags are placed within the <UL> and </UL> tags for each item in the list. Ordered lists display numbers and are created by using <OL> and </OL> instead of <UL> and </UL>.
Displaying an Image	<img src = "image.gif">	Place the name of the image in "image.gif."
Creating Hyperlinks	<a href = "http://whereto.com"> location></A>	Place the location's address in "http://whereto.com" and link information in "location."
Playing Movies and Sounds	<a href="file_name">instruction </a>	Place the filename of the sound or movie in "file_name" and directions (such as "click here") in "instruction."

Creating a web page may appear to be intimidating, but many elementary school students are developing pages every day. In some cases, they learn a few basic HTML tags and then gradually expand their "vocabulary" as they become more experienced. In other cases, they do not learn HTML at all; instead, they use a word processor or web editor that allows them to create web documents without typing in any command codes.

There are several ways to create a web page, including the following:

- Create an HTML page "by hand" by typing HTML code into a text editor.

- Use a web editor, such as Adobe DreamWeaver or KompoZer (see http:// kompozer.net/).

- Use a web app such as Weebly, Google Sites, Webs, Wix, Yola, and others.

- Use a mobile app such as SimpleDifferent, Simpl, or inWeby. These are free apps; others are available for purchase.

- Use an application program, such as Microsoft Word or PowerPoint, and *Save As . . . Web Page*.

Creating a Web Page with a Text Editor

One of the least expensive methods for creating web pages is to use the free text editors that come with a computer, such as *SimpleText* on Macintosh and *NotePad* on Windows machines. An advantage of creating HTML in these simple text editors is that they save the files in text-only format—exactly the format needed for the web pages. A disadvantage is it can be the most time-intensive method of creating a web page.

To create HTML files in a text editor, you type in all of the required codes (as illustrated in Figure 6.9). Then save the file with an .htm or .html extension. Note that the images and media elements will be separate files (usually saved in the same directory). When you are finished, test the file by displaying it through a web browser.

Keep in mind that no matter how a web page is created, it is stored in HTML code. Even though there are many other options, it is wise to understand at least the basics of HTML; that way, you and the students will be able to make minor changes to web pages no matter how or where they were created.

Creating a Web Page with a Web Editor

Several web editors are available that provide users with a *WYSIWYG* (what you see is what you get) environment. These include Adobe DreamWeaver and KompoZer. KompoZer is a free download and DreamWeaver is relatively inexpensive for educational use.

These programs allow users to type text on their web pages just as they would in a word processing program. Styles, such as bold, are added by highlighting the text and selecting a style on the menu bar. Users do not have to see the HTML code; it is generated "behind the scenes" and will be interpreted by the web browser. It is possible to insert graphics, include lists, create tables, and insert forms with these programs as well (see Figure 6.11).

After a web page is created, it (and all relevant media files) must be uploaded to a web server so the rest of the world can see it. To upload files to a web server, you may need special permissions and passwords. Most webmasters and administrators are extremely cautious about granting

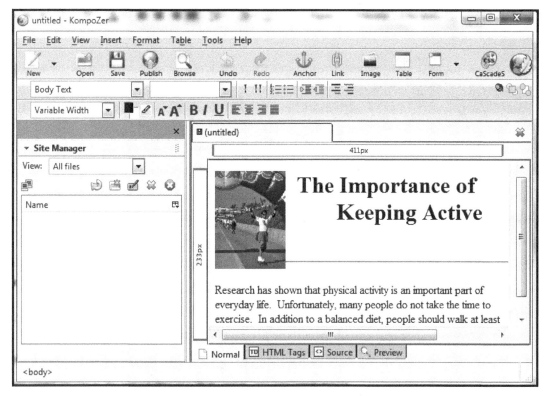

Figure 6.11. KompoZer interface.

permission to upload files because of the prevalence of hackers and viruses. You may be asked to send the files to the administrator, and he or she will place them on the server.

Creating a Web Page with a Web App

Another way to create web pages is to use a web app (see Figure 6.12 for an example). Web apps provide templates or online forms—you simply fill in the forms and a web page is generated. There are several websites (some are especially designed for teachers) that provide free templates. Many of these websites will also host your pages and store them on their web server, so you do not have to worry about uploading or storing them on a local web server.

The following websites offer templates and other tools to allow you to build and store a website easily:

- Google Sites at http://sites.google.com/ provides a wealth of free templates.

- SchoolRack at http://www.schoolrack.com/ provides a free service for teachers to create and host their website and has features specifically designed for teachers.

- TeacherWeb at http://teacherweb.com/ provides a straightforward design. Options are available to create school websites with areas for a calendar, announcements, links, frequently asked questions, and assignments. A small subscription fee is required.

Figure 6.12. Interface for Weebly template.

- Webnode at http://www.webnode.com/ provides an easy-to-use, drag-and-drop interface.

- Webs at http://www.webs.com/ provides free web tools, templates, and hosting.

- Weebly at http://www.weebly.com/ provides free web templates, tools, and hosting. Weebly has features built specifically for education.

- Wix at http://wix.com/ provides free templates, tools, and hosting. It also supports HTML5, meaning the websites are accessible by all devices, including the iPad.

- Yola at https://www.yola.com/ provides templates and tutorials and forums for first-time users.

Creating a Web Page with Application Programs

Web pages have become so popular that many of the standard word processing programs, spreadsheets, presentation programs, desktop publishing, and other tools include an option to save the file as a web page (in HTML format). These programs offer a fast, efficient way to create web documents from existing documents. For example, students could write stories in Microsoft Word, then use the "Save As . . . Web Page" to convert it into HTML. At that point, it can be uploaded to a web server and accessed via a web browser. Application programs are a great way to get started on large, text-intensive projects.

DIGITAL VIDEO PROGRAMS AND EDITORS

Even though today's technology makes it easy to capture video, producing a video project involves a great deal of planning, organizing, and creative energy. As illustrated in Table 6.2, the phases in a video production project are often referred to as preproduction, production, and

Table 6.2. Phases of Digital Video Projects

Preproduction	Production	Postproduction
• Select project idea/goal • Outline project • Write scripts and storyboards • Assign roles • Design sets (if necessary)	• Shoot video • Record audio • Create graphics	• Import video into editing software • Edit video clips • Add transitions • Add title slides • Combine the clips into movie file

postproduction. The video files can be used in a stand-alone mode (as a DVD, for example), or they can be integrated into a hypermedia, presentation, or web program.

In the past, editing the video clips into a finished movie was a complex process that involved high-end, expensive equipment, consisting of multiple videotape players, recorders, and control devices. Thanks to advancements in hardware and software, it is now possible to do sophisticated editing with a classroom computer or on a mobile device. Popular video-editing programs for schools include iMovie by Apple and Movie Maker by Microsoft, as well as web-based products such as Animoto. If your students need more features, there are several "high-end" editors on the market, such as Adobe Premier and FinalCut Pro. Another tool that should be mentioned is Quick-Time Pro. Although this is not a video editor per se, it does allow you to record and convert video to different formats. It also provides you with access to simple editing tools (e.g., you can shorten a movie). Simple editing tools are also available on a variety of smartphones.

iMovie

iMovie is a digital editor is included on Macintosh computers and is also available as an app on the iPad. Figure 6.13 shows the editing window in iMovie. Note that the clips that

Figure 6.13. Editing digital video in iMovie.

have been imported are displayed on the left. A large preview window appears on the right. Students can easily add titles, narration, transitions, and special effects, as well as edit the audio and video clips.

Microsoft Movie Maker

Movie Maker is a similar video-editing program that can be downloaded free from the Microsoft website. Figure 6.14 shows the editing window in Movie Maker. Note that the features are basically the same as iMovie, although they are arranged a little differently. Both iMovie and Movie Maker offer tutorials and abundant Help features to get started.

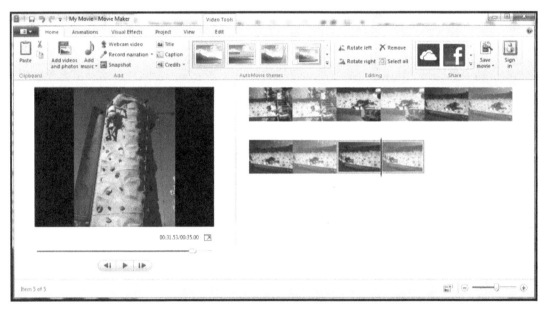

Figure 6.14. Editing digital video in Movie Maker.

Animoto

With Animoto, users can easily create and share their videos online. First, users are asked to create a style (choose a template) for their video. Next, users upload photos and videos from a computer or Facebook, Picasa, Flickr, Dropbox, or other locations. Users can also add text, music, narration, and other features to their video. Videos can be downloaded or shared via Facebook, YouTube, Vimeo, Twitter, and others. Students can create 30-second videos for free; additional time, styles, and features are for sold at various prices. Figure 6.15 shows the online interface for creating a free video in Animoto.

Screencasts are another way students can produce a video. A screencast is a video recording of the computer screen. For example, students can use screencasts to demonstrate different features of a particular program, show how to create or draw something, model a solution to an algebra problem, and so on. Screencast programs include CamStudio, Screencast-o-matic, and screenr.

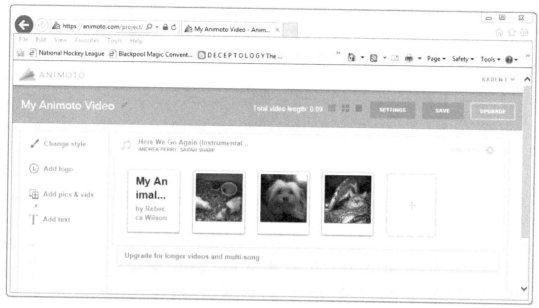

Figure 6.15. Animoto interface for creating a free online video.

eBOOKS

eBooks (electronic books) are another way students may choose to share their work. There are a variety of free programs available as web apps or downloads, such as Pubb Soft, Interact Builder, and iBooks Author. Additional eBook programs are available for purchase, including eBook Maestro PRO and Desktop Author.

There are many forms of eBooks, including ePubs, iBooks, and PDF (Portable Document Format). ePub is a distribution and interchange format established by the International Digital Publishing Forum. The format is used by publishers of digital books and other online publications. It is an open (free) standard for eBooks, although not all eBooks use the ePub standard. ePub is vendor independent; several eBook formats are not. In other words, an ePub is not platform specific and will look the same regardless of the platform. The latest ePub standard supports embedded video, audio, and media overlay—the ability to synchronize audio with text.

Students can create their own ePubs by using the export feature in Apple's Pages. The ePub option supports changes in text size, font, and device orientation (landscape or portrait), embedded video, iBook notes, and navigation using an automatically created table of contents. It does not support content created in page layout templates. More information about creating ePubs with Pages can be found at http://support.apple.com/kb/ht4168.

Book Creator, by Red Jumper Studio, is another resource for creating interactive, multimedia-rich eBooks that support the ePub3 standard. Book Creator is available for the iPad and Android tablets. Users can submit their eBooks to Apple's iBooks Store or Google Play Books.

Conversion tools and websites are also available to convert documents to ePubs. Calibre can be downloaded for free and can convert numerous file formats to an ePub format, including docx, HTML, Mobi, PDF, rtf, and txt. Simply upload the document (Add books) and choose the output format (Convert books). Figure 6.16 shows a Word document (docx) converted to an ePub format. By clicking on the menu options on the right of the eBook viewer, users can increase or decrease the text, access the table of contents, view the eBook full screen, move forward and back through the pages, create bookmarks, and more. Calibre can also manage eBook collections, sorting

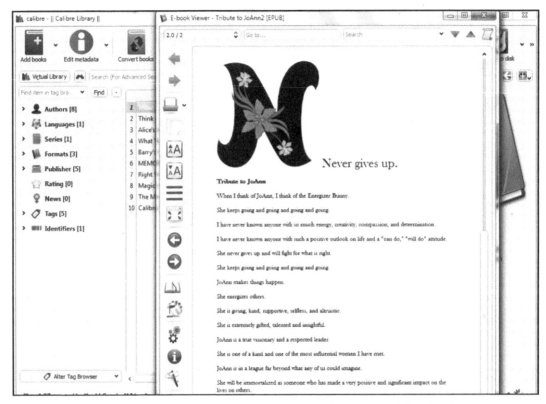

Figure 6.16. A Word document converted to an ePub in Calibre.

books in your library by title, author, date, rating, and so on. In addition, it provides searchable meta-data, allowing users to include tags and comments to personalize information. Calibre allows users to download eBooks and news from the web, access their eBooks from anywhere, and much more.

Apple's iBooks Author is an eBook format that is currently platform specific. It is a proprietary Apple file format that is not universally readable or editable as an ePub document. Designers can create content using only Apple hardware, and the final product (iBook) can be viewed only on a Macintosh or iPad, or exported as a PDF. Advantages of the iBook are its ability to embed a range of multimedia, including video and audio, as well as its numerous interactive features. Other commercial software, such as eBook Maestro PRO and Desktop Author, are Windows specific. Desktop Author lets users output eBook files in Windows, Mac, and Android formats.

PDF is another eBook format that is not vendor specific. PDFs can be viewed on different devices using a PDF reader, but do not have the same ability to reflow text to accommodate the viewing size of different sized screens. For example, an ePub can be seen on a 3.5-inch smartphone without having to keep zooming in and out and scrolling around to see the entire document, as one would have to when viewing a PDF. Similar to other eBook formats, PDF files can contain clickable links and buttons, video, and audio. Most application programs support saving files to PDF. Adobe Acrobat is also available to create PDFs.

eBooks may be web specific, too. For example, FlipHTML5 converts PDFs and other documents to HTML5, allowing users to publish interactive, media-rich eBooks on the web. Content can be viewed across a variety of devices and platforms. PDF to Flipbook, 3D PageFlip Standard, and simplebooklet are similar conversion programs.

Graphic novels are another way students can express their ideas via an eBook. Several applications are available on the Internet to help students combine graphics with text to create their own comic strips. These include Graphix, MakeBeliefsComix.com, Pixton, and ToonDoo. Each vary in

Figure 6.17. Make Beliefs Comix interface and sample comic strip.

their simplicity and options. For example, MakeBeliefsComix.com by Bill Zimmerman and Tom Bloom is an easy-to-use program that provides a library of resources to help students create their own comics. Resources include characters, objects, backgrounds, word bubbles, and so on. Characters are available in different poses and can be flipped and resized. One strip is created at a time, so students need to create each panel separately, printing or sending it to themselves to create their final graphic novel. Figure 6.17 shows the MakeBeliefsComix.com interface and a sample comic strip (printed with permission of MakeBeliefsComix.com). There is also a free Make Beliefs Comix app for the iPad.

ToonDoo provides users with an extensive clip art library, word bubbles, and the option to draw their own images, as well as import graphics. It also features a novel format, allowing users to store their strips in a book format. Users can keep their work private, share their work with a specific group of people, or publish their work so everyone can view it. Options also include the ability to let others edit the comic strips, something that may be useful in team projects. Figure 6.18 (p. 134) shows the interface and the development of a comic strip in ToonDoo.

Novels can be printed or shared via the Internet. Mobile apps are available, also. For example, ComicLife is available for the iPad, iPhone, and iPod, as well as Macintosh and Windows computers. Similar to Pixton and ToonDoo, ComicLife allows students to easily import photographs, scanned drawings, and other images.

SELECTING A DEVELOPMENT TOOL

Each of the development tools described in this chapter has features that are useful for digital content creation. The following guidelines may help determine which type of tool is best for a particular situation:

- If cost is a factor, there are many free programs that can be downloaded or used on the web. These include Google Apps, Prezi, Glogster, Tux Paint, Scratch, KompoZer, Weebly, Wix, Animoto, Calibre, and others. Free apps are available for mobile devices as well.

Figure 6.18. Interface and the development of a comic strip in ToonDoo.

- For maximum interactivity, hypermedia programs may be the best. Hypermedia programs are designed to contain hyperlinks to graphics and media elements. In addition, they usually contain question formats and scoring techniques.

- For ease of use, application programs are typically the best; however, many programs designed specifically for children have easy to use interfaces. See Table 6.3 for a comparison of the development tools presented in this chapter.

Table 6.3. Comparison of Development Tools

Attribute	Application	Hypermedia	Web Pages	Digital Video	eBooks
Learning curve	Low	High	Medium	High	Low
Cost	Low	Medium	Low	Low	Low
Amount of interactivity	Low	High	Medium	Low	Low
Amount of multimedia	Medium	High	Medium	High	Medium

FACILITATING MULTIMEDIA PROJECTS IN THE CLASSROOM

As the students enter the DEVELOP phase of the project, they compile the media elements based on the information in their flowcharts and storyboards. At this point, the teacher's role is that of a facilitator. This includes the following activities:

- Ensuring that all of the necessary equipment, batteries, software, Internet, and so on are available

- Reviewing necessary prerequisite skills related to the technology or concepts related to the content

- Circulating the room, assisting students as they need it

- Monitoring the progress of each group or student, ensuring that students stay on task

- Troubleshooting hardware and software issues

- Conducting formative assessments and providing ongoing feedback for students' progress

- Being aware of the time allotted for the activity in relation to the progress

- Having a backup plan (or two) in case the technology crashes

- Emphasizing the relationship to the lesson's goals

Digital content creation activities in the classroom can be exciting, effective, and motivating. Unfortunately, they also offer opportunities for students to be distracted, off-task, and disruptive. Students may misbehave because they become bored, frustrated, or misdirected. There are, however, several techniques that can assist in keeping students on task and engaged with the activity and the lesson's goals. These techniques include the following:

1. Present clear goals and expectations.

2. Provide adequate structure.

3. Keep students actively involved.

4. Assign "tech buddies."

5. Be flexible and ready to adapt.

6. Teach, model, and enforce time management.

Present Clear Goals and Expectations

For some teachers, the thought of having students working cooperatively with multiple technology tools leads to nightmares, as they imagine off-task behavior and chaos in the classroom. However, if students are engaged in activities that they find meaningful, the discipline problems can actually decrease or disappear entirely! Begin by developing a set of expectations that you and the students can live with—rules that are enforceable. These expectations might include issues such as how to handle the equipment, an appropriate volume level for voices, strategies for seeking help (such as placing a paper cup on their desk), and so on. Be patient and consistent—you will be amazed at how captivated the students will become with their activities!

Provide Adequate Structure

Whether your students are first graders or seniors in high school, you must provide a clear framework for them. In other words, "set the stage" in the beginning, telling the students the procedure, exactly what is required (such as writing storyboards), how the activity will be assessed (if you have a rubric, share it with them, or let them help you create one), and how much time is allowed for each phase of the activity. If students are working in groups, the roles of the team members should be clear, as well as how the group will be assessed (individually or collectively).

One way to provide structure and assign computer use (including tablet and other devices) is by using a Jigsaw cooperative learning approach. For example, each team's graphic artists can work with the graphic artists from other teams to select and review each other's media needs on the class computers. If there are eight groups of students, one person from each group could be designated as the group's graphic artist. These students would form their own group to help create and research each other's graphics on the classroom computers. Similarly, the programmers from each group could work together to produce the templates for the projects.

Keep Students Actively Involved

It has been said that the cure for boredom is curiosity. If students are waiting for their turn with a camera, tablet, or laptop, chances are they may become bored and look for diversions. Activities must be designed to keep all students engaged at all times. When designing a multimedia project for groups using limited resources, always include supplemental activities that can be completed without hardware. For example, if students are waiting to use a computer, they can conduct research through traditional means (books), work at a learning center that has related manipulatives, evaluate their peers' projects, or write the script for a project.

If limited peripherals (such as a scanner, camera, microphone, etc.) and software are available, you may rotate student groups so that they are assigned a different "station" each day. For example, a scanner might be attached to computer 1; Adobe Photoshop might be installed on computer 2; a video editor might be installed on computer 3; and computer 4 may have a connection

to the Internet. Rotating assignments allows student groups to plan their time using a scanner, a single copy of Adobe Photoshop, or other limited resources. Students may also use a sign-up sheet to use a particular computer or other digital device.

Assign Tech Buddies

Many teachers have found that assigning tech buddies helps to reduce the amount of questions and off-task behavior. By working together, tech buddies can help each other solve problems and troubleshoot. This approach has also been referred to as the "Ask Three Before Me" rule—students must ask three classmates for assistance before seeking the teacher. Student involvement provides valuable assistance for the teacher and helps build students' self-esteem.

Be Flexible and Ready to Adapt

Teachers should accept the fact that technology may not fit neatly into traditional paradigms. For digital projects to foster collaboration, cross-discipline explorations, and complex problem solving, the school schedules may have to be adjusted—some activities may require 30 minutes; others three hours. In addition, Murphy's Law may strike at any time—always have a backup plan (or two).

Teach, Model, and Enforce Time Management

At first, this may seem to be a direct contradiction of the previous guideline (Be flexible and ready to adapt). Flexibility and time management are both important. For example, suppose you have restructured your class schedule to allow three hours for a cross-curricular, multimedia activity. The students, however, are being very creative, and they are experimenting with every font that PowerPoint allows. The three hours are almost over; one group is finished; one is almost done; and the other three groups would need an additional two hours! Possible solutions to this dilemma include setting a kitchen timer to allow specific amounts of time for substeps. For example, you could announce, "You will have 45 minutes to select your background, fonts, and clip art for the project" (assuming that the planning of the project was previously completed). If computers must be shared by various groups and students, computer logs with "time in" and "time out" are also helpful, along with a strict rotational schedule (refer back to Scheduling Computer Time in Chapter 3).

SUMMARY

The final step in the development process is to combine the text, graphics, audio, video, and other media elements with a development tool. There are many alternatives available. This chapter focused on several inexpensive and free options for students and teachers: multimedia documents, presentation and image programs, hypermedia, web pages, digital movies, and eBooks. As you are planning the curriculum tools for your classroom, consider these tools and others that will allow your students to produce and deliver their products in a timely fashion.

RESOURCES

Multimedia Documents

- **Microsoft Office Products:** http://www.microsoft.com/

- **Numbers:** http://www.apple.com/mac/numbers/

- **Pages:** http://www.apple.com/mac/pages/

- **Google Apps:** http://www.google.com/intl/en/about/products/

- **Mobile Apps:** CloudOn, Word Offline, Textilus, Office2 HD, Microsoft Office Mobile Apps, Pages, Numbers, iSpreadsheet, and Permanent 2

Presentation and Image Programs

- **Microsoft PowerPoint:** http://office.microsoft.com/en-us/powerpoint/

- **Keynote:** http://www.apple.com/ios/keynote/

- **Prezi:** https://prezi.com/

- **Glogster:** http://www.glogster.com/

- **KidPix 3D:** http://www.mackiev.com/kidpix/

- **Tux Paint:** http://www.tuxpaint.org/

- **Picasa:** http://picasa.google.com/

- **iPhoto:** http://www.apple.com/ios/iphoto/

- **Mobile Apps:** Keynote, ShowMe, Bitsboard, SlideShark, Prezi, Haiku Deck, Photo Reflection Editor, Photo Editor by Aviary, Photo Editor by Fotoir, Split Pic Photo Editor, and PicShop Lite

Hypermedia Programs

- **HyperStudio:** http://www.mackiev.com/hyperstudio/

- **Scratch:** http://scratch.mit.edu/

- **Adobe Captivate:** http://www.adobe.com/products/captivate.html

Web Page Production

- **Adobe DreamWeaver:** http://www.adobe.com/products/dreamweaver.html

- **Google Sites:** http://sites.google.com/

- **KompoZer:** http://kompozer.net/

- **SchoolRack**: http://www.schoolrack.com/

- **TeacherWeb:** http://teacherweb.com/

- **Webnode:** http://www.webnode.com/

- **Webs**: http://www.webs.com/

- **Weebly:** http://www.weebly.com/

- **Wix:** http://www.wix.com/

- **Yola:** https://www.yola.com/

Digital Video Programs and Editors

- **Adobe Premier:** http://www.adobe.com/products/premiere.html
- **Animoto:** http://animoto.com/
- **CamStudio:** http://camstudio.org/
- **FinalCut Pro:** http://www.apple.com/final-cut-pro/
- **iMovie:** http://www.apple.com/ios/imovie/
- **Movie Maker:** http://windows.microsoft.com/en-US/Windows-Live/movie-maker#t1=overviewrosoft.com/
- **QuickTime Pro:** http://www.apple.com/quicktime/extending/
- **Screencast-o-matic**: http://www.screencast-o-matic.com/
- **screenr:** http://www.screenr.com/

eBooks

- **3D PageFlip Standard:** http://www.3dpageflip.com/
- **Adobe Acrobat:** http://www.adobe.com/products/acrobat/create-pdf-creator.html
- **Adobe Reader:** http://www.adobe.com/products/reader.html
- **Book Creator:** http://www.redjumper.net/bookcreator/
- **Calibre:** http://calibre-ebook.com/
- **ComicLife:** http://comiclife.com/
- **Creating ePub Files with Pages:** http://support.apple.com/kb/ht4168
- **Desktop Author:** http://www.desktopauthor.com/
- **eBook Maestro PRO**: http://www.ebookmaestro.com/
- **FlipHTML5:** http://fliphtml5.com/
- **Graphix:** http://www.scholastic.com/graphix/createcomic.htm
- **iBook Author:** http://www.apple.com/ibooks-author/
- **Interactive Builder:** http://www.interactbuilder.com/
- **International Digital Publishing Forum:** http://idpf.org/epub
- **MakeBeliefsComix:** http://www.makebeliefscomix.com/Comix/
- **PDF to Flipbook:** http://www.boxoft.com/pdf-to-flipbook/
- **Pixton:** http://www.pixton.com/

- **Pubb Soft**: http://pubbsoft.com/
- **simplebooklet**: http://simplebooklet.com/
- **ToonDoo:** http://www.toondoo.com

Additional Resources and Tips

- **Adobe Captivate Tutorials:** http://blogs.adobe.com/captivate/adobe-captivate-tutorials
- **Educational Technology Clearinghouse:** http://etc.usf.edu/
- **Free Technology for Teachers:** http://www.freetech4teachers.com/
- **Free Web Building Tutorials (HTML and CSS):** http://w3schools.com/
- **KidsVid (Video production tips for kids):** http://kidsvid.4teachers.org/
- **Media Resources for Teachers and Students:** http://www.uen.org/general_learner/multimedia_resources.shtml

Chapter 7

EVALUATE

A SCENARIO

Mr. Clark, Ms. Barry, and Mrs. Orville sat at their grade-level meeting, contemplating how they could make the standard "Use equivalent fractions as a strategy to add and subtract fractions" more interesting to their students. In the past, they felt students relied too much on rote procedures to solve the equations instead of demonstrating their conceptual understanding of adding and subtracting fractions with unlike denominators. "I love math," commented Ms. Barry. "The last thing I want to do is making it boring, rote, and abstract for my students."

"Why don't we try incorporating technology this year?" asked Mrs. Orville. "Kids love it when we bring out the laptops. They've done excellent work illustrating and writing their stories, poetry, and reports. Why can't we use the same idea for math?"

"Great idea!" said Mr. Clark. "We can place the students in cooperative groups like we do when we have them create reports and assign them to illustrate how to solve a specific equation."

"Yes," interjected Ms. Barry, "and we need to make sure they show how to solve the problem conceptually, not abstractly. We can have the students create a story about the problem, too, giving it context and meaning."

"I bet we can modify our current story rubric to address the content and requirements of this lesson," added Mrs. Orville.

"Let's make sure we have the students provide input into the revised rubric as well," noted Mr. Clark.

The three teachers continued to discuss their ideas and plan their lesson, addressing how they would ensure their students had the necessary background knowledge, prerequisites skills, and list of expectations to successfully complete the project.

OVERVIEW

To ensure digital projects are purposeful, educators need to identify the projects' specific objectives and how these support district, state, or national standards. In addition, teachers must correlate the objectives with specific assessment measures to ensure students are learning what has been specified in each objective. Assessment criteria can be clarified and categorized using rubrics. Rubrics can provide feedback about the effectiveness of instruction and provide benchmarks for measuring and documenting students' progress. In addition, rubrics let students know what is expected of them. They serve as a grade contract. Based on the expectations outlined in a rubric, students can plan their time accordingly. For example, if video is not a requirement for a project, students should not spend time incorporating it into their work unless it is appropriate or they have extra time on their hands. Rubrics can help students set their priorities and better manage their projects, as well as help teachers assess students' progress throughout the development of their projects.

Poor learning experiences can be avoided through well-planned and frequently assessed projects. Formative assessment provides constructive feedback at each phase of the DDD-E process. Without it, students may encounter unnecessary obstacles, extra work, frustration, unfinished products, and fragmented learning. Ongoing assessment helps educators teach for understanding and ensures that students are ready to move on to the next step of a project. This chapter defines several assessment techniques and their relationship to digital content creation. In addition, this chapter provides information on creating rubrics and provides sample rubrics for each phase of the DDD-E process. Topics include the following:

- Alternative assessment techniques
  - The role of digital content creation in alternative assessment
- Assessment strategies
  - Resources for creating and finding sample rubrics
  - Using rubrics
  - Additional rubric options
- Assigning grades
- Reflections and future goals

ALTERNATIVE ASSESSMENT TECHNIQUES

There are a variety of ways to evaluate students' learning. With the implementation of Common Core State Standards, schools are using a computer-based, shared assessment system to provide benchmark, formative, and summative assessments. The assessments include nonperformance- and performance-based items. Unlike standardized tests of the past, the Common Core State Standards focus on authentic learning experiences, conceptual understanding, career and college readiness, and what it means to be a literate person in the 21st century. Emphasis is on real-world learning and competencies like reasoning, critical thinking, communication, and collaboration. Students must be able to apply what they have learned. Traditional tests (e.g., true/false, multiple choice, matching) tend to reveal only what a student can recall or recognize, often focus on low-level knowledge objectives, and can be culturally biased, distorting student performance. Alternative assessments focus on students' ability to produce or perform, mastery and application of learning, and higher-order thinking skills (Hardiman and Whitman 2014; Kingsley and Brinkerhoff 2011; Norton and Hathaway 2010).

Alternative assessment is assessment in some form other than the true or false, multiple-choice, matching, and fill-in-the-blank responses often associated with standardized or "traditional" tests. Performance-based assessment, authentic assessment, and portfolio assessment are forms of alternative assessment. Many of these terms overlap and are used interchangeably. They are defined as follows.

Performance-based assessment requires teachers to evaluate a student's knowledge and skills by observing the student do something (e.g., participating in a debate, playing an instrument, dribbling a basketball) or create something that results in a tangible product (e.g., a model or drawing, a video production, a blouse).

Authentic assessment includes performance tests, observations, interviews, exhibitions, and portfolios. The goal of authentic assessment is to involve students in activities that better represent what they are likely to face outside the school setting. The context, purpose, audience, and constraints of the task *must* connect to real-world situations and problems. For example, students might be asked to identify the chemical composition of a given solution by conducting various analyses, or they might take samples from local rivers and lakes and identify pollutants. Both tasks would be performance based, but the latter would be considered authentic because it involves and addresses a real-world problem.

Portfolio assessment is a systematic collection of a student's best work and may include narrative descriptions, records of observation, test results, student reflections or self-evaluations, and so on. Portfolios show growth over time, focusing on a student's progress rather than on a finished product. A portfolio provides a broad view of a student's achievements. E-portfolios (electronic portfolios) may be used to blend technology, accountability, and assessment. They may be housed online or stored on disc.

Based on the needs of the learner, alternative assessment techniques have the advantage of providing teachers and parents with directly observable products and clear evidence of students' performance. Alternative assessments support a Common Core Approach, focusing on students' performance, real-world learning experiences, and higher-level thinking skills. Assessment results are both meaningful and useful for improving instruction. The following guidelines can be used for creating, monitoring, and implementing alternative assessment in the classroom.

- Plan assessment alongside instruction, not as an afterthought. Your assessment plan should represent what is valued instructionally.

- Ensure assessments benefit all learners and inform teaching practices.

- Make expectations clear.

- Collect examples of alternative assessments and activities.

- Include peer assessment techniques. This can enhance students' evaluation skills and accountability.

- Use assessment results to develop learner profiles.

The Role of Digital Content Creation in Alternative Assessment

Creating digital content provides ample opportunities for performance-based assessment, authentic assessment, and portfolio assessment. Table 7.1 identifies project ideas for each of these assessment techniques. Evaluating students on their performance places greater emphasis on comprehension, critical thinking, reasoning, problem solving, metacognitive processes, and the construction of knowledge (Colley 2008; Jonassen 2006; Kingsley and Brinkerhoff 2011; Norton and Hathaway 2010; VanTassel-Baska 2014), all of which support 21st-century learning and a Common Core Approach to learning.

Table 7.1. Project Ideas for Various Assessment Techniques

Assessment Technique	Relationship to Digital Content Creation
Performance-Based Assessment	Digital projects can be used to demonstrate students' proficiency in specific computer skills; it also serves as a forum for demonstrating and presenting the students' knowledge and skills. For example, using a variety of digital media elements, students may create a project that demonstrates their knowledge of the water cycle, different body systems, plate tectonics, or other topics.
Authentic Assessment	Digital projects may be similar to what students are likely to encounter as professionals. For example, students may create projects that are designed to gather data for analysis (such as a web page that collects information from probes), create documentaries, or present a comparative analysis.
Portfolio Assessment	A multimedia database or e-portfolio can be designed to house digitized samples of a student's work. This includes reading samples (a recording of a student reading aloud), handwriting samples, homework, writing samples, artwork, and performances. Items may be entered into the computer by keyboard, scanner, microphone, video, or digital camera. Students may also create multimedia resumes.

In addition to evaluating students on the final outcome of their performance, it is important to assess students' progress through each step of the DDD-E process. To create successful projects, assessment must be ongoing. It begins with the DECIDE process and ends with an evaluation of the final product.

ASSESSMENT STRATEGIES

Checklists, narrative or anecdotal approaches, and rubrics are ways to evaluate a student's performance. Checklists indicate whether certain elements are present, narrative reports consist of a teacher's written notes or documentation of students' progress, and rubrics are used to evaluate designated performance criteria with a rating scale. Each of these can be used to guide students through each step of their project. In addition to teacher observations and anecdotal notes, daily journals (see Chapter 3) can help teachers diagnose each group's progress, problem-solving skills, and social skills. Checklists and rubrics help students know what is expected, leaving the teacher more time to advise and assist students with specific questions.

Creating a Rubric

Before developing a rubric, you must ask yourself the following questions:

- What national, state, or district standards am I addressing?

- What knowledge, skills, or concepts am I trying to assess?

- At what level should my students be performing?

- What criteria should be used to judge students' performance?

After identifying the standards and instructional goals, consider the qualities that need to be displayed in a student's work to illustrate proficient or "top level" performance of these goals. For example, "The student lists and describes the contributions of four people associated with the California Gold Rush." After developing the criteria for the highest level of performance, define the criteria for the lowest level of performance. For example, "The student is unable to list or describe the contributions of anyone associated with the California Gold Rush." After developing the high- and low-level criteria, compare and contrast the two to arrive at the middle level of performance. For example, "The student correctly identifies and describes the contributions of two people associated with the California Gold Rush." If additional distinctions are necessary, make comparisons between the existing criteria to arrive at other score levels.

Researchers discuss the validity, reliability, and benefits of rubrics (Jonsson and Svingby 2007; Moskal and Leydens 2000; Panadero and Jonsson 2013; Reddy 2011; Rezaei and Lovorn 2010). Validity includes the following:

- Content-related evidence—the extent to which the assessment instrument reflects students' knowledge in a particular content area

- Construct-related evidence—the extent to which the assessment instrument measures students' reasoning, problem-solving, or other processing skills

- Criterion-related evidence—the extent the assessment instrument identifies how well a student's performance can be generalized to other, more relevant activities (e.g., how well the student will perform outside of school or in a different situation)

Moskal and Leydens (2000) note that "since establishing validity is dependent on the purpose of the assessment, teachers should clearly state what they hope to learn about the responding students (i.e., the purpose) and how the students will display these proficiencies (i.e., the objectives)" (p. 4). They list three steps for evaluating the appropriateness of scoring categories to a stated purpose:

1. State the assessment purpose and objectives.

2. Develop score criteria for each objective.

3. Reflect on the following:

   - Are all of the objectives measured through the scoring criteria?

   - Are any of the scoring criteria unrelated to the objectives?

Teachers should avoid making vague statements such as, "The student covers the topic completely and in depth." What does "in depth" mean? What are the criteria for such an accomplishment? What has the student learned? In addition to validity issues, vague or general statements reduce the reliability of the rubric.

Reliability refers to the consistency of assessment scores. Two forms of reliability are interrater reliability and intrarater reliability. Interrater reliability is based on how well or how closely different evaluators or "raters" assess the same scores. If evaluators come to the same conclusion, then the assessment has "interrater reliability." It is important to have set criteria to guide the rating process. Intrarater reliability focuses on outside factors that may influence the scoring of students' work. For example, a rater's fatigue level, mood, or bias may influence the scoring process if the criteria are too subjective. Reliability can be improved by providing clear descriptions of the criteria, assigning a specific score to each task, and using topic-specific rubrics (Jonsson and Svingby 2007; Moskal 2003; Moskal and Leydens 2000; Reddy and Andrade 2010).

The use of rubrics can support improved student performance in many ways. Rubrics can increase transparency (i.e., letting students know what is expected of them), reduce anxiety, aid in the feedback process, improve student self-efficacy, and support student self-regulation (Panadero and Jonsson 2013). When designing a rubric, consider the age and ability level of the students. Note the simplicity of the primary rubric at the end of this chapter (see Primary MM Rubric blackline). Encourage student input. This allows students to work toward individual goals and to create their own learning experiences. Keep rubrics short, simple, and to the point. Categorize topic areas or provide separate rubrics for each area, depending on the project's sophistication. For beginning projects, focus on only a few outcomes.

Numbers or words (e.g., deficient, novice, apprentice, intermediate, proficient) may be used as a scale to evaluate learning outcomes. It is important that the criteria for each rating is established and listed on the rubric. For example, expanding upon the Gold Rush example noted earlier, a student would be given a score of "4" if she were able to list and describe the contributions of four people associated with the California Gold Rush; a "3" if she correctly identified and described the contributions of three people associated with the California Gold Rush; a "2" if she were able to list and describe the contributions of two people associated with the California Gold Rush; and a "1" if she correctly identified and described the contributions of only one person associated with the California Gold Rush. A score of "0" would be assigned if she was not able to do the task. Listing the criteria on the rubric or having it readily available for students provides them with clear expectations and performance standards.

In addition to content, teachers may assess students' projects according to required media elements, design, and so on. These would be considered in the construction of the rubric as well and are discussed in more detail under Using Rubrics.

Resources for Creating and Finding Sample Rubrics

Sample rubrics can be found on the Internet at a variety of websites. In addition, there are online tools available to help teachers construct their own rubrics. Examples include the following:

Kathy Schrock's Guide for Everything: Assessment and Rubrics (available at http://www.schrockguide.net/assessment-and-rubrics.html) lists multiple links to rubric resources, including Common Core-specific resources, presentation rubrics, digital story rubrics, and more.

Midlink Magazine Teacher Resource Room (available at http://www.ncsu.edu/midlink/ho.html) provides links to rubrics, evaluation resources, and downloadable rubric templates.

Rubistar (available at http://rubistar.4teachers.org) provides sample rubrics for a variety of topics, as well as an online rubric generator where teachers can create or customize their own rubrics. Both English and Spanish versions are available.

Rubrics allow teachers to clarify criteria in specific forms and make project assessment more objective and consistent. In addition, rubrics allow students to begin their projects with clear and consistent guidelines through which they will be evaluated. Students know what is expected of them and their peers. Rubrics are useful for providing feedback and documenting students' progress.

Using Rubrics

To help students understand how rubrics will be used to evaluate their projects, review several existing projects. These may be teacher created for demonstration purposes, samples included with the software, projects from previous classes, or examples on the web. Review projects that are comparable to your students' ability levels. Encourage students to discuss what they like and dislike about the projects, the projects' strengths and weaknesses, and what they might do to make the project better. Decide what criteria might be used to evaluate the projects. Review sample projects before the DESIGN stage.

As mentioned, rubrics ensure that the students and teacher understand how the project will be evaluated. It is important to provide students with a list of evaluation criteria and standards for the assigned project at the onset of their digital project. Students will know what is expected of them and may put more effort into their projects because of it. Encourage students to use the rubrics to guide them during the learning process and to explain the rubrics to their parents.

Rubrics can be designed to address each step of the DDD-E process and the desired outcome or focus of the assigned projects. As noted in previous chapters, the steps include:

- DECIDE—Brainstorming and researching

- DESIGN—Planning and designing

- DEVELOP—Gathering and creating media

- EVALUATE—Continual assessment of projects

Figure 7.1 depicts the evaluation stages of the DDD-E process. Each item in Figure 7.1 is included as a blackline master at the end of this chapter. As previously noted, the teacher may also review daily journals to ensure the groups' progress and to help the teacher facilitate instruction. The daily journal entry sheet is in Chapter 3. Additional checklists can be found in Chapter 4.

DECIDE. Assessment begins with the groups' original idea and their ability to define the major sections of their reports, as well as how these sections relate to each other. Students should be able to articulate their research question, explain why it is important, and discuss how they intend to pursue it. Following the students' initial research, the teacher may decide to collect, review, and discuss each group's brainstorming or KWL Knowledge Chart (see Chapter 3), as well as their research findings. Teachers can check the accuracy of the information, ensure that students are using a variety of resources, and verify that the students are addressing the stated questions. Note that the

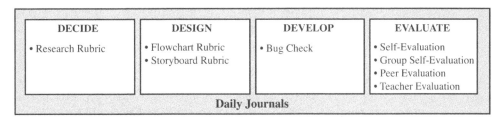

Figure 7.1. Evaluation stages of the DDD-E process.

criteria for each score need to be defined by the teacher (and students, if they helped create the rubric). A sample Research Rubric blackline master appears at the end of this chapter.

DESIGN. After their research has been verified, students need to map and define their ideas through flowcharts. After reviewing the flowcharts, the teacher should meet with each group to discuss the anticipated links, sequences, and section relationships identified in their flowcharts. Assessment may be based on the flowchart's structure, links, clarity, symbols, and labels. See the Design Rubric blackline master at the end of this chapter for an example.

Storyboard production can begin after the flowcharts have been approved. Storyboards help students plan how their computer screens will look and relate to each other. Students should make their storyboards as clear and complete as possible. This allows the teacher to provide guidance before the students invest a great amount of time in the final production phase. Teachers may want to provide students with a list of design guidelines (see Chapter 4). The Flowchart Rubric blackline master at the end of this chapter can be used as an example. Again, the criteria for each score need to be defined by the teacher (and students, if they helped create the rubric). The final production phase takes place after the groups' storyboards have been approved.

DEVELOP. In the DEVELOP phase, students construct their final product to meet the standards and criteria set at the beginning of the assignment. Before students submit their projects for final evaluation, projects should go through a review and debugging phase. This is best performed by their peers. Students can check each other's projects to see whether they meet the required criteria, as well as check for programming, spelling, and punctuation errors. A Bug Stops Here blackline master is available at the end of the chapter.

EVALUATE. Self-, peer-, and teacher evaluations occur after the projects are complete. These evaluations provide students with multiple levels of feedback. Self-evaluation encourages students to reflect on what they have learned as well as how it was learned. In addition, it provides students with the opportunity to elaborate on what went well and what they might have done differently. Peer evaluation offers students another audience for their projects. It allows students to measure the extent to which they were able to explain their work and ideas successfully to each other. In addition, peer evaluations allow students to practice their evaluation skills, provide ideas and constructive feedback, and help each other with the projects. Peer evaluations may also be used within groups (intragroup evaluation) to evaluate each member's cooperative efforts. (See Group Self-Evaluation blackline master at the end of this chapter.) Teacher assessment provides ongoing support and guidance, as well as a final evaluation of the project. The teacher's evaluation should reflect the criteria established during the beginning stages of the project.

The project's final evaluation may be based on one or more of the following: content learning, technology skills, design skills (see Additional Rubric Options section), as well as media appropriateness, social skills, or self-reflection, depending on the purpose of the project. The depth and scope of the evaluation should be consistent with the students' age and ability level. Sample evaluation forms are reproduced at the end of this chapter.

Additional Rubric Options

Depending on the project's goal and the students' ability level, teachers may wish to employ multiple rubrics to evaluate various outcomes. For example, a content rubric may be used to evaluate the students' understanding of a particular topic, as well as how well they communicated their knowledge. A technical rubric may review defective links, inoperative media (e.g., video or audio clips), and so on. A design rubric may critique the clarity and consistency of the layout, purpose of the media and navigation options, contrast between text and background, text readability (including fonts, sizes, colors, and styles), types of feedback, and whether the students followed their storyboards and flowchart.

A presentation rubric may provide students with feedback on their speaking skills, appearance, organization, professionalism, ability to capture and hold the audience's attention, and so on.

One or more of these rubrics may be provided to the students and attached to the teacher's final evaluation form to aid in the summative evaluation of the students' projects. Examples of each of these rubrics are available at the end of this chapter.

ASSIGNING GRADES

Groups may receive a grade based on the combined, averaged scores of the teacher and peer evaluations (see Figure 7.2). Sample teacher and peer evaluation forms appear at the end of this chapter.

Teacher evaluation forms may include an overall rating of a group's journal entries and bibliography information, as well as the average rating of the group's storyboard, design, content, and mechanics rubrics. For example, using the sample teacher evaluation form located at the end of this chapter, a group may have averaged a rating of 2 on their storyboards, design, and technical rubrics, and the teacher may have rated the group's content, journal entries, and bibliography information as 3s (see Figure 7.3). The teacher's evaluation equals 15 points, or an average score of 2.5.

Teachers may choose to insert their own categories for final evaluation. In addition to the sample form presented in Figure 7.3, a blank form is included at the end of this chapter.

Using the Peer Evaluation blackline master, students can evaluate each other's projects. The sample form available at the end of this chapter provides space for students to comment on a project's content and design. It also asks that students rate the project on a scale of 0 to 3. Teachers can evaluate the students' comments and weight them appropriately, transferring the students' average rating to the final grades evaluation form (see Final Grades blackline master). For example, if three groups evaluated a project, and groups 1 and 2 gave the project a 3 and group 3 gave the project a 2, the average score transferred to the final grades sheet would be 2.67. Figure 7.4 shows the final grade sheet with transferred scores from the teacher's evaluation and average peer evaluation. In this example, the group grade equals 2.59, the average of the teacher and peer evaluations. The letter grade depends on the teacher's grading scale.

Individual grades may be based on the combined and averaged scores of students' self-assessment, the group's self-evaluations, and the group grade (see Figure 7.5). This ensures individual accountability within groups. Sample self-evaluation and group self-evaluation forms appear at the end of this chapter.

Using the Self-Evaluation blackline master, students reflect on what they learned. The teacher uses the student's comments to rate the evaluation on a scale of 0 to 3 and adds his or her rationale for the score on the back of the evaluation. For example, if a student is specific and notably

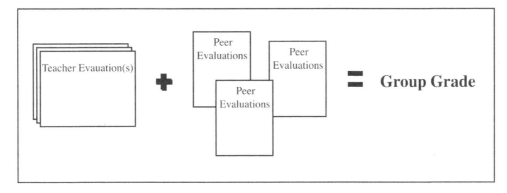

Figure 7.2. Assigning group grades.

Teacher Evaluation

CRITERIA	0 to.99	1 to 1.99	2 to 2.99	3
Storyboards (see Storyboard Rubric)			2	
Design (see Design Rubric)			2	
Content (see Content Rubric)				3
Technical (see Technical Rubric)			2	
Daily journal entries				3
Bibliographical information				3

Good job! You effectively organized your project and demonstrated excellent teamwork! You averaged 2.5 on your project.   Total __15__

Figure 7.3. Sample teacher evaluation form.

Final Grades

CRITERIA	0 to.99	1 to 1.99	2 to 2.99	3
Group Self-Evaluations				
Self-Evaluation				
Peer Evaluations			2.67	
Teacher Evaluation			2.5	

Group Grade __2.59__   Individual Grade _____

Figure 7.4. Final grade sheet with two transferred scores.

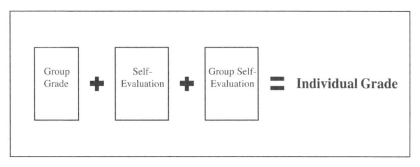

Figure 7.5. Assigning an individual grade.

reflective on each of the questions, the teacher may score the evaluation a 3. This score is transferred to the final grade sheet.

The Group Self-Evaluation blackline master provides group members with the opportunity to rate the participation and contributions of their teammates, as well as their own. The average score of each student is transferred to his or her final grade sheet. For example, if Samantha received ratings of 3, 2, and 2 from her teammates and rated herself a 3, her average group self-evaluation score would be 2.5. The average of the self-evaluation, group self-evaluation, and group grade determine an individual's final grade. In Figure 7.6, the self-evaluation and group self-evaluation scores have been transferred to the final grade sheet, along with the scores from Figure 7.4. The final individual grade equals 2.70: the average of the group self-evaluation (2.5), self-evaluation (3), and the group grade (2.59). Again, the letter grade depends on the teacher's grading scale.

Teachers are encouraged to make their own evaluation forms designed to meet the needs and ability levels of their students. Teachers can determine the point scale (0–3, 5–10, etc.) and decide how to weigh the various scores for final evaluation. This chapter provides several examples of various rubrics; teachers may pick and choose those that are applicable to their students and projects. Additional forms for specific projects are included in Chapters 8, 9, 10, 11, and 12.

Final Grades

CRITERIA	0 to .99	1 to 1.99	2 to 2.99	3
Group Self-Evaluations			2.5	
Self-Evaluation				3.0
Peer Evaluations			2.67	
Teacher Evaluation			2.5	

Group Grade __2.59__   Individual Grade __2.70__

Figure 7.6. Final grade sheet with transferred scores.

REFLECTIONS AND FUTURE GOALS

Learning does not end with a grade. Teachers need to provide time for students and themselves to reflect on what went well and how they would change or improve upon the assignment in the future. Students have an opportunity to assess their own learning and contributions on the self-evaluation form, but their feedback about the learning experience may help teachers improve the organization, management, timelines, and so on for the next project. Teachers are encouraged to solicit feedback from students, having them write or discuss what helped them complete the project, where they may have encountered confusion or frustration, and what changes they would recommend for the next project. Student feedback as well as the teacher's own reflections and analyses of student learning should be used to improve future learning experiences associated with the development of digital content.

SUMMARY

The multifaceted nature of digital content creation encourages many types of assessment. Assessment is ongoing and determines whether a group is ready to proceed to the next stage of development. Checklists, rubrics, and other assessment tools ensure that students know what is expected of them. In addition, rubrics allow teachers to clarify criteria in specific forms and make project assessment more objective and consistent. Teachers need to ensure the validity and reliability of their assessment tools, including rubrics.

The DDD-E model poses several levels of assessment. In the DECIDE stage, students should be able to articulate their research question, explain why it is important, and discuss how they intend to pursue it. Next, they should demonstrate their ability to gather, organize, and synthesize information through brainstorming activities and research. In the DESIGN stage, students need to display how they intend to map and link their ideas together. In addition to examining the project flowcharts, students can explain the anticipated links, sequences, and section relationships identified in their flowcharts with the teacher. Afterward, students can begin producing their project's storyboards. The completed set is assessed by the teacher before the students continue to the DEVELOP stage. The DEVELOP stage includes review and debugging by the students' peers. Final projects include self-, peer, and teacher evaluations. Daily journal entries (see Chapter 3) that assess the group's progress and ability to work together can be collected and submitted with the group's final project. Groups may receive a grade based on the combined scores of the teacher and peer evaluations, and a final individual grade may be based on students' self-assessment, group self-evaluations, and group grade. Rubrics ensure that both students and teacher understand how each step of the project will be evaluated. At the end of the project, student feedback, teacher reflection, and analyses of student learning can be used to improve future digital projects and learner outcomes.

BLACKLINE MASTERS

This chapter includes an assortment of blackline masters designed to help teachers and students review and evaluate digital projects. Blackline masters include:

- Research Rubric: used in the DECIDE phase to ensure that students are ready to move on to the DESIGN phase

- Flowchart Rubric: a form used to evaluate a group's flowchart before the students proceed to the storyboard stage of the DESIGN phase

- Storyboard Rubric: a final evaluation form for a group's storyboards; a storyboard checklist is provided in Chapter 4

- The Bug Stops Here: a review sheet used to help students debug projects during the DEVELOP phase, before the projects are submitted for final evaluation

- Self-Evaluation: one way in which students can reflect on their participation and learning at the end of a multimedia assignment

- Peer Evaluation: one way in which student groups can evaluate other groups' work

- Group Self-Evaluation: a sample of how students may evaluate their own group's performance (intragroup evaluation)

- Teacher Evaluation: a sample of how teachers may evaluate a group's project

- Blank Evaluation: a template for creating your own rubrics

- Content Rubric: a sample rubric for evaluating the content of a project (Note: Educators will need to fill in the objectives and list the performance criteria.)

- Technical Rubric: a sample rubric for reviewing defective links, inoperative media (e.g., video or audio clips), the use of technology (scanners, digital camera, video camera)

- Design Rubric: a sample rubric for evaluating a project's design

- Presentation Rubric: a sample rubric for evaluating project presentations

- Primary MM Rubric: a simple rubric designed for young children

- Final Grades: an accumulating score sheet for determining an individual's final grade, as well as a group grade

REFERENCES

Colley, K. 2008. Performance-based assessment. *The Science Teacher*, 75(8), 68–72.

Hardiman, M., and Whitman, G. 2014. Assessment and the learning brain. *Independent School*, 73(2), 36–41.

Jonassen, D. H. 2006. *Modeling with technology: Mindtools for conceptual change* (3rd ed.). Upper Saddle River, NJ: Prentice-Hall.

Jonsson, A., and Svingby, G. 2007. The use of scoring rubrics: Reliability, validity and educational consequences. *Educational Research Review*, 2(2), 130–144.

Kingsley, K., and Brinkerhoff, J. 2011. Web 2.0 tools for authentic instruction, learning, and assessment. *Social Studies and the Young Learner*, 23(3), 9–13.

Moskal, B. M. 2003. Recommendations for developing classroom performance assessments and scoring rubrics. *Practical Assessment, Research & Evaluation*, 8(14). Available at: http://PAREonline. net/getvn.asp?v=8&n=14. Retrieved on August 3, 2014.

Moskal, B. M., and Leydens, J. A. 2000. Scoring rubric development: Validity and reliability. *Practical Assessment, Research & Evaluation*, 7(10). Available at: http://pareonline.net/getvn.asp? v=7&n=10. Retrieved on August 3, 2014.

Norton, P., and Hathaway, D. 2010. Video production as an instructional strategy: Content learning and teacher practice. *Contemporary Issues in Technology and Teacher Education*, 10(1), 145–166.

Panadero, E., and Jonsson, A. 2013. The use of scoring rubrics for formative assessment purposes revisited: A review. *Educational Research Review*, 9, 129–144.

Reddy, M. 2011. Design and development of rubrics to improve assessment outcomes: A pilot study in a master's level business program in India. *Quality Assurance in Education: An International Perspective*, 19(1), 84–104.

Reddy, Y., and Andrade, H. 2010. A review of rubric use in higher education. *Assessment & Evaluation in Higher Education*, 35(4), 435–448.

Rezaei, A., and Lovorn, M. 2010. Reliability and validity of rubrics for assessment through writing. *Assessing Writing*, 15(1), 18–39.

VanTassel-Baska, J. (2014). Performance-based assessment. *Gifted Child Today*, 37(1), 41–47.

Research Rubric

CRITERIA	0	1	2	3
Clarity of research question	There is no research question stated.	Question is vague and hard to understand.	Question is somewhat clear, but could be more precise.	Question is clear and specific.
Supportive answers	There are no answers to the stated question.	Few of the answers support the research question.	Most of the answers support the stated question.	The answers directly support the stated question.
Resources	No or only one reputable resource is used.	Two reputable resources are used.	Three reputable resources are used.	Four or more reputable resources are used.
Accuracy	Information is lacking and is inaccurate.	The information contains more than one inaccurate statement.	The information contains one inaccurate statement.	The researched information is accurate.
Bibliographical information	Information is lacking and is inaccurate.	The information contains more than one inaccurate statement.	The information contains one inaccurate statement.	The information is correct.
Brainstorm (or KWL Knowledge Chart)	Activity was not started.	Activity is missing more than one required element.	Activity is missing one required element.	The information is complete.
				Total _____

Flowchart Rubric

CRITERIA	0	1	2	3
Structure	The flowchart is incomplete or missing.	The flowchart does not have any structure.	Structure is not aligned with the project's goals and content.	Structure is aligned with the project's goals and content.
Branching	There is no branching.	Branching is incomplete.	Branching is complete, but it is not clearly depicted.	Branching is complete and clearly depicted.
Labels	None of the elements of the flowchart are labeled.	More than one of the elements is not labeled.	All elements are labeled, but not easy to understand.	Each element is clearly labeled and easy to understand.
Symbols	No symbols are used.	More than one incorrect symbol is used.	One incorrect symbol is used.	All symbols are correct.
Ease of use	Flowchart cannot be followed.	Flowchart is difficult to follow; it's easy to get lost.	Flowchart is somewhat easy to follow; it could be clearer.	Flowchart is easy to follow and understand.
				Total _____

Storyboard Rubric

CRITERIA	0	1	2	3
Screens	More than two of the required screens are not included.	Two of the required screens are not included.	All but one of the required screens are included.	All required screens are included.
Links	No links are indicated or described.	More than one link or description is incomplete.	One link or description is incomplete.	All links are indicated and described.
Content	Content is missing or incomplete.	Content is complete, but inaccurate.	Content is complete, but difficult to read and understand.	Content is complete, factual, interesting, and easy to understand.
Layout	The design is inconsistent in more than one area.	The design is inconsistent in one area.	The design is consistent, but not clear.	The design is consistent and clear.
Media elements	Media elements are not included.	Some of the media elements are included and described.	All media elements are included, but not all are described.	Required media elements are included and described.
Font, background, and transition	Font, background, and transition information is incomplete.	Two of the requirements are incomplete.	One of the requirements is incomplete.	All font, background, and transition information is provided.
				Total _____

The Bug Stops Here

Name of group being reviewed: _____

Project title: _____

Reviewed by: _____

Spelling Corrections

Word	Page		Word	Page
_____	_____		_____	_____
_____	_____		_____	_____
_____	_____		_____	_____

Punctuation and Grammar Corrections

Problem	Page	Problem	Page
_____	_____	_____	_____
_____	_____	_____	_____
_____	_____	_____	_____

Link and Media Corrections

Problem	Page	Problem	Page
_____	_____	_____	_____
_____	_____	_____	_____
_____	_____	_____	_____

List design and content comments on back.

Self-Evaluation

Name of group: _____

Project title: _____

Group member: _____

How did you contribute to the project?

What did you learn about your topic in the process of developing this project?

What did you learn about multimedia development in the process of developing this project?

What did you learn about yourself in the process of developing this project?

Teacher's Rating: _____   (Comments on back)

Peer Evaluation

Name of group being reviewed: _____

Project title: _____

Reviewed by: _____

Content

What did you learn about this topic that you did not know before?

In terms of content, what are the strengths of this project?

How might the presentation of information be improved?

Design

What are the strengths in the design of this project?

What improvements in the design would you suggest?

On a scale of 0 to 3 (3 being the highest),
how would you rate this project?   _____

Group Self-Evaluation

Name of group being reviewed: _____

Project title: _____

Group member: _____

What were your group's strengths?

What were your group's weaknesses?

What are some of the things that you learned about working with others?

What would you do better the next time your group works together?

On the back of this form, list yourself and your group members. Rate yourself and each of your group members' level of participation in the project. 0 = not enough, 1 = fair, 2 = a lot, 3 = did most of the work. Explain your ratings.

Teacher Evaluation

CRITERIA	0 to .99	1 to 1.99	2 to 2.99	3
Storyboards (see Storyboard Rubric)				
Design (see Design Rubric)				
Content (see Content Rubric)				
Technical (see Technical Rubric)				
Daily journal entries				
Bibliographical information				
			Total _____	

CRITERIA	0	1	2	3
				Total _____

Content Rubric

CRITERIA	0	1	2	3
Objective:				
Objective:				
Objective:				
Structure: Begins with an introduction, uses students' own words, and ends with a conclusion.	Does not use students' own words.	Uses students' own words, but intro and conclusion are missing.	Uses students' own words, but intro or conclusion is missing.	Meets all of the require-ments.
Flow: Chunks information in a meaningful way, text is easy to follow and understand.	Information is scattered and difficult to understand.	Information is somewhat organized, but difficult to understand.	Information is somewhat organized and easy to understand.	Meets all of the require-ments.
Mechanics: Spelling, grammar, and punctuation are correct.	More than four spelling, grammar, or punctuation mistakes are made.	Three or four spelling, grammar, or punctuation mistakes are made.	One or two spelling, grammar, or punctuation mistakes are made.	Meets all of the require-ments.
				Total _____

Technical Rubric

CRITERIA	0	1	2	3
Navigation links	More than two of the links do not work correctly.	Two of the navigation links do not work correctly.	One of the navigation links does not work correctly.	All links work correctly.
Menu links	More than two of the menu links do not work correctly.	Two of the menu links do not work correctly.	One of the menu links does not work correctly.	All links work correctly.
Media elements	More than two of the media elements are not working.	All but two of the media elements are working.	All but one of the media elements are working.	All media elements operate correctly.
Text boxes	More than four text boxes aren't "read-only" or locked where appropriate.	All but three or four text boxes are "read-only" or locked where appropriate.	All but one or two text boxes are "read-only" or locked where appropriate.	All text boxes are "read-only" or locked where appropriate.
Use of different technology tools (e.g. digital camera, scanner, video camera, microphone, etc.)	Project is lacking more than two of the necessary tools.	Project incorporates all but two of the necessary tools.	Project incorporates all but one of the necessary tools.	Project incorporates all of the necessary tools.
				Total _____

Design Rubric

CRITERIA	0	1	2	3
Continuity	Project does not follow storyboards or flowchart.	Project follows some of the storyboards.	Project follows the storyboards but not the flowchart.	Project follows the storyboards and flowchart exactly.
Layout	The layout is not clear and is inconsistent.	The layout is clear but is inconsistent.	The layout is somewhat clear and is consistent.	The layout is very clear and consistent.
Purpose of media elements	More than two media elements are not meaningful.	All but two of the media elements are meaningful and add to the project.	All but one of the media elements are meaningful and add to the project.	All media elements are meaningful and add to the project.
Text clarity	Text is not easy to read and doesn't contrast with the background.	The text is not easy to read but contrasts with the background.	The text is easy to read but doesn't contrast with the background.	All text is easy to read and contrasts with the background.
Navigation buttons	None of the navigation buttons are easy to understand.	Some of the navigation buttons are easy to understand.	Most of the navigation buttons are easy to understand.	Navigation buttons are clearly marked and identified.
Feedback	Feedback is not consistent or appropriate.	Feedback is consistent but not appropriate.	Feedback is not consistent, but it is appropriate.	Feedback is consistent and appropriate.
				Total _____

Presentation Rubric

CRITERIA	0	1	2	3
Clarity	Presenter(s) did not speak clearly and did not speak loud enough.	Presenter(s) spoke loud enough, but did not speak clearly.	Presenter(s) spoke clearly but not in a loud enough voice.	Presenter(s) was articulate and spoke in a loud enough voice.
Attire	Presenter's attire was not appropriate.	Most of the presenter's attire was appropriate.	Presenter's attire was appropriate, but not well kept.	Presenter(s) was well groomed and dressed for the presentation.
Professionalism	Presenter(s) was rude and disrespectful.	Presenter(s) seemed indifferent and not attentive to the audience.	Presenter(s) acted professional most but not all of the time.	Presenter(s) was polite, professional, and attentive to the audience.
Organization	Presenter(s) was very disorganized, distracting the presentation.	Presenter(s) was somewhat organized but needs to improve a lot.	Presenter(s) was well organized most of the time.	Presenter(s) was well organized throughout the presentation.
Appeal	Presenter(s) did not captivate or hold my attention.	Presenter(s) held my attention for a short period of time.	Presenter(s) held my attention for most of the time.	Presenter(s) captured and held my attention the whole time.
Outcome	I did not learn anything from this presentation.	I did not learn that much from this presentation.	I learned a lot, but I feel more could have been presented.	I learned a lot from this presentation; it was very thorough.
				Total _____

From *Digital Content Creation in Schools: A Common Core Approach* by Karen S. Ivers and Ann E. Barron. Santa Barbara, CA: Libraries Unlimited. Copyright © 2015.

Primary MM Rubric

The project starts with a title screen.

Directions are provided.

Enough information is provided.

The information is correct.

There are no spelling or punctuation errors.

___ pictures and ___ sounds were used.

The screens are linked together so the project makes sense.

Final Grades

CRITERIA	0 to .99	1 to 1.99	2 to 2.99	3
Group Self-Evaluations				
Self-Evaluation				
Peer Evaluations				
Teacher Evaluation				

Group Grade _____   Individual Grade _____

Chapter 8

Digital Content Creation Projects: Presentation Tools

A SCENARIO

Ms. Timassy just celebrated her 25th year as a teacher. Teaching and expectations had changed over the years, but Ms. Timassy was shocked when she learned her first-grade students would now be required to create their own PowerPoint presentations. Ms. Timassy had just learned PowerPoint herself a few years ago. "How can six- and seven-year-olds be expected to create a PowerPoint presentation?" she thought. She discussed this with her colleagues who assured her that, given a set of templates, her students were very capable. Ms. Timassy began with a small group of her high-ability students and provided them with a template and instructions on how to add text, pictures, and add additional slides. They developed a short, five-slide presentation together. Unlike Ms. Timassy when she first learned PowerPoint, her students were not apprehensive and enjoyed "playing" with the tool. "Wow," she thought, "I have really underestimated my students' capabilities. Their world is so much different from mine. Technology is natural and fun for them." Ms. Timassy took advantage of her student experts and teamed them with her other students as they created their PowerPoint slides. Next, she had student pairs practice presenting their presentations to each other. It was a humbling yet exciting experience for Ms. Timassy.

OVERVIEW

Presentation projects can be used across grade levels to address a variety of standards, including those related to listening and speaking skills, writing, and so on. Students learn to work together, apply their research skills, plan and organize content, select appropriate media and layouts, and deliver professional-looking presentations. Designing and presenting presentation projects provide students with invaluable real-world learning experiences; many professions and activities require presentation and public-speaking skills.

Although professional-looking presentations can be created with hypermedia and web tools, there are several tools on the market especially designed for creating large-group presentations. Microsoft PowerPoint, Apple's Keynote, Google Slides, Glogster, and Prezi are some of the many tools available (see Chapter 6). Most presentation programs provide the option of using predesigned templates. Some programs also have "wizards" or other guides that prompt users through the design process.

This chapter presents several ideas for digital projects that can be created with presentation tools. A lesson description and the DDD-E process are provided for each activity.

SAMPLE PROJECTS

The following projects can be created with most presentation tools. Teachers should choose the most appropriate tool for their students and ensure that they are familiar with the tool before beginning the project. Students should also be familiar with guidelines for presentations (see Guidelines for Presentations blackline master at the end of this chapter). See Chapter 3 for computer scheduling options.

Persuasive Automotive

Lesson Description: The goal of this lesson is to engage older students in persuasive speaking and writing strategies. Students structure ideas and arguments in a sustained, persuasive, and sophisticated way and support them with precise and relevant examples. In this lesson, students research, compare, and analyze real-world considerations of purchasing an automobile. Each group of students is assigned a different automobile (e.g., a sports utility vehicle—SUV) from different manufacturers. As part of their research assignment, student groups must try to persuade classmates that their assigned automobile is the best. For example, students researching a Subaru Forester would create a presentation highlighting what they believe are its benefits—gas mileage, price, warranty, options, aesthetics, safety, buying options (current percentage rates and leasing options), and so on. Audience members would have the chance to ask questions and debate the presented issues. Other topics for persuasive speaking include school rules, laws, best places to eat or shop, the most influential person who ever lived, and so on. For younger students, teachers can have them try to persuade one another of Goldilocks's guilt or innocence in trespassing, what makes the best pet, and so forth. Students have the opportunity to state a clear position in support of a proposal, support a position with relevant evidence, follow a simple organizational pattern, and address reader concerns.

DECIDE. As a class, determine what students know about buying an automobile (use the KWL Knowledge Chart in Chapter 3). Ask students what they know about their own or their parents' cars and why they purchased them. Complete the second column of the KWL Knowledge Chart by asking students what they would like to know about purchasing cars. Introduce the project by assigning students to teams as described in previous chapters. Explain that groups will randomly choose an SUV to research and share with the class. As part of the assignment, explain that they will be required to present an overview and the benefits of the SUV via a presentation tool. Continue to explain that the purpose of the presentation is to persuade classmates that their SUV is the best. Groups must be prepared to answer questions and to debate the presented issues. As a group, design an evaluation form for the presentation. For an example, see the Persuasive Presentation Evaluation blackline master at the end of this chapter.

Provide student groups with the opportunity to brainstorm and research topics about their SUV. Check their progress and bibliography sheets (see Chapter 3) before letting them move on to the DESIGN phase.

DESIGN. After the students' research has been approved, provide class time to create their storyboards. To expedite the process, teachers may provide the students with a standardized

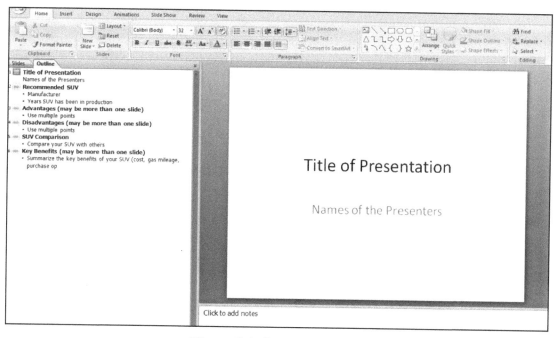

Figure 8.1. Sample template.

template (see Figure 8.1). A limit of 15 screens could be imposed, if desired. Remind students of the purpose of bulleted text and the printout options available in the presentation tool.

DEVELOP. After the students' storyboards have been approved, team members discuss and assign each other specific "lead" roles in the development of the project. For example, job responsibilities may include project manager, graphic artist, editor, instructional designer, and so on. Depending on the resources available, students may work together to find or create graphics and other media, conduct additional research, or begin scripting their presentation. Team members should review and practice their presentation before presenting it to the class.

EVALUATE. Teachers and students use the evaluation form created during the DECIDE phase of the project. Students may be evaluated on the effectiveness of their presentation, its organization and structure, its content and accuracy, their speaking skills, and so on. The evaluations are collected and averaged by the teacher. Students may also choose to conduct self- and intragroup evaluations (see Chapter 7).

Famous People in History

Lesson Description: The goal of this lesson is to engage students in an informative presentation about a famous person in history, a common requirement across grade levels, addressing social studies and language arts standards. Student groups have the opportunity to choose a famous person and to share their findings with the class. Media elements can be added to the presentations to highlight certain aspects of the famous person. For example, if students choose to do a presentation on Scott Joplin, music can be added to demonstrate his work. If Neil Armstrong were chosen, students might opt to include an audio segment of his first words on the moon. In any case, the goal of the presentation should be to inform viewers about a particular person in history. Presentations should be clear, well organized, and interesting and should address the content criteria established by the teacher.

DECIDE. Assign students to teams. Ask what makes a person famous. Students may discuss current celebrities. Ask them what makes these people different from others or debate whether they really are different. Discuss how celebrities or famous people of today compare with famous people of yesterday. Discuss what made people in history famous.

Following this discussion, have the groups decide on a famous historical person to research and present to the class. Ensure that each group chooses a different person. After their selection is approved, students conduct research on the person they have chosen. Evaluate their research before letting students continue the DESIGN phase.

DESIGN. Students need to examine their research findings and organize the information for their presentation. Make sure they understand the importance of planning and the development of storyboards. Provide groups with a list of design guidelines, a presentation storyboard template (see Chapter 4), and the journal entry form and project checklist. Explain each form. In addition, provide groups with the storyboard, design, content, and technical rubrics (see Chapter 7). Multiple copies of the journal entry form and the bibliography form should be available. Remind students of the purpose of bulleted text and the printout options available in the presentation tool (see Chapter 6). Teachers may choose to set a minimum and maximum number of screens in the presentation.

DEVELOP. After the students' research and storyboards have been approved, team members assume specific roles in the development of the project. If resources are limited, students may work on the following while they are waiting for time on a computer:

- Creating a Venn diagram that compares the life of their famous person to their own lives

- Drawing a portrait of their famous person

- Creating a diorama depicting a prominent event in the person's life

- Creating a timeline of their famous person's life

EVALUATE. Peers and the teacher can evaluate group presentations by using the content, technical, and presentation rubrics in Chapter 7. The students receive a group grade based on combined scores. Students receive an individual grade based on their group, self-, and intragroup evaluations. The teacher may present a whole-class quiz to assess what was learned from each presentation.

Scientific Follow-Up

Lesson Description: The goal of this lesson is to engage students in reporting their scientific findings. This is one way to assess students' knowledge of what they have learned and can be applied to science projects across grade levels.

Following small-group science experiments, organize student groups into design teams to present their findings to the whole class. Talk about how they think such presentations might relate to real life. Discuss the importance and purpose of presentations in the business world, in the scientific community, and in education.

DECIDE. In the DECIDE phase, student groups must decide how to best represent and discuss their findings by reexamining their data and methods. Students should organize their ideas with a planning sheet (see Chapter 4) before continuing to the DESIGN phase.

DESIGN. Depending on the experiment, students may want to incorporate a variety of media (e.g., charts, photos, animations) into their presentations to illustrate their methods and findings (see Figure 8.2).

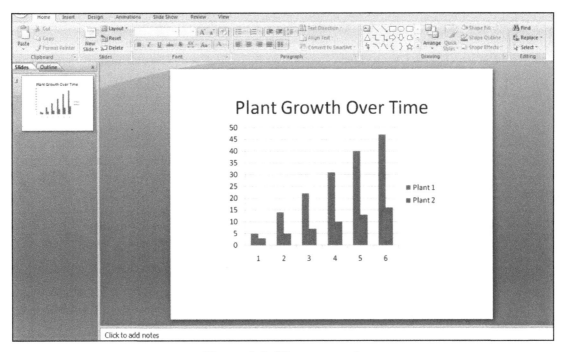

Figure 8.2. Chart example.

Provide groups with a list of design guidelines, a presentation storyboard template (see Chapter 4), and the journal entry form and project checklist available in Chapters 3 and 4. Explain each form. In addition, provide groups with the storyboard, presentation design, content, and technical rubrics available in Chapter 7. Remind students of the purpose of bulleted text and the printout options available in the presentation tool (see Chapter 6). Teachers may choose to set a minimum and maximum number of screens in the presentation.

DEVELOP. After the students' storyboards have been approved, teams work together using the available technology resources. Team members should review and practice their presentation before presenting it to the class.

EVALUATE. Peers and the teacher can evaluate group presentations (see Chapter 7). The students receive a group grade based on the teacher and peer evaluations. Students receive an individual grade based on their self- and intragroup evaluations. The two grades can be averaged for a final score (see Final Grades in Chapter 7).

How To

Lesson Description: The goal of this lesson is to encourage students to teach each other how to do something and addresses standards related to listening and speaking skills. For example, students need to be able to give precise directions and instructions, restate and perform multiple-step instructions and directions, and so on. There are many advantages to using a presentation tool for instruction: step-by-step instructions can be bulleted, enlarged photographs can show procedures close up, video and animation can show a sequence of events, and learners can be provided with screen-by-screen handouts to assist them in the learning process.

DECIDE. Assign student teams. Introduce the project, explaining that the goal of the presentation is to teach their classmates how to do something. You may begin by asking the students to tell you how to make a peanut butter and jelly sandwich. Have a loaf of bread, a jar of peanut butter, a jar of jelly, a plate, and a spoon on a table in front of you. Depending on the age of the students, this can be quite funny. Do exactly as they say. For example, if the students say, "Put the peanut butter on the bread," pick up the jar of peanut butter and place it on the loaf of bread. Students will quickly discover the importance of precise and properly sequenced directions. Discuss different strategies for communicating how to do something and the advantages of using different media elements. Following the discussion, let groups decide on something to teach. Next, students should brainstorm different ways to teach the procedure to the class.

DESIGN. When students are ready to move on to the DESIGN phase, make sure they understand the importance of designing their presentation on storyboards. Discuss the design issues explained in Chapter 4 and, if possible, show the students samples of "how-to" presentations. Again, review the significance of certain media elements.

DEVELOP. Once the students' storyboards are approved, they can begin developing their presentations. Team members assume designated roles and take turns using the available technology resources. If each student has their own laptop or tablet, students can work individually or in pairs, based on their assigned roles and content responsibility. The project manager ensures each member is on task and understands his or her responsibility to the team.

EVALUATE. How-to presentations may be evaluated by the rubrics in Chapter 7 or by a customized rubric designed by the class. For an example, see the How-to Evaluation blackline master at the end of this chapter.

SUMMARY

In addition to planning and organizational skills, presentation tools provide students with the opportunity to practice speaking in front of a group and conveying their ideas verbally. Presentation tools can help support a presenter's train of thought, as well as provide visual cues for learners. Creating and delivering presentations through presentation tools provides students with valuable real-world and authentic learning experiences.

BLACKLINE MASTERS

Presentation projects provide students with opportunities to practice their speaking and presentation skills. This chapter includes additional evaluation forms for assessing specific student projects. Blackline masters in this chapter include:

- Presentations Guidelines

- Persuasive Presentation Evaluation: a rubric designed to rate the presenter's ability to persuade his or her audience

- How-to Evaluation: a rubric designed to rate the presenter's ability to teach members of the audience a procedure.

Presentation Guidelines

These guidelines can help you make effective presentations.

Computer Display

Keep the presentation simple and easy to follow.
Make sure the text is readable to everyone (about 24 pt font).
Mix upper- and lowercase letters for the bullets.
Keep consistent headings (titles) and subheadings.
Provide plenty of space between bullets.
Use a maximum of five colors.
Include a maximum of six bullets.
Each bullet should only have about six words.
Include key phrases in bullets -- not the entire presentation.
Use high contrast between the text color and the background.
Do not place text on a highly textured/patterned background.
Make sure your graphics are large enough for everyone to see.
If you include charts, make large labels and legends.

Media: Audio and Video

Use audio and video only when necessary and appropriate.
Test the speakers and projection unit before the presentation.
Make sure everyone can hear and see the media.

Presentation Techniques

Rehearse the speech before presenting it.
Make notes to yourself on cards or on the computer.
Face the audience -- not the projection screen.
Start with a brief introduction and overview of the topic.
Don't read the bullets to the audience; expand on them.
Always plan a little extra in case you talk too fast.
Don't talk too fast -- pause and let the audience reflect.
Stand tall and speak directly to the audience (don't slouch)!
Don't fidget with keys, coins, pens, pencils, etc.
End the presentation with a summary and conclusion.
Smile!

From *Digital Content Creation in Schools: A Common Core Approach* by Karen S. Ivers and Ann E. Barron.
Santa Barbara, CA: Libraries Unlimited. Copyright © 2015.

Persuasive Presentation Evaluation

CRITERIA	0	1	2	3
Clarity	Presenter(s) did not speak clearly and did not speak loud enough.	Presenter(s) spoke loud enough, but did not speak clearly.	Presenter(s) spoke clearly but not in a loud enough voice.	Presenter(s) was articulate and spoke in a loud enough voice.
Supporting facts	Presenter(s) did not provide facts to support his or her opinion.	Presenter(s) provided one or two facts to support opinion.	Presenter(s) provided three or four facts to support opinion.	Presenter(s) provided five or more facts to support his or her opinion.
Viewpoints	Presenter(s) did not consider other opinions and didn't provide compelling reasons for own opinion.	Presenter(s) did not consider other opinions, but provided compelling reasons for own opinion.	Presenter(s) considered other opinions, but didn't provide compelling reasons for own opinion.	Presenter(s) considered other opinions and provided compelling reasons for own opinion.
Organization	Presenter(s) was very disorganized, distracting the presen-tation.	Presenter(s) was somewhat organized but needs to improve a lot.	Presenter(s) was well organized most of the time.	Presenter(s) was well organized throughout the presentation.
Appeal	Presenter(s) did not captivate or hold my attention.	Presenter(s) held my attention for a short period of time.	Presenter(s) held my attention for most of the time.	Presenter(s) captured and held my attention the whole time.
Persuasiveness	Presenter(s) did not change my opinion; he or she reinforced my other beliefs.	Presenter(s) did not change my opinion.	Presenter(s) changed my opinion, but I'm not completely convinced.	Presenter(s) changed my opinion; I'm completely convinced.
				Total _____

How-to Evaluation

CRITERIA	0	1	2	3
Clarity	Presenter(s) did not speak clearly and did not speak loud enough.	Presenter(s) spoke loud enough, but did not speak clearly.	Presenter(s) spoke clearly but not in a loud enough voice.	Presenter(s) was articulate and spoke in a loud enough voice.
Directions	Presenter(s) did not provide clear or step-by-step directions.	Presenter(s) provided step-by-step directions, but they were not clear.	Presenter(s) provided clear directions, but they were not step-by-step.	Presenter(s) provided clear, step-by-step directions.
Organization	Presenter(s) was very disorganized, distracting the presen-tation.	Presenter(s) was somewhat organized but needs to improve a lot.	Presenter(s) was well organized most of the time.	Presenter(s) was well organized throughout the presen-tation.
Instructional approach	Presenter(s) did not use a variety of instructional approaches.	Presenter(s) used two different instructional approaches.	Presenter(s) used three different instructional approaches.	Presenter(s) used four or more different instructional approaches.
Appeal	Presenter(s) did not captivate or hold my attention.	Presenter(s) held my attention for a short period of time.	Presenter(s) held my attention for most of the time.	Presenter(s) captured and held my attention the whole time.
Outcome (Fill in the blank based on the topic.)	I did not learn anything about how to ____.	I learned a little about how to ____.	I learned a lot about how to ____.	I successfully learned how to ____ and I could teach someone else.
			Total _____	

From *Digital Content Creation in Schools: A Common Core Approach* by Karen S. Ivers and Ann E. Barron. Santa Barbara, CA: Libraries Unlimited. Copyright © 2015.

Chapter 9

Digital Content Creation Projects: Hypermedia

A SCENARIO

Lynn loved creative writing and was excited to work with her teammates to create a hypermedia choose-your-own-adventure story. Her teacher, Mr. Watanabe, provided the class with a flowchart, showing the layout of the story structure. The first screen was the title page, followed by a screen that provided an introduction and instructions for the user. Next, users would be taken to the beginning of the story, which covered three more screens. The next screen was a menu that allowed users to choose the next part of the story. There were four possible choices. Each choice branched to a different storyline. In addition, some storylines had additional choices or branches. While it sounded complicated at first, the flowchart made it easy to follow. The challenging part would be to come up with different storylines and make the adventures engaging and exciting. The target audience for the adventure stories was fourth graders. Lynn had to ensure her team wrote their story at a fourth-grade reading level and that it would appeal to fourth graders' interests. Each of her team members took responsibility for one of the branches. They discussed the use of fonts, the layout, and other design issues to ensure the story looked consistent. Creating storyboards helped. As they work individually on their laptops, they met frequently to proofread each other's work, share ideas, and ensure everyone was making progress. The students used a flash drive to help construct the final product on Lynn's laptop. Mr. Watanabe praised their work, but the team's greatest accolade came from the students using their hypermedia product. "This is so cool!" said one fourth grader.

"I want to learn how to make one of these!" declared another.

"What a fun way to read and experience different story possibilities," commented another.

OVERVIEW

Ideas for digital projects are endless, limited only by the imagination of teachers and students. Digital projects can be integrated across the curriculum, and they can help students share their knowledge in many ways. In addition to engaging students as they learn specific content standards, digital projects may be designed to focus on specific student skills (learning how to use a particular hypermedia tool), selected media formats (animation), or social skills (cooperative learning).

As with any other curricular unit, planning is an essential part of successful digital projects. Limited computer resources may require educators to facilitate several activities at once. This idea is not new; many educators find themselves managing multiple activities in the classroom on a daily basis. For example, during a social studies unit on the Gold Rush, some students may be panning for gold, others may be working on a model of a mining camp, some may be working on written reports, and more may be weighing and evaluating the value of gold nuggets. During digital projects, the only difference is that some students may be working on computers or other digital devices while others are working on non-computer-related activities. The computer provides the students with yet another mode of learning—one that provides new insights into organizing, synthesizing, evaluating, and presenting information. This chapter presents several ideas for digital projects that can be created with hypermedia tools such as HyperStudio by Roger Wagner (http://www.mackiev.com/hyperstudio/), Scratch by the MIT Media Lab (http://scratch.mit.edu/), and others (see Chapter 6). The tool is not as important as the process; just make sure you choose a tool that fits the ability level of your students.

SAMPLE PROJECTS

The following projects address various areas of the curriculum and can be created with a variety of hypermedia tools. Several of the suggested projects may be completed using the button features within presentation tools such as PowerPoint, too. For more complex and interactive projects (use of drag-and-drop features, scripting options, and so on), hypermedia tools such as Hyper-Studio, Scratch, or Captivate are recommended.

Students should be familiar with the chosen tool before engaging in the digital project. Design teams consist of four students, and periods may consist of 30 to 45 minutes. If one-to-one laptops or tablets are not available, refer to Chapter 3 for computer-scheduling options. Wikis, blogs, Google Apps, learning management systems (e.g., Blackboard, Moodle, etc.), and other online tools may be used for group collaboration, journal entries, sharing of information, and so on.

All About Me

Lesson Description: This project is designed for beginners to provide them with the opportunity to focus on planning, design issues, and the hypermedia tool. It also addresses standards related to reading and writing. In one-to-one laptop or tablet environments, instructors may consider having students work independently on their own "all about me" presentation, following a class template so projects may be combined into one class project at the end. The benefit of having students work in cooperative groups is that it provides them with an opportunity to focus on social and team-building skills, as well as collaboration and communication skills.

The content of the project is information about the students. Each student team creates an eight-screen (or card) project consisting of the following screens: title, information, main menu, student 1, student 2, student 3, student 4, and credits. (All About Me blackline masters are provided at the end of this chapter).

DECIDE. Assign student teams as described in previous chapters. As a class, brainstorm what makes people interesting, what information students might find in an autobiography, and other related questions. Generate a class list of 10 items (e.g., name, date and place of birth, hobbies, and favorite books, among other things). Assign each student the responsibility of providing information about him or herself for each of the 10 items.

DESIGN. The next period, provide student teams with a copy of a flowchart (see the All About Me: Flowchart blackline master). Discuss the flowchart's layout and how the screens will be connected. Next, distribute copies of the All About Me: Storyboard Templates (see the blackline masters at the end of this chapter). Explain how the students should complete the storyboards, and how they will use them to create the computer screens of their digital projects. Discuss design issues (e.g., contrasting background and text, consistency), and, if possible, show some sample All About Me projects. These sample projects may be created by the teacher or be projects from previous classes. Use the projects to show good and bad examples of design, and let the students discuss what they observe. For example, a bad example might have navigation icons in inconsistent places on the screens, unreadable text, links that do not work, and spelling mistakes. Following the class discussion, provide students with a list of design guidelines (see Chapter 4) and a checklist of expectations (see All About Me: Project Checklist blackline master). During the next period, students work on their team's storyboards, including the storyboards about themselves. Each self-storyboard should contain a paragraph describing the 10 items that the student has answered about him or herself. Teams' storyboards should be assessed and approved by the teacher before students are allowed to work on the computers. Students can track their progress by using the Journal Entry form discussed in Chapter 3.

DEVELOP. After the students' storyboards have been approved, students create their project on the computer. If one-to-one laptops or tablets are available, students may be assigned to create their own card or slide, as well as the title, information, main menu, or credit slide. Students will need to designate a teammate's computer as the location where all of the elements will come together. Or, if transferring information is an issue, one computer may be designated for the project and students can take turns entering and supporting each other in the process. Supporting or concurrent activities that students may complete when they are not working on the computer include reading an autobiography or biography of a famous person of their choice and working with a Venn diagram to compare differences and similarities between the person they are reading about and themselves, or creating a self-portrait using pastels, papier-mâché, clay, or other medium. In addition, students may research, gather, and organize information for a class newspaper or magazine that describes what occurred during the years students were born, as well as provide interesting facts about each student's birthplace and identify it on a map.

As students complete their digital projects, another team reviews the project for problems or errors (see Chapter 7). The corrected project, along with the group and self-evaluations and journal entries, is submitted to the teacher.

EVALUATE. In addition to the teacher's evaluation, peers may be asked to evaluate each other's projects (see the All About Me: Teacher Evaluation and All About Me: Peer Evaluation blackline masters). The students receive a group grade based on the teacher and peer evaluations. Students receive an individual grade based on their group, self-, and intragroup evaluations. The two grades can be averaged for a final score. A class Jeopardy game or quiz may be provided to see how well students know their classmates.

Pollution Solution

Lesson Description: This project focuses on the students' ability to research, synthesize, and present information about the hazards of pollution. Other topics are possible, based on the grade level and science standards that need to be addressed. In this example, students are required to use a variety of media formats to help them emphasize the importance of finding solutions to pollution. For instance, they may incorporate digitized photographs and video segments into their projects to illustrate the outcomes of pollution or animations that illustrate a recycling process.

DECIDE. Assign student teams as described in previous chapters. As a class, brainstorm what students already know about pollution and what they want to learn about it (see the KWL Knowledge Chart in Chapter 3). For example, they may know that pollution is harmful, but they may not know the extensive effects of pollution on the environment, what regulations are in effect to help stop pollution, what causes smog, how and what items are recycled, the dirtiest cities in the world, and steps they can take to help stop pollution. Assign or have each group select a different topic to research. Distribute and explain the BrainStorm activity sheet and the Bibliography Information sheet (see Chapter 3). Before groups brainstorm and begin research about their specific topic, stipulate that groups need to incorporate photos, video segments, or animations to illustrate their points. Ask the students why pictures are important when discussing a topic like pollution. Discuss (or demonstrate) how a picture of dead fish in a river has a stronger impact on people than the text "dead fish in a river" has by itself.

DESIGN. Students may take two or three class periods to research their specific topic. As students are finishing their research, discuss the concept of flowcharts and storyboards. Students need to examine their research findings and organize the information by chunks and meaningful links. Students may want to use index cards to create and manipulate a rough draft of their flowchart and storyboard ideas. Discuss the design issues explained in Chapter 4. View sample projects that contain video, animations, and photographs and have students discuss what makes the projects effective or ineffective. Discuss various levels of interactivity. Depending on the ability level of your students and hypermedia tool being used, require students to embed drag-and-drop and other interactive features within their projects. Students may incorporate mini-quizzes, pop-up fields, rollover features, and so on. Provide groups with a list of design guidelines; a toryboard template (see Chapter 4); and the Journal Entry form, Project Checklist, and Bibliography Information sheet available in Chapters 3 and 4. Explain each form. In addition, provide groups with the storyboard, design, content, and technical rubrics available in Chapter 7. Groups should keep these forms in a binder or store them online in Dropbox, Google Docs, or other shared location. Multiple copies of the Journal Entry form and the Bibliography Information form should also be available. Allot enough time for students to complete their flowchart and storyboards.

DEVELOP. After the students' flowchart and storyboards have been approved, teams begin working on their projects. Depending on the number of computers available, students will be working on different tasks. For example, a couple of students may be in charge of finding or designing the graphics and video for the project, one may be designated as the lead instructional designer, and another may serve as the subject matter expert.

As students complete their projects, another team reviews the project for problems or errors (see Chapter 7). The corrected project, along with the project's rubrics, group and self-evaluations, bibliography sheets, and journal entries, is submitted to the teacher.

EVALUATE. Following the teacher's evaluation of the projects, peers need to evaluate each other's projects, too (see Chapter 7). The students receive a group grade based on the teacher and peer evaluations. Students receive an individual grade based on their group, self-, and intragroup evaluations.

When the grading is complete, a main menu can be developed that links the projects together (see Figure 9.1, p. 185). Students can view the entire multimedia presentation and answer each other's quiz questions for additional content evaluation. The remaining column on the KWL Knowledge Chart can now be completed.

Community Concerns

Lesson Description: This project focuses on the students' ability to develop and issue a survey, organize and interpret the collected information, discuss issues with members of the community, and participate in an authentic learning experience. Students are required to research and

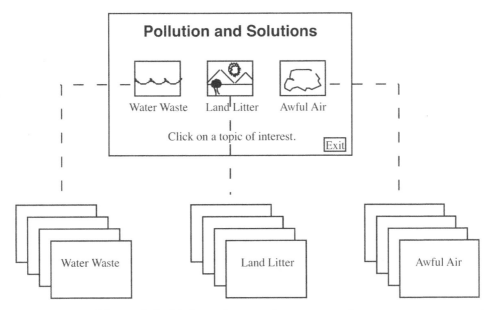

Figure 9.1. Link student projects to a main menu.

address community concerns by reading the local newspaper, watching the local news, and interacting with members of the community. Findings are presented in a digital project. Authentic learning experiences are the result of conducting interviews, making video recordings and audio tracks of community members, and compiling the data. Multiple standards across different subject areas can be addressed through this and similar activities.

DECIDE. Assign student teams. As a class, discuss the concept of a community and what issues their community may be facing. Topics may include the homeless, curfews, the elderly, crime, education, and other concerns. Assign or have each group select a different topic to research. Explain that their research should include local newspaper articles and television news, as well as interviews with community members. Distribute the BrainStorm activity sheet (see Chapter 3) to help students organize the possibilities of their topic. During the next two or three class periods, discuss how to construct a survey and, if possible, distribute sample surveys. Students should think about questions that are important to their particular topic. For example, students researching the concerns of the elderly may ask the elderly questions regarding health care, Social Security, transportation, recreation services, and family concerns. This student group may contrast and compare answers they receive from the elderly with answers they receive from other age groups. All of the data are accumulated, synthesized, and evaluated. The teacher should approve the surveys before students begin their interviews. During the interviews, students should ask for written permission to record, video, or photograph the person being interviewed. Students can keep track of their sources using the Bibliography Information sheet (see Chapter 3).

DESIGN. Discuss the concept of flowcharts and storyboards. Students need to examine their research findings and organize the information by chunks and meaningful links. Students may want to use index cards to create and manipulate a rough draft of their flowchart and storyboard ideas. Discuss the design issues explained in Chapter 4. View sample projects that contain audio tracks, video, and photographs, and have students discuss what makes the projects effective or ineffective. Provide groups with a list of design guidelines, a storyboard template (see Chapter 4), and the Journal Entry form and Project Checklist available in Chapters 3 and 4. Explain each form. In addition, provide groups with the storyboard, design, content, and technical rubrics available in Chapter 7. Groups should keep these forms in a binder or stored online. Multiple copies of the Journal Entry form and the

Bibliography Information sheet should be available. Provide students enough time to complete their flowchart and storyboards. Remind students to complete daily journal entries (see Chapter 3).

DEVELOP. Help students define their roles and activities within their cooperative group so they can start their projects after their flowchart and storyboards have been approved. Roles may include project manager, instructional designer, graphic artist, program author, and so on. Students may extend their work to include proposing a club, fund-raising campaign, or service learning project that supports their specific topic or writing letters to their local representatives about their findings and concerns.

As students complete their projects, another team reviews the project for problems or errors (see Chapter 7). The corrected project, along with the project's rubrics, group and self-evaluations, bibliography sheets, and journal entries, is submitted to the teacher.

EVALUATE. Students may choose to share their projects with local community members. Peers and teachers can also evaluate the projects. Students may receive a group grade based on the average score of their peer, teacher, and community evaluations. Individual grades are calculated by the group grade, self-, and intragroup evaluations.

All That Jazz

Lesson Description: This project focuses on the students' ability to research, synthesize, and present information about different styles of music. In addition to standards related to reading and writing, students have the opportunity to address standards related to the historical and cultural context of music. Students are required to incorporate audio clips of a selected music style into their projects to help teach other students about music. For example, students creating a project about ragtime could include audio clips of *The Entertainer* and the *Maple Leaf Rag* while discussing the contributions and history of Scott Joplin. Each team chooses or is assigned a specific music style and generates a project that reports assigned information about that style. Educators may choose to impose a specific layout and style for student storyboards and flowcharts; hence, the projects will contain the same topics and can be connected at the end of the project.

DECIDE. As a class, generate a list of different types of music (e.g., rock-and-roll, ragtime, classical, jazz, country-western). Discuss what students already know about certain types of music and what they would like to learn about the types of music (see the KWL Knowledge Chart in Chapter 3). For example, they may know that Elvis Presley is considered the "King of Rock and Roll," that Beethoven wrote classical music, and that ragtime was popular during the 1920s. Students may want to learn the origins of country music or find out more about New Age music. Assign students to teams based on their interests. Ask student teams to research the following information: the music's history and peak(s) of popularity, at least three musicians and their history and contribution to the music style, and additional music titles and interesting facts. Distribute the BrainStorm activity sheet from Chapter 3. To adhere to a specific project format, explain that each group's BrainStorm sheet should contain the following information: the music type should be placed in the Main Idea bubble, and Related Idea bubbles should contain music history, musicians, music titles, and interesting facts. Students can create additional Related Idea bubbles for other topics. Branches from the Related Idea bubbles will contain more specific information about the topic. Allow students enough time for research, reminding them that audio clips are required for the project. Assist students with their research by bringing in a variety of music recordings in CD, MP3, or other audio formats.

DESIGN. As students are finishing their research, discuss the concept of flowcharts and storyboards. As a class, discuss how the gathered information might best be organized, chunked, and linked together. Create a flowchart for everyone to follow (see Figure 9.2).

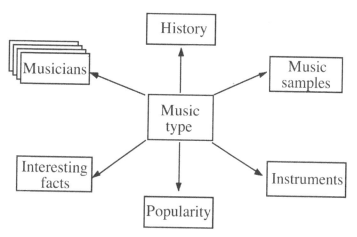

Figure 9.2. Sample flowchart.

Next, discuss the design issues explained in Chapter 4. View sample projects that contain music clips and have students discuss what makes the projects effective or ineffective. Discuss various levels of interactivity. Depending on the ability level of your students and hypermedia tool being used, require students to embed drag-and-drop and other interactive features within their projects to reinforce specific content and engage learners. Discuss storyboard designs and decide on a standard layout for everyone to use. Distribute the Journal Entry form and Project Checklist available in Chapters 3 and 4. Explain each form. In addition, provide groups with the storyboard, design, content, and technical rubrics available in Chapter 7. Allow students enough time to complete their flowchart and storyboards.

DEVELOP. After the students' flowchart and storyboards have been approved, teams begin developing their projects on their computers or tablets. Ensure students are familiar with various audio formats and compression techniques (see Chapter 5). Extension or concurrent activities may include students creating a persuasive report or presentation for a future debate explaining why their music style is the best, developing quiz questions about their project for other students, reading a biography of a composer and designing a diorama depicting and explaining an important event in the composer's life, learning and interpreting the lyrics to a particular song, creating a watercolor or acrylic painting that depicts the mood or feelings associated with a particular piece of music, learning to play a music selection, or creating a composition of their own.

As students complete their projects, another team reviews the project for problems or errors (see Chapter 7). The corrected project, along with the project's rubrics, group and self-evaluations, bibliography sheets, and journal entries, is submitted to the teacher.

EVALUATE. Both students and teachers evaluate the projects. The students receive a group grade based on the teacher and peer evaluations. Students receive an individual grade based on their group, self-, and intragroup evaluations. When the grading is complete, a main menu can be developed that links the projects together. The remaining column on the KWL Knowledge Chart can now be completed. Teachers may want to create a quiz or short essay exam that assesses students' knowledge of the presented projects.

Sherlock Project: A Problem-Solving Adventure

Lesson Description: This project focuses on the students' ability to solve problems, research, and develop interdependent clues to produce a digital project that demonstrates their processing skills. In addition, graphics and pop-up text boxes can be required components of the project. Students are required to create a mystery that is solved by finding and deciphering the various clues within the project. For example, a group may use the theme of a haunted house and tell the story of how the only way out of the house is to enter the correct combination into the passageway door. Throughout the project, students create mathematical and logic problems that will help users determine the correct code. For example, in the first room of the house, the following clue could be discovered when users click on a ghost (see Figure 9.3):

It happened on a scary night,
One I know was full of fright;
Yet Joey Jones, as calm as could be,
Said, "Divide 800 by the answer in Room 3."

A text box may appear, the clue may be recorded audio, or both. Room 3's clue might appear when users click on a book (see Figure 9.4, p. 189):

Weary travelers visit here;
Guess how many times a year?
(7 * 8) − (10 + 21)

By combining the clues in Rooms 1 and 3, the answer to Room 1 is 32. Room 6's clue may indicate that this is the first number in the combination. For example, upon visiting Room 6, the users may find the following scrawled on the wall (see Figure 9.5, p. 189):

Room 1 = 1st number to combination

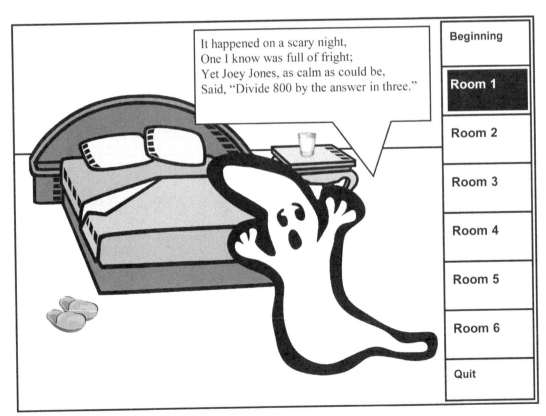

Figure 9.3. Sample screen design for Room 1.

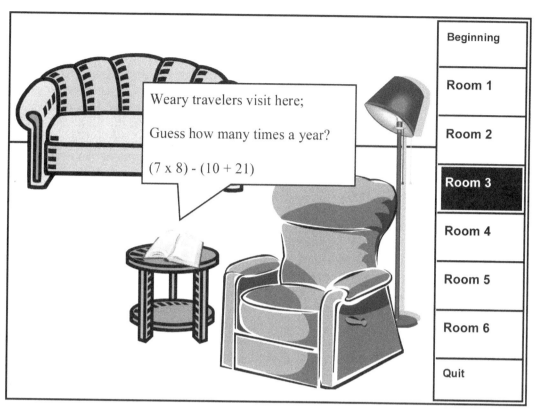

Figure 9.4. Sample screen design for Room 3.

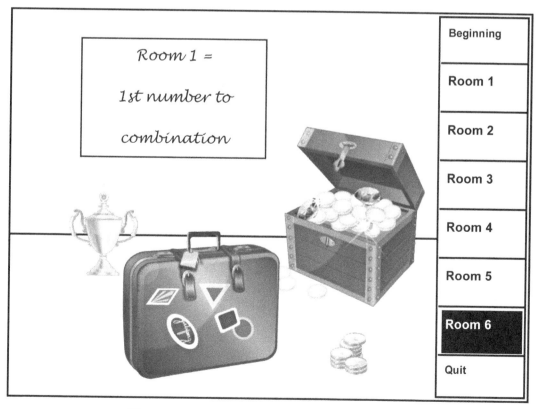

Figure 9.5. Sample screen design for Room 6.

Projects can be made much more complex and sophisticated by integrating current areas of study, incorporating outside research into the answers to the clues, making answers to clues dependent on more than one other clue, including different media that become part of the clues, and embedding more interactive features into the design. To begin, limit students to six clues in the puzzle.

DECIDE. Assign student teams as described in previous chapters. As a class, discuss the different strategies students can use when solving a math problem, as well as the basic problem-solving steps: (1) understanding the problem, (2) devising a plan, (3) carrying out the plan, and (4) looking back. Discuss the importance of gathering all information before coming to a conclusion about a problem. Illustrate this by distributing one puzzle clue to each different student group (see the Introductory Puzzle blackline master at the end of this chapter). Ask the students if they can solve the puzzle. Obviously, they cannot, because they each hold only one piece to the puzzle. Randomly select groups to read their puzzle pieces aloud, while everyone else takes notes. Inquire whether students can solve the puzzle after each clue. Note that some clues may not make any sense until other clues are read, and that some clues are interdependent (they rely on other clues for additional information). Some clues may have to be repeated. After all of the clues are read, discuss the answer and how students arrived at it. Reflect on the interdependent puzzle pieces and the importance of gathering and understanding all the clues.

Explain that students are going to create a digital project based on the puzzle example. Their project should contain a theme (e.g., a haunted house, a pirate's treasure, outer space, the jungle) and their clues should be hidden (pop-up text boxes) or part of the graphic environment. Users should experience traveling from room to room or place to place.

Let student teams brainstorm about a specific theme and a mystery to go along with it. For example, using an outer space theme, the story might involve the crash of a spaceship on an unknown planet; the clues might spell the name of the planet or give its position from the sun. Or, using a pirate theme, the story might involve the location of a buried treasure; the clues could provide the *x* and *y* coordinates to a location on a treasure map. Themes may also address current units of study (e.g., Ancient Civilizations, American Revolution, or other topics). After a theme and a story have been decided, students can discuss the solution to their mystery and create clues that users will need to solve the mystery. Remind students to make some of their clues interdependent. Provide students with enough time to complete this first step.

DESIGN. Once student teams have finished their puzzles, review the concepts of flowcharts and storyboards. Each clue should have its own storyboard, and the flowchart should show the navigation possibilities throughout the project. Clue cards or screens may be linked to a central location, accessible from every clue card, or found attached to another clue card. Discuss the design issues explained in Chapter 4. If possible, view sample problem-solving projects for additional design ideas. Provide groups with a list of design guidelines, a storyboard template (see Chapter 4), and the Journal Entry form and Project Checklist available in Chapters 3 and 4. Explain each form. Also provide groups with the storyboard, design, and technical rubrics available in Chapter 7 and the Puzzle Rubric blackline master at the end of this chapter. Groups should keep these forms in a binder and complete daily journal entries.

DEVELOP. After the students' flowchart and storyboards have been approved, team members define their computer roles, including who will be responsible for the graphics, layout, and so on. One member may be responsible for creating a record-keeping sheet for users to keep track of their notes as they attempt to solve the team's completed project. Concurrent or extension activities may include student teams working on problem-solving puzzles provided by the teacher or brought in by other students.

As students complete their projects, another team reviews the project for problems or errors (see Chapter 7). The corrected project, along with the project's rubrics, group and self-evaluations (see Chapter 7), and journal entries, is submitted to the teacher. Provide the students with enough time on the computer to finish a 10-card or screen project, especially because some of the students will spend their development time creating and researching different pictures for their project's theme. Clip art libraries should be made available to the students.

EVALUATE. Following the teacher's evaluation of the project, peers need to evaluate each other's projects as well (see Chapter 7), remembering that specific content may or may not be an integral part of the project. Emphasis should be placed on the clarity of information, sophistication of the puzzle, use of graphics, and overall design. For alternative evaluation forms, see the Puzzle Rubric and Peer Puzzle Evaluation blackline masters at the end of this chapter. Each Sherlock project should be shared and solved by the different groups.

SUMMARY

The possibilities for digital projects are endless, and emphasis on student learning outcomes can be placed in a variety of areas. This chapter presented sample projects that focus on different areas of the curriculum and learning outcomes. Projects can be completed in one-to-one device classroom settings or in classrooms with limited computer access. More complex and interactive projects can be created by embedding drag-and-drop features, quizzes, pop-up text boxes, and other interactive options available in most hypermedia tools. Extension activities for the projects presented in this chapter include sharing projects with peers over the Internet or with the school and community at local conferences. Projects may also be recorded to DVDs for student distribution and archival purposes.

BLACKLINE MASTERS

This chapter contains variations on several blackline masters presented in other chapters, providing teachers with additional ideas for creating their own checklists and evaluation forms that are specific to the students' projects and ability levels. Specific forms have been designed for the All About Me and Sherlock projects. References are also made to the checklists and evaluation forms in other chapters. Blackline masters in this chapter include:

- All About Me: Flowchart: a flowchart for All About Me projects

- All About Me: Storyboard Template: an alternative storyboard layout

- All About Me: Project Checklist: a specific checklist for All About Me projects

- All About Me: Teacher Evaluation: a simplified evaluation sheet for All About Me projects

- All About Me: Peer Evaluation: a specific evaluation sheet for All About Me projects

- Introductory Puzzle: a story problem containing independent clues

- Puzzle Rubric: one way of evaluating problem-solving adventure projects

- Peer Puzzle Evaluation: an alternative peer evaluation form for problem-solving adventures.

All About Me: Flowchart

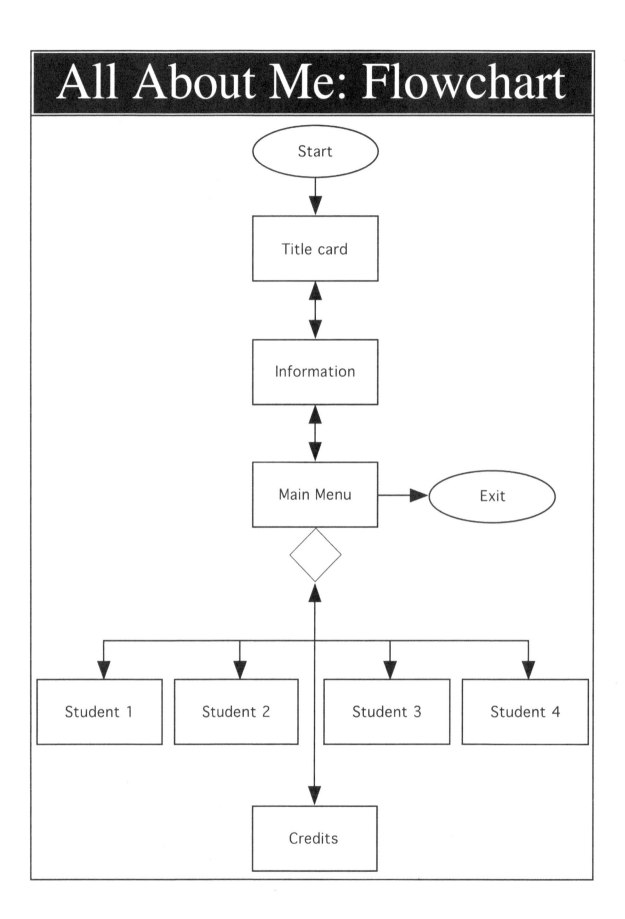

All About Me: Storyboard Template

Background: _____

Border: _____

Pictures: _____

	Font	Size	Style	Justification	Color
Title					
Text					

Button	Go to	Transition	Other

All About Me: Project Checklist

Team Name _____

Before developing your project at the computer, complete the following:

☐ Flowchart   ☐ Storyboards

Make sure your project has:

☐ A minimum of _____ pages (or cards).

☐ A maximum of _____ pages (or cards).

☐ A Title page (or card).

☐ An Information page (or card).

☐ A Main Menu.

☐ A page (or card) with a paragraph description for each member in your group.

☐ A Credits page (or card).

☐ Appropriate navigation options.

☐ Text that is easy to read and is accurate.

☐ Complete sentences with correct punctuation, grammar, and spelling.

☐ The assigned media requirements:

_____ Clip art

_____ Original drawings (use of paint tools)

_____ Audio

☐ Other: _____

All About Me: Teacher Evaluation

CRITERIA	0	1	2	3
Continuity	Project does not follow storyboards or flowchart.	Project follows some of the storyboards.	Project follows the storyboards but not the flowchart.	Project follows the storyboards and flowchart exactly.
Content and mechanics	Project does not contain paragraphs about each team member.	Project contains paragraphs about each team member, but there are many errors.	Project contains paragraphs about each team member, with one or two errors.	Project contains paragraphs about each team member, without any errors.
Media elements	None of the media elements have been incorporated.	Two or more media elements don't work, or few are incorporated.	All media elements are incorporated, but one does not work.	All media elements are incorporated and work.
Navigation buttons	None of the navigation buttons are functioning correctly.	Some of the navigation buttons are functioning correctly.	Most of the navigation buttons are functioning correctly.	All navigation buttons are functioning correctly.
Design	None of the design guidelines were followed.	Some of the design guidelines were followed.	Most of the design guidelines were followed.	All design guidelines were followed.
Daily journal entries	Journal entries are missing for three or more days.	Journal entries are missing for two days.	Journal entries are missing for one day.	No journal entries are missing.
				Total _____

From *Digital Content Creation in Schools: A Common Core Approach* by Karen S. Ivers and Ann E. Barron. Santa Barbara, CA: Libraries Unlimited. Copyright © 2015.

All About Me: Peer Evaluation

Name of group being reviewed: _____

Project title: _____

Reviewed by: _____

What are the strengths of this stack?

How might the presentation be improved?

What improvements in the design would you suggest?

On a scale of 0 to 3 (3 being the highest), how would you rate this project? Why?

Introductory Puzzle

Help Mr. Alfonzo calculate the average number of pages read in one week by a group of his students: Fred, Ethel, Lucy, Ricky, Wilma, and Betty.

Both Fred and Ethel read two books with 70 pages each. In addition, Fred read a 20-page book about frogs.

Lucy read the same frog book as Fred, the same cat book as Barney, and half of the dog book that Ricky read.

Ricky read a 20-page book about dogs.

Barney read a 60-page book about cats and two 30-page books.

Both Wilma and Betty read the same books as Ethel.

Answer: 115 pages. [Fred: (2x70) + 20 = 160; Ethel: 2x70 = 140; Lucy: 20 + 60 + (20÷2) = 90; Ricky: 20; Wilma: 140; Betty: 140] Divide total pages by 6.

Extension Activities:
- Calculate each student's average number of pages read in one week.
- Determine the range, mode, and medium of the group. Compare and contrast this to the group mean.
- Track and calculate the average number of pages read in one week by individuals and the class. Compare this with other classes and age groups.
- Create a bar graph that illustrates the favorite genre of the class. Compare this with other classes and age groups.

From *Digital Content Creation in Schools: A Common Core Approach* by Karen S. Ivers and Ann E. Barron. Santa Barbara, CA: Libraries Unlimited. Copyright © 2015.

Puzzle Rubric

CRITERIA	0	1	2	3
The project presents users with the goal(s) and objectives of the puzzle.	Project does not have goals or objectives stated.	Project presents a goal, but no objectives.	Project presents objectives, but no clear goal.	Project presents clear goals and objectives for the puzzle.
The group uses several interdependent clues.	The project does not have interdependent clues.	The project has one interdependent clue.	The project has two interdependent clues.	The project has three or more interdependent clues.
The group includes all of the necessary info to solve the puzzle, and the design of puzzle is appealing.	Not enough information is included, and the design is not appealing.	Not enough information is included, but the design is appealing.	Enough information is included, but the design is not appealing.	Enough information is included, and the design is appealing.
The puzzle challenges the user's thinking skills, yet it isn't too difficult to complete.	The puzzle is too simple.	The puzzle is too difficult to complete.	The puzzle is somewhat challenging, but not challenging enough.	The puzzle is challenging, but not too difficult to complete.
It is easy to navigate through the puzzle - buttons are easy to understand and work.	Buttons are not easy to understand and some do not work.	Buttons are easy to understand, but some do not work.	Buttons are not easy to understand, but they all work.	Buttons are easy to understand, and they all work.
				Total _____

Peer Puzzle Evaluation

Name of group being reviewed: _____

Project title: _____

Reviewed by: _____

What are the strengths of this stack?

How might the presentation be improved?

Explain why you were able or unable to solve the puzzle.

On a scale of 0 to 3 (3 being the highest), how would you rate this project? Explain your answer.

Chapter 10

Digital Content Creation Projects: Web Pages

A SCENARIO

Brenda, Julie, Sang, and Marco are seniors in high school, preparing for careers in marketing. The culminating project for their marketing course is to create an online presence for an assigned company.

Brenda's group has been assigned an organic baby food company, called Best for Baby. Their business strategy includes a creating a website that highlights the products and provides free shipping of the baby food. They were hopeful that their strategy would prove beneficial for mothers who want quality food for their babies, but do not have the time or energy to run to the grocery store.

As the students worked through the DDD-E process, they conducted research via Google and located images on the web that could be used on their site. They also reviewed other company websites related to baby food to learn how the "competition" marketed their products online. Finally, they structured their content into four major areas (About Us; Products and Prices; Benefits of Organic Baby Food; and Contact Us).

To develop the website, they chose to use WIX.com because anyone over 13 can register for a free account; it provides a wide array of professional templates; no coding is required; and the websites are hosted on the WIX server. Since they had already specified their content during the DESIGN phase, it did not take long to fill in the template with text and images. Throughout the process, they were reminded that they should be careful about using images without permission, and that the images should be compressed so they would download in a timely manner. They were excited to see that WIX even offered options for a shopping cart and a checkout button for e-commerce.

When the projects were ready for review, Mr. Cheng used a rubric to assess the websites and provide feedback to the students. He emphasized that issues such as the content, writing style, ease of use, and navigation would be important to clients in the students' future endeavors in 21st-century marketing.

OVERVIEW

The World Wide Web is a powerful resource for K–12 education. Never before has the educational community had such an inexpensive, easily accessible method of communicating, researching, and distributing information. It opens doors to multicultural education, establishes real-world learning experiences, promotes higher-order thinking skills, enables social networking, and helps increase motivation and writing skills.

The web offers a wonderful environment for students to create and publish multimedia projects and documents. Besides sharing their artwork and stories with others, students can collect data for original research projects and produce reports that are linked to authentic, dynamic information sources. They can also post school news for the community, create websites for public service or special interests, or produce interactive lessons and WebQuests.

The projects outlined in this chapter are examples of school-based activities that involve web-based design and development. The first (School Newsletter) and second projects (Our Town) require that the students interact with others to acquire the information needed, then design and develop an appropriate website to convey the information.

The web is also a great place for students to publish research reports on a variety of topics that they can investigate and share. By creating a web-based report, they can include audio, video, images, and links to resources available at other sites. The "Learning through Reflections" project is an example of a report that incorporates data from archival sites, but also includes original interviews and information that has been synthesized by student groups.

The final project in this chapter focuses on designing, developing, and implementing Web-Quests in the classroom. WebQuests are designed to guide learners as they research and synthesize a specific issue and incorporate the results into an authentic product or project. They are excellent tools for students at all grade levels and in all content areas.

SAMPLE PROJECTS FOR WEB-BASED DEVELOPMENT

The following projects can be created with tools ranging from text editors and word processors to sophisticated web creation programs (such as Kompozer or DreamWeaver). Online web editors with multiple templates and free hosting are also available at Weebly, WIX, Google Sites, etc. Teachers should choose the most appropriate tool for students and ensure that their students are familiar with the tool before beginning the project (see Chapter 6 for more information on web authoring tools).

The sample projects can be designed and developed by individual students or by groups of up to six students. In all cases, it is important to maintain a thorough review cycle before uploading the pages, particularly if they will be accessible through the web.

School Newsletter

Lesson Description: Producing an online newsletter or magazine is an ideal project for student groups and can integrate skills from language arts, social science, mathematics, and life sciences. Each group can be assigned one particular aspect of student life, such as sports, clubs, drama, scheduling, faculty profiles, upcoming events, and so on. Alternatively, the entire class can work together on producing an online magazine that highlights stories and news events written by the students. In this case, the students could be divided into groups based on tasks such as writers, editors, web designers, graphic artists, marketing (advertising), etc. For an example of a magazine project in middle school, see http://fcit.usf.edu/matrix/lessons/active_infusion_languagearts.

DECIDE. As a class, brainstorm potential topics that could be included in an online newsletter or magazine. Allow time for the students to investigate resources available at school, such as statistics for sports, electronic files of school history, photographs, or other archival information.

Assign student teams that will assume a variety of roles in the development of the project. Allow plenty of time for the students to review other school websites and investigate the format and layout of other online newspapers and magazines.

DESIGN. Discuss the overall flow of the lesson with the entire class. Emphasize the need for a consistent interface for the entire project, as well as the need for each section to be unique. Discuss navigation and format options. For example: What content will be included? How will the content be organized? Should the final layout be in a two- or three-column format? Should the final product be accessible in HTML, PDF, or both formats? Other ideas might include the following:

- Using the school mascot and colors as a theme

- Taking photos at school events

- Including audio clips with interviews

- Podcasting audio and/or video news

- Highlighting stories and articles written by students

- Creating a visual tour of the school

- Linking to the district website

- Including coupons for local merchants

Remind the students that they must be careful not to include personal information (such as names, photos, or home addresses) about individual students. Also, emphasize the need to involve the school's administrators in the review cycle.

DEVELOP. After the students' concept map, flowcharts, storyboards, etc., have been approved, the production process can begin. Help students to determine the best tools and service provider for the product—editors such as KompoZer or DreamWeaver can be used if there is a web server at school (see Figure 10.1 for a three-column template on DreamWeaver). Alternatively, hosting services with web templates (such as Weebly, Wix, or Google Sites) provide good options.

EVALUATE. If possible, the pages should be tested on different computers and operating systems (Macintosh and PC), as well as with different browsers. Be sure to include as many administrators, teachers, coaches, and students as possible in the review cycle. The club's president or faculty sponsor should authorize all content that relates to a particular club or organization before being uploaded to the Internet.

Our Town

Lesson Description: This project focuses on research, interactions with community members, and students' ability to organize, interpret, and convey information. Students are required to create a website for the community that is related to the town's history, economy, attractions, etc.

DECIDE. As a class, discuss the community and possible topics for a website. Brainstorm in small groups to generate as many ideas as possible for consideration. For example, they might create a website for the local park, conduct research on the air or water quality, or create a website

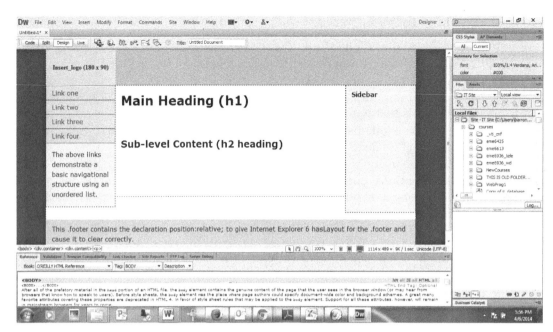

Figure 10.1. Three-column DreamWeaver template.

to attract tourists. The project could focus on the broad history of the town, or on a specific aspect, such as the railroads, an economic era, or a historical building, event, or person. The possibilities are limitless.

As the students conduct their field research, they should ask for written permission to record, video, or photograph anyone whom they want to include on the website. If existing graphics are used, they should seek permission to scan the images. Students can keep track of their sources using the Bibliography Information sheet in Chapter 3.

DESIGN. Allow time for the students to review websites that have similar content to what they are targeting. For examples of community projects, see the School Websites section of *Emerging America: Teaching and Learning American History* at http://emergingamerica.org/windows-on-history/school-sites/. As the students outline their intended content, remind them that they must keep the scope within the constraints allowed. In other words, if this is a short-term project, they may be limited to creating only one or two pages. They should also consider the target audience for the website—it might include local people or a worldwide audience.

DEVELOP. Teams can alternate between data collection, media production, and the creation of the web pages. The website can be created with a variety of tools, ranging from web templates (such as Weebly, Wix, and Google Sites) to web editors (such as KompoZer and DreamWeaver). The focus should be on community involvement and focus. Tasks may include:

- Researching the town's history and maps

- Interviewing senior community members about the community's evolution

- Photographing pertinent sites

- Recording unique sounds and videos

- Interviewing the mayor or other elected officials

Advanced students may want to include some interactivity into the website, in the form of a quiz or game. There are many quiz- and game-generating programs available on the web

Table 10.1. Game- and Quiz-Generating Programs on the Web

Website	Address
Classtools Net	http://classtools.net/
Content Generator	http://www.contentgenerator.net/
Eclipse Crossword	http://www.eclipsecrossword.com/
Game Zone	http://reviewgamezone.com/
Hot Potatoes	http://web.uvic.ca/hrd/halfbaked
QUIA	http://www.quia.com
QuizBox	http://www.quizbox.com/builder/
Quiz Game Master	http://cybertrain.info/quizman/qmhome.html

(see Table 10.1). After the quiz or game is created, it can be embedded into the website. For example, within a website relating to the town's history, students could include a crossword puzzle or game about major events.

EVALUATE. As students complete their websites, the teacher, other students, and the community members who were involved should review the projects. It is important that each page be thoroughly reviewed before it is uploaded to the Internet. In addition, the copyright releases for all media elements should be documented and filed for future reference.

Learning through Reflections: A Research Project about Conflicts and War

Lesson Description: In the past 70 years, the world has seen many conflicts and wars. Some of these, such as the Vietnam War and Korean Conflict, are mysteries to current students. This research project requires students to integrate primary and secondary resources as integral parts of a history website focusing on the following topics:

- Cold War
- Korean Conflict
- Vietnam War
- Operation Desert Storm
- War on Terror
- War in Afghanistan
- War in Iraq

DECIDE. Assign teams and allow the students to select a topic from the list of conflicts/ wars. As a class, brainstorm what students already know about their assigned conflict and what they need to know (see the KWL Knowledge Chart in Chapter 3). For example, they may know which countries were involved in the conflict, but not understand the triggering events that led American troops to be involved. Next, inform the students that there are several topics that should be included in their research, including (see Figure 10.2):

1. OVERVIEW. A brief overview of the conflict, including maps and other relevant images.

2. CASUALTIES. A synopsis of the casualties related to the conflict. This should include charts depicting national, state, and, if possible, local mortalities. This information can be retrieved from governmental archives, such as those found at http://www.archives.gov/research/military/korean-war/casualty-lists/me-alpha.pdf.

3. PERSONAL REFLECTIONS. It is feasible that students may know a veteran of some of the conflicts. For example, Vietnam veterans are now in their 60s and 70s, and many in the same age bracket may have served on the DMZ in Korea. Students should be encouraged to locate and interview a veteran in their family or community. If unable to locate a veteran, there are oral histories available online, such as the one at http://fcit.usf.edu/vietnam/.

4. OUTCOME AND AFTERMATH. This section should answer questions such as: How did it end? Why did it end? What controversies surround the cost (in lives and money) of the conflict?

As students conduct their research, emphasize the need to ascertain the validity and accuracy of the content. Ask them to fill out the Fact or Fiction sheet (see the blackline master at the end of this chapter) when they are analyzing the reliability of the sources.

DESIGN. Flowcharts and storyboards are extremely important to help students map out their ideas and provide a structure for each section of their website. Remind them that writing for the web differs from writing a research paper. Reading from a computer screen, etc., generally takes longer than reading from paper. Also, people are used to scanning web pages for pertinent information (Diehl 2014). On the web, the writing style must be very clear and concise, with short paragraphs and bulleted lists (Redshaw 2003).

Provide copies of the Web Design Guidelines and a storyboard template. Also, discuss using media elements in the project. Point out that graphics that are not optimized for the web (as far as size, resolution, etc.) may be slow to load. Encourage students to check the file size of images— if they are more than 50K, they should probably be compressed.

Remind students of copyright restrictions. Publishing on the web is different from producing a multimedia project that will be used only within the classroom. All graphics, music, text, and video should be original or should be part of the public domain. If students locate a graphic or another media element on the web, they should read the copyright statements to make sure that they can place that element on a web page that will be accessible through the Internet.

DEVELOP. After the students' design documents have been approved, they can begin the development of their website with an appropriate tool. If teams are not working on the computers, students can be:

■ Conducting research about the topic in textbooks, videos, and encyclopedias to continue verifying the content found on the web

■ Asking teachers, parents, etc., about their recollections of the time period

Figure 10.2. Personal Reflections area for Vietnam War website (created with Weebly).

- Identifying and contacting veterans about an interview

- Writing interview questions

- Reviewing maps related to the conflict

- Creating charts and graphs related to the casualties of the war

As students complete the development of their website, they should ask one or two of their peers to review their work, noting any usability issues, grammatical errors, etc. If possible, student review teams should also note any graphics or media elements that take too long to download, and they should test the site with different browsers and computers. The content of the report should be original and should provide proper citations for any references.

EVALUATE. Follow the general procedure for project evaluations (teacher evaluation, peer evaluation). If the projects are going to be accessible throughout the world, an additional review-and-revision cycle may be necessary. After the teacher has noted changes, students should revise the content as necessary before uploading the projects to the server. All class websites can be linked via a class page that explains the project and the parameters.

Classroom WebQuests

Lesson Description: A WebQuest is an inquiry-oriented activity that provides an excellent example of how the various resources on the Internet can be effectively integrated for a classroom project. WebQuests are designed to guide learners as they research and synthesize a specific issue and incorporate the results into an authentic product or project.

There are two major levels of WebQuests—short-term and long-term. A short-term Web-Quest is designed to be completed in one to three class periods. It focuses on a specific domain of knowledge, with limited reference sites. A long-term WebQuest may require several weeks to complete. It involves a significant amount of information, and may include an extensive final product, such as a presentation, website, or multimedia production.

WebQuests are appealing because they provide structure and guidance both for students and for teachers. The following six components are essential for implementing WebQuests:

1. Introduction: Background on the activity to be completed

2. Task: Description of main research question and anticipated end product

3. Process: Steps for completing the task

4. Resources: Websites that provide information relative to the task

5. Evaluation: Guidelines for evaluation (often includes a rubric)

6. Conclusion: Opportunities for reflection and extension

DECIDE. WebQuests can be created by the teacher or by student groups. To become familiar with the structure, the entire class could participate in a WebQuest such as "A WebQuest about WebQuests" at http://webquest.sdsu.edu/webquestwebquest-hs.html. This WebQuest was created as an introduction to the WebQuest strategy (Dodge 2009). Students work in groups, each of which analyzes five websites from different perspectives (Efficiency Expert, Affiliator, Altitudinist, and Technophile). This exercise not only introduces students to the structure of WebQuests, it also helps them to understand how the same information can be interpreted very differently from various perspectives.

WebQuests can be implemented in the classroom as individual, small-group, or whole-class activities—with only one computer or with many digital devices. There are thousands of WebQuests on the web that can be used "as is" or adopted for a specific class. For example, at WebQuestGarden, you can search by subject area and grade level to access multiple WebQuests that have been created by educators (see http://questgarden.com/author/examplestop.php). Likewise, Zunal posts almost 20,000 WebQuests on their subject/grade matrix at http://zunal.com/index-matrix.php.

DESIGN. After reviewing and/or completing several WebQuests, it is time to create one or have students groups work together to create a WebQuest. Since the structure of a WebQuest is predefined (Introduction, Task, Process, Resources, Evaluation, and Conclusion), the design can focus on the curricular goals and the content. This is by far the most difficult part of designing a WebQuest. In his article "WebQuest Taskonomy: A Taxonomy of Tasks," Dodge (2002) outlined several strategies used in including, journalistic, compilation, consensus building, mystery, persuasion, creative product, and judgment tasks. WebQuests should not be simple "cut and paste" activities where students merely look for answers on the web (March 2004). Instead, WebQuests should require that students use their problem-solving and creativity skills to synthesize, analyze, and interpret information.

DEVELOP. Although WebQuests can be developed with a variety of tools, one of the easiest methods is to use the templates on Zunal.com and similar sites. After you register on Zunal, you can fill in each section of the WebQuest, add images, complete a rubric, link to other websites, and embed videos (see Figure 10.3). When the WebQuest is finished, it will be hosted on the Zunal server.

EVALUATE. Most WebQuests specify the production of an end product to present the results of students' research/investigation. For example, students may be asked to write a persuasive essay, build a model of a volcano, create a presentation, produce a video, or author an eBook. These products are generally assessed with a rubric that focuses on the content.

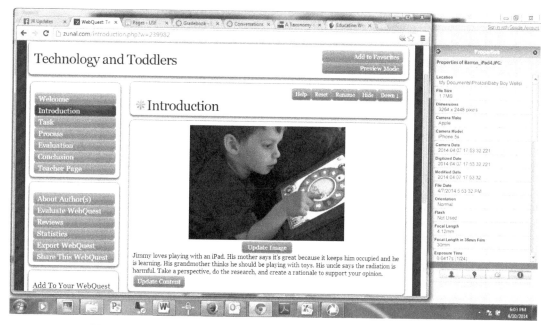

Figure 10.3. WebQuest development structure at Zunal.com.

SUMMARY

Authentic web-based projects can be designed for all grade levels and content areas. As the web continues to proliferate in our homes and schools, the development of web-based programs will become an increasingly important tool for students.

BLACKLINE MASTERS

The web is an invaluable resource for sharing and researching information. This chapter described several activities and two blackline masters for assisting students with their web projects. Blackline masters in this chapter include:

- Web Design Guidelines: a list of guidelines specific to web projects

- Fact or Fiction: a means to record and analyze information on the web

REFERENCES

Diehl, A. Web writing style guide. Available at: http://www.hampshire.edu/web-writing-style-guide.htm. Retrieved on August 3, 2014.

Dodge, B. (2002). WebQuest taskonomy. Available at: http://webquest.sdsu.edu/taskonomy.html. Retrieved on August 3, 2014.

Dodge, B. (2009). A WebQuest about WebQuests. Available at: http://webquest.sdsu.edu/webquestwebquest-hs.html. Retrieved on August 3, 2014.

March, T. (2004). The Learning Power of WebQuests. Available at: http://tommarch.com/writings/ascdwebquests/. Retrieved on August 3, 2014.

Redshaw, B. (2003). Scannability and readability in web writing. Available at: http://www.kerryr.net/webwriting/structure_scan-read.htm. Retrieved on August 3, 2014.

Web Design Guidelines

The following guidelines can help make your Web pages more user-friendly for the visitors to your site.

General

Carefully plan your pages before you create them.
Place a descriptive title on the top of all pages.
Include the date of the last revision on the pages.
Limit the length of Web pages to three screens.
Test the pages with several different browsers and computers.
Check all pages for correct spelling and grammar.

Graphics

Make sure the graphics are relevant to the page.
Limit the file size of the graphics to less than 30K each.
Limit the number of graphics on each page.
Use GIF graphics for line drawings and simple graphics.
Use JPG graphics for photographs.
Limit the width of graphics to less than 470 pixels.

Text

Make sure there is high contrast between background and text.
Limit the length of text lines.
Include blank space between paragraphs.
Limit the use of blinking text.

Media: Audio and Video

Use audio and video only when necessary.
Include information about audio and video file sizes.
Include information about format (e.g., wav, avi, quicktime)

From *Digital Content Creation in Schools: A Common Core Approach* by Karen S. Ivers and Ann E. Barron. Santa Barbara, CA: Libraries Unlimited. Copyright © 2015.

Fact or Fiction

Because anyone can create a Web page, it is important to try to determine if the information presented there is true or not. Fill out this form for Web sites that you are including in your project.

Web Site #1

Title of Site _____

Address (URL) _____

Author _____

Date last modified _____

Clues that help to determine if the information is Fact or Fiction

_____

Web Site #2

Title of Site _____

Address (URL) _____

Author _____

Date last modified _____

Clues that help to determine if the information is Fact or Fiction

_____

Web Site #3

Title of Site _____

Address (URL) _____

Author _____

Date last modified _____

Clues that help to determine if the information is Fact or Fiction

_____

Chapter 11

Digital Content Creation Projects: Video

A SCENARIO

"Lights! Action! Cameron—get over here! You're supposed to be in this shot!" yelled John. Cameron had stepped aside to practice his lines. John, the director of the group's video project, noticed that they were falling behind schedule and did not want to have to rush their project. "This is important!" emphasized John. "The community board meeting is in two weeks and unless we have a convincing, professional, and finished product, we'll have to wait another month to present our idea." John and his team were working on a class project that involved helping the community. John's team decided to focus on the idea of creating a community garden. There was a vacant lot near the school that would serve as an ideal planting spot. Each member had expressed concern over the fact that most families living in the community lived in apartments with no yard, or had small yards that were mostly cement. The team's project was a documentary and proposal. The team had captured video of other community gardens, their supporters, and the impact it had on the members of the community. In addition, the team had conducted surveys, done interviews, and gathered petitions to demonstrate the need and desire for a community garden. Last, the team had a plan to get the community garden started, including funding. It was a huge project, but something the students had been working on since the beginning to the school year. "I'm ready," said Cameron. "Let's keep going. Cue the camera."

OVERVIEW

Students live in a visual world, watching television, going to movies, playing video games, logging on to the Internet and engaging in social media sites, and more. Video is everywhere—even in grocery store checkout lines. It is a "natural" part of today's world, accessible on mobile devices, in automobiles, and more. Creating a video project can help make learning more meaningful to students because it is a part of their everyday life—how they play, interact, and learn. Now, thanks to video-editing programs that are inexpensive and easy to learn, video projects are feasible for students in all grades. As discussed in Chapters 5 and 6, today's technologies make it easy to capture video. Video can be captured on cell phones, digital cameras, smartphones, computer webcams, and innovative devices such as Google Glass.

Video projects can be created from a variety of sources with popular, easily available programs and apps such as iMovie, Movie Maker, and Animoto (see Chapter 6). Projects can be shared on the web, including YouTube (http://www.youtube.com), TeacherTube (http://www.teachertube.com), Vimeo (https://vimeo.com/), SchoolTube (http://www.schooltube.com/), and many social media sites.

Integrating video production into classroom activities has many benefits for students. Similar to other digital projects, video production encourages collaboration and requires students to be active and constructive. It can be used across the curriculum and to support students' communication and presentation skills.

SAMPLE PROJECTS

Video projects can range from a simple, one-shot video of a demonstration, interview, or event to a complex, multiple-edit production. For example, students may take a camera on a field trip to record their experiences; they can make video yearbooks; they can create book trailers; or they can produce the school news programs. Videos can also be produced as screencasts (such as how to edit a document) or still images with audio and transitions (see Chapter 6). Visit SchoolTube (http://www.schooltube.com/) and TeacherTube (http://www.teachertube.com/) for more ideas.

The sample projects included in this chapter offer a variety of approaches for video. Video may be recorded or imported using digital cameras, smartphones, tablets, and so on. Final products may be recorded on a DVD, uploaded to the web, or stored and displayed on a computer, smartphone, or tablet.

Before assigning a video product, carefully analyze the skills and experiences of your students. Obvious differences in requirements and outcomes should be expected based on students' understanding of the technical and design aspects of video production (video-scripting guidelines are presented at the end of this chapter). Remember, however, that although the quality of the finished product may be higher with a high school media production class than an elementary class, the learning benefits can be the same or even greater for the latter.

As with other digital projects, you will want to assess your resources. If you have three computers in your classroom, you may want to designate one for video editing and use the others to design graphic logos or other elements that can be incorporated into the students' videos. Scheduling and rotation lists will depend on the number of computers and video cameras available in the classroom. As groups take turns shooting their video segments, other groups can be using the computers for research, graphics, or digital editing. Those who are not working with computers or cameras can be assigned other tasks that are related to the project. In one-to-one computer or tablet classrooms, student groups can designate each student's device for a particular task, aligned with each student's role in the project. The following projects are designed to give you ideas of how to incorporate digital video into your classroom.

Show and Tell

Lesson Description: A good, introductory video project is one in which the students can concentrate on the process rather than new content. This project focuses on compiling a video that demonstrates how to do a particular task. For example, students could create video shots that demonstrate different dance steps. The final product can be created so viewers can pick and choose which dance steps they would like to see demonstrated, the order in which they would like to see them, and how often they want to see each segment.

DECIDE. Have students explain what is meant by "a picture is worth a thousand words." Discuss the advantages and disadvantages of text, pictures, and video. Have students share experiences of how they learned something by watching someone else or give examples of how they could learn something by watching someone else. Discuss what makes it easy or difficult to learn by watching someone.

Place students in groups and have them brainstorm ideas of what could be learned by watching someone do something—for example, how to swing a bat, dribble a basketball, bowl, tie a knot, make a balloon animal, knit, and so on. Remind students that learning is the first step before doing —just because someone *knows* how to ride a bike (get on the seat, balance oneself, and pedal) does not mean he or she can do it without practice! Some learning tasks are more difficult than others.

Have student groups select a multistep task (like making a balloon animal or origami) or variations of a single task (e.g., multiple ways to shuffle a deck of cards, different tennis swings, and so on). Have students share what would make a "how-to" video useful—types of shots (e.g., close-up, angles), pace, clarity, and so on. Create a rubric based on the criteria defined by the class.

Discuss how text and pictures may be used to enhance or support the video clips. Create a rubric with the students that includes the important elements of the assignment. See the How-to Evaluation blackline master in Chapter 9 for more ideas.

DESIGN. Assist students in the preproduction phase: outlining their project, creating a shot list, and writing the script (if applicable) for the video. If the videos will be incorporated into a PowerPoint presentation, website, or other program, students will also need to develop a flowchart and storyboards. These should indicate the placement of the video clips. Flowcharts, storyboards, and the video outline and shot list are reviewed before teams are allowed to go to the next stage.

DEVELOP. When it is time to shoot the video, team members should assume various roles, such as actors, lighting technicians, camera operator, and producer. After the video is imported into an editing program, students can be assigned various roles within their group—for example, project manager, audio technician, lead editor, and so on.

EVALUATE. Use the class-created rubric(s) to evaluate the projects. Class projects may be uploaded to YouTube, TeacherTube, iTunes, etc. (after review by the teacher and permission from the parents). For privacy issues, make sure students are not identified by name if sharing the projects publically.

If this is an initial video project, have students discuss lessons learned by answering the following questions:

- Which part or parts of the project were easier than originally thought?

- Which part or parts of the project were more difficult to complete?

- How did the video contribute to the effectiveness of this project? In other words, could a PowerPoint presentation have been as effective?

- What are two "lessons learned" that you would like to share with your classmates?

Conceptual Understanding

Lesson Description: Similar to "Show and Tell," another option is to have students create a video that demonstrates a concept. For example, rather than using or explaining a rote procedure for adding fractions with unlike dominators or how to create an improper fraction, students develop video segments that use visuals to conceptually explain how to add fractions with unlike denominators or how to create an improper fraction. Videos can be created for classmates or designed to assist younger learners. This option is more complex than the "Show and Tell" dance example, supporting the need for students to explain their thinking and understand mathematics conceptually.

DECIDE. Have students share experiences of how they learned different concepts in mathematics. Did they learn through memorization, with manipulatives, through stories and songs, by drawings or formulas, or other strategies? Chances are they learned mathematics through a combination of different strategies. Discuss the difference between conceptual understanding and rote procedures. Have students share why it is important to be able to understand and make meaning of what is learned and apply it in other situations.

As a class, brainstorm different mathematical concepts that students may currently, or did in the past, find difficult. Assign groups by mathematical concepts (e.g., place value, division, adding unlike denominators in fractions, creating improper fractions or mixed numerals, etc.) and ensure there is at least one "expert" in the group who has a clear understanding of the concept.

Have students share what would make a teaching video useful —types of shots (e.g., close-up, angles), pace, clarity, visuals and models, conceptual examples, engagement, and so on. Discuss how the design of their video will differ, depending on the target audience (e.g., younger learners or their peers). Create a rubric based on the criteria defined by the class. See the How-to Evaluation blackline master in Chapter 9 for more ideas. Make sure students understand that their video must teach conceptual understanding, not memorization.

DESIGN. Assist students in the preproduction phase: outlining their project, creating a shot list, and writing the script for the video. The teacher should monitor student work and answer questions during the DESIGN stage to ensure students' conceptual understanding is correct.

DEVELOP. Once student scripts have been approved and the preproduction phase is complete, groups can assign members specific roles and begin shooting the video. After the video is imported into an editing program, students can be assigned various editing and management roles.

EVALUATE. Use the class-created rubric(s) to evaluate the projects. Projects may be used to assist classmates or younger learners, as well as shared on the web (with parent permission).

Creating a Convincing Commercial

Lesson Description: Students are very familiar with commercials on television. However, have they ever stopped to analyze commercials and consider the persuasive tactics that are employed? This project involves student groups in creating a short commercial that could be used to convince others to purchase a specific product.

DECIDE. Begin the assignment by showing examples of television commercials. You may have access to prerecorded commercials on DVD or the web. Video clips of commercials can be found by searching YouTube (http://www.youtube.com) for "commercials" or specific search terms like "old commercials" or "cereal commercials." You can also find clips at ClipLand (http://www.clipland.com/). Discuss the concepts of marketing and persuasion.

As the commercials are being viewed (either individually or as a group), have the students note the following:

- The length of time each ad runs

- How many edits (different scenes) are used in each commercial

- Where and how the commercials "imprint" the company—either by logo, by jingle, or by words and actions

- The emotions that are evoked by the commercial

- The targeted audience—children or adults; males or females; local, national, or international audiences

Form groups of four to six students, and have them continue the discussion by brainstorming possible products that they could target for the commercials. These products can be real or fictional; however, do not allow them to target a product that is already being advertised on television. For example, students may decide to market a book, a fictional invention, or a local event like an environmental cleanup. Ask each group to generate at least 20 ideas of possible content items. Help them select a product that is feasible, based on their interests and the availability of props, images, and resources. Encourage innovation, creativity, and fun.

DESIGN. Discuss general design issues for commercials. Emphasize the need to convey a persuasive position in a short period of time. Encourage them to search the web for information about producing commercials and possible lessons learned by marketing companies.

Students should create storyboards or video scripts, or both, that detail the types of video shots needed, along with the narration. Continually remind them of the short length of the final video; encourage them to brand the product with a logo, a jingle, or a phrase. Review the following design guidelines that apply to commercials:

- The most important portion of the commercial is the visual aspect. Even if the sound is turned off or down, a message should be conveyed.

- Commercials aim to motivate viewers and to touch their emotions. Concentrate on one or more emotions.

- Grab the viewer's attention quickly. Within a couple of seconds, the viewers may decide (consciously or unconsciously) to leave the room if they are not "hooked" by the commercial.

- Keep the message simple and visual. Include the name of the company and logo visually on the screen.

- Be repetitive. Repeat the product name several times in the commercial.

- Keep it short. Commercials are often designed for 30-second slots; however, many are only 10 or 20 seconds.

At this time, it may be a good idea for the class to design a rubric for evaluating their commercials. Criteria may include the appeal of the commercial (how well it motivates or touches the viewer's emotions), how well the message is conveyed and remembered, how well it grabs the viewer's attention, whether it convinced one to purchase the product, and so on.

DEVELOP. When it is time to shoot the video, team members should assume various roles, such as actors, lighting technicians, camera operators, and producers. After the video is imported into an editing program, ensure that all students have input into the appropriate cuts and transitions.

EVALUATE. Record the projects to DVD for class evaluation. Students use the rubric designed in the DESIGN phase to evaluate and discuss each group's commercial. A sample rubric appears at the end of this chapter.

Digital Storytelling

Lesson Description: The term *digital storytelling* can be used to refer to many approaches and content areas. For example, in the literal sense, students write a story and "act it out" via video. This is one method for integrating video projects into the language arts curriculum and meeting standards addressing speaking, reading, writing, and other skills. Video storytelling can also refer to producing documentaries. Whether the video story is fiction or nonfiction, it provides students with a means to act out or convey what they know through an interactive environment.

Depending on the grade level and topic to be addressed, select or have your students create a story to act out on video. For example, students may act out a play about the famous ride of Paul Revere or write the script themselves based on research. Students may reenact the Boston Tea Party or other historical event; act out fairy tales, nursery rhymes, or chapters of books they are reading; or create and act out a story of their own. They may document the day of a teacher, a student, or school custodian; document the growth of a plant over time, the life cycle of a butterfly, and so on.

DECIDE. Make sure the selected topic is relevant and is aligned with your state or district standards. For example, if you are a fourth-grade teacher in California, you may want to design a timeline of the events that led up to the California Gold Rush and group your students to research and act out one of the events. The recorded events can be imported, edited, combined, and sequenced inside the computer and burned onto a DVD about the California Gold Rush.

Students can work in teams toward one topic, as described earlier, or perhaps work on different documentaries or stories that will be made accessible through a DVD or embedded into another project. For example, younger students may act out and record short nursery rhymes, and the teacher may link these within PowerPoint. Older students may be assigned to document specific concerns relative to their community and produce a community-based DVD to share with city council members. Whichever approach you decide to take, make sure your students understand what will be required of them (define the criteria) and assign them to appropriate teams.

DESIGN. Assist students in the preproduction phase: outlining their project, creating a shot list, and writing the narration. Emphasize that they should use a variety of shots—some close up and some wide angle to add interest and variety. Define the evaluation criteria for the design of their project.

DEVELOP. When it is time to shoot the video, team members should assume various roles, such as actors, lighting technicians, camera operators, and producers. After the video is imported into an editing program, ensure that all students have input into the appropriate cuts and transitions.

EVALUATE. The evaluation of the selected project will be based on the criteria defined during the DECIDE and DESIGN stages. Projects can be presented during Open House or shared with other classes studying the same topics.

Historical Movie

Lesson Description: Digital storytelling can also be used to illustrate historical documents or recreate historical events. Several examples can be found at http://digitalstorytelling.coe.uh.edu/. In this lesson, students create a digital story using images of the Civil War to support their narrative of the Gettysburg Address.

DECIDE. Introduce the topic and provide background information for the students. Use a KWL chart to list what students know and want to learn about the document and the related historical events. Have students brainstorm ideas of where to locate information about the Gettysburg Address and the history of the Civil War. Create a rubric for the project, based on desired content or facts and the project design. Give students time to conduct the necessary research.

DESIGN. Divide the class into pair groups and assign a section of the Gettysburg Address to each group to memorize and recite. Have students choose pictures from a Civil War website that can be used to illustrate the document. Students should have enough pictures to cover their narration, with each picture displaying no more than eight seconds. Such criteria should be added to the rubric for evaluation.

DEVELOP. Have each group read and record its assigned section of the document into an assigned video-editing program (e.g., iMovie, Movie Maker, or Animoto). Team members can take turns reciting or they can recite their part together. Import and combine all of the audio clips into a master file. Distribute the master file to all groups. Each group will then add the photographs to the sound track to create their final movie. Groups can designate specific roles for each team member.

EVALUATE. Record the projects to DVD for class evaluation. Evaluate the projects based on the rubric created in the DECIDE and DESIGN stage. Optimize the videos for the web and post them on the school or other secure website. Make sure you have parents' permission and do not identify the students by name.

SUMMARY

Today's technologies make it easy and relatively inexpensive to create, edit, and produce video. Video projects may be recorded to DVD, made into podcasts, uploaded to the web, or incorporated into other digital projects (e.g., PowerPoint presentations or hypermedia projects). Creating videos is a powerful addition to a student's arsenal of learning tools, creating opportunities for high-level thinking, organization, planning, and management skills that can be applied in the "real world." Developing digital videos encourages creative thinking, multiple perspectives, and teamwork. They can be implemented across the curriculum for meaningful learning and provide a real-world way to actively engage students in the learning process.

BLACKLINE MASTERS

Blackline masters in this chapter include:

- Video Guidelines: a list of guidelines specific to writing video scripts

- Commercial Evaluation: a sample rubric for evaluating student commercials

Video Guidelines

The following guidelines can improve your digital videos.

Pre-Production

Make sure you have charged batteries or an electrical connection.
Obtain talent and copyright releases.
Label all tapes and log all shots.
Record with the best possible camera -- digital, if possible.
Use external microphones instead of built-in camera microphones.
Target the scripts at the intended audience.
Carefully plan your shots to tell a story.
Keep the script simple -- include only one or two main points.
Create a shot list and use it to sequence the recording.
Consider impact of distribution media (videotape or DVD vs. Web).

Production

White-balance the camera before shooting.
Shoot with your back to the light.
Use natural lighting; avoid fluorescent lighting.
Beware of cluttered backgrounds and excess movement.
"Set the stage" for the video with a wide shot of the area.
Shoot people interacting with each other, not the camera.
Use a tripod (or stand still and keep the camera very still).
Minimize panning, tilting, tracking, and other movements.
Shoot excess footage at both ends of a shot (to be edited out later).
Continue recording until the audio portion ends.
Carefully frame your shots and "lead" the eye of the viewer.
Use over-the-shoulder shots to draw the audience into the action.
Minimize harsh, close-up shots of people.
Maintain a continuous time code.

Post-Production

Minimize special effects and transitions.
If in doubt, leave it out.
Smooth sound is more important than smooth video.
Keep an archival copy of the source video.

From *Digital Content Creation in Schools: A Common Core Approach* by Karen S. Ivers and Ann E. Barron. Santa Barbara, CA: Libraries Unlimited. Copyright © 2015.

Commercial Evaluation

CRITERIA	0	1	2	3
The commercial's length was appropriate.	Commercial's length was way too short.	Commercial's length was way too long.	Commercial's length was almost appropriate.	Commercial's length was appropriate.
The commercial struck a variety of my emotions.	Commercial did not strike my emotions.	Commercial struck one of my emotions.	Commercial somewhat struck a variety of my emotions.	Commercial struck a variety of my emotions.
The commercial's message was clearly conveyed and is rememberable.	Commercial's message was not conveyed.	Commercial's message was somewhat conveyed, but it is not something I will remember.	Commercial's message was clearly conveyed, but it is not something I will remember.	Commercial's message was clearly conveyed and is something I will remember.
The commercial motivated me to purchase or support its product.	It made me not want to purchase or support this product.	It did not motivated me to purchase or support its product.	I'm unsure whether or not I will purchase or support this product.	It motivated me to purchase or support this product.
The commercial captured and held my attention.	Commercial did not captivate or hold my attention.	Commercial held my attention for a short period of time.	Commercial held my attention for most of the time.	Commercial captured and held my attention the whole time.
The commercial included the company logo and repeated the product names several times.	Commercial excluded logo and didn't repeat product name.	Commercial included logo but didn't repeat product name.	Commercial excluded logo but did repeat product name several times.	Commercial included logo and repeated product name several times.
			Total _____	

Commercial Evaluation

From *Digital Content Creation in Schools: A Common Core Approach* by Karen S. Ivers and Ann E. Barron. Santa Barbara, CA: Libraries Unlimited. Copyright © 2015.

Chapter 12

Digital Content Creation Projects: eBooks

A SCENARIO

Betty recently moved to a new school that provided tablets to its students. Even better, thought Betty, was that fact that all of their textbooks were eBooks—no more lugging around a backpack full of heavy books! Most assignments required students to use their tablets; Betty's favorite assignment thus far was the creation of an eBook for possible inclusion in the school library. She and her teammates had signed up for a school competition, featuring a variety of genres from which students could choose. Betty and her team decided to use one of their social studies assignments, one in which they had to write an essay about the different branches of government. Writing the text was easy, but making it interesting to their peers would be challenging. In addition, to be chosen as a school eBook, the project had to meet specific guidelines in regard to the design, credits, citations, and content. Betty and her team used the checklist created by the library staff to guide their project. Each member of Betty's team assumed a specific role in the design and development process. Together they designed storyboards and a flowchart to organize their ideas and assigned additional roles and responsibilities within the team. They chose an eBook tool that met the needs of their project. The tool had to provide allow users to incorporate video, sound, and graphics; include clear and multiple navigation options; and allow the final product to be accessible through the web across multiple devices. Betty's team had received an "A" on their social studies assignment; now it was a matter of time to see whether or not their eBook met the needs of and was worthy enough to be included in the school library.

OVERVIEW

We live in a world where digital media is at our fingertips at all times. We no longer need to physically visit the library to check out a book or read a magazine; the library comes to us through our smartphones, tablets, and computers in the form of electronic books (eBooks) and other electronic publications. Textbooks are becoming eBooks as well, enriching students' learning by incorporating links, videos, audio, and other multimedia. Many magazine and newspaper subscriptions are electronic, available on the web and through mobile apps.

As much as many of us may enjoy the feel of a book or magazine in our hands, the trend to digital publications is here to stay. It is cost effective, reduces our dependency on paper, and certainly reduces the weight of a student's book bag! As mentioned, several eBooks, like other digital media, are accessible from any digital device and can provide users with features not available in traditional books. While there are numerous benefits for consumers of eBooks, there are many benefits for creators of eBooks as well. For example, similar to other digital content creation projects, creating eBooks provides students with the opportunity to communicate their knowledge in multiple ways, using multimodalities to support meaning making. eBooks provide students with an easy way to share their work with a wider audience.

SAMPLE PROJECTS

Writing is one way we ask students to share what they know. Creating eBooks allows students to enhance what they have written and to share what they know by incorporating multimedia. In addition, they can share, catalog, and publish their books online. As mentioned in Chapter 6, not all eBooks are created equal. iBook Author is the best example of an interactive, multimedia platform for eBooks, but it has platform limitations. Book Creator is an excellent, interactive app for tablets. Other eBook programs allow users to incorporate multimedia such as video and audio, but the interactivity and design may be limited. Based upon the hardware and software available, it is up to the teacher to decide which development tool is best for the intended purpose, archiving, and distribution of the proposed project.

Students may create eBooks that focus on fictional stories, poetry, historical events, famous people, a science or mathematics concept, life stories, and so on. Working in cooperative groups provides students with the opportunity to share ideas with each other, balance their strengths and weaknesses, and prepare them for real-world environments. In one-to-one laptop or tablet classrooms, teachers may be tempted to assign individual projects. It is best not to use technology as a means to isolate students; instead, use technology to provide students with real-world learning opportunities to collaborate, communicate, and share ideas. Students are still responsible for their individual work; working cooperatively, they are also responsible to the team. Group and self-evaluations (see Chapter 7) and journal entries (see Chapter 3) can be used to support student groups.

Things You Need to Know About

Lesson Description: This activity can be tied to any curriculum area or other topic of interest. For example, a teacher may have student groups write a 10-page eBook expressing things people need to know about different drugs, alcohol, and smoking. Student groups are assigned a specific topic and conduct research based on categories designated by the class and the teacher. For example, categories may include the history of the product, related statistics, dangers, abuse, and so on.

DECIDE. Assign student teams a topic to research. As a class, brainstorm what categories should be included to provide readers with the most relevant and important facts about the topic. Limit group eBooks to 10 pages and have students discuss what they can do to engage the reader, including the use of media. The 10 pages should include the cover, table of contents, and credits. Decide on a development tool for creating the eBook (see Chapter 6). The development tool will depend on the available technology, media choices, and how the product will be shared.

Figure 12.1. eBook and sample page created in Word and converted into an ePub.

Have students assist you with the creation of a rubric that includes the important elements of the assignment, as well as spelling, sentence structure, grammar, crediting resources, and so on, or use the What You Should Know Rubric at the end of this chapter. Figure 12.1 shows a sample of a document created in Word and converted into an ePub using Calibre.

DESIGN. Instruct students how to create storyboards to represent the layout and sequence of their pages. Student teams can designate leaders for specific tasks, but each team member should be involved in the research and design process. If computer resources are limited for conducting research, refer to Chapter 3 for scheduling options. Once the research is completed and the storyboards have been approved, students can begin the next stage.

DEVELOP. Provide students with the necessary instructions to use the chosen eBook development tool. Student groups should assign members to specific roles (e.g., editor, graphic artist, project manager, and so on). As students complete their eBooks, another team reviews the eBook for clarity, spelling, and so on. The corrected project, along with the project's rubrics, is submitted to the teacher.

EVALUATE. Following the teacher's evaluation of the project, peers can evaluate each other's projects as well (see Chapter 7). Select projects may be shared via eBook websites or stored within a Calibre class library (see Chapter 6). Teachers may quiz students on the content of the eBooks, also.

Limerick Stories

Lesson Description: Group eBooks can be created to showcase students' creative writing through the use of limericks. Students work together in small groups to create a story using a series of limericks. Students write, illustrate, and record their story.

Figure 12.2. Sample eBook page created in Interact Builder.

DECIDE. Assign student teams. Review the rhyming pattern of a limerick and share several examples. Next, explain that students will be working in their small group to write a story created out of limericks. Discuss that the story must contain at least four sets of limericks, connected to make a story. One example you may use is the "Terrible Talky Not-Quite" by Ann McGovern, available in *Squeals & Squiggles & Ghostly Giggles.* Another is "The Erratic Rat" by Carolyn Wells (see http://www.dltk-kids.com/crafts/miscellaneous/cwells-erraticrat.htm). You may choose to increase or decrease the number of limericks for the story dependent on the ability level of your students. Provide students with an opportunity to brainstorm what they want to write about and to create their story. You may use the rubric at the end of this chapter (see Limerick Story Rubric) or design your own rubric with the students to evaluate final submissions. Figure 12.2 provides a sample page created in Interact Builder. Note the options at the bottom for incorporating different media elements. Audio is available as an Action item within the different media elements.

DESIGN. Once student groups have written their limerick story, students create storyboards to layout the design of their eBook. Remind students that they will be narrating their story, and will need to create separate audio clips for each of their pages. Discuss how the tone, pace, pitch, inflection, and so on of how we read a poem or story can change how it is perceived. Provide an example by reading a passage in a monotone voice, and then again with thought and emotion.

DEVELOP. Use an interactive eBook tool such as Interact Builder or iBooks Author to create the multimedia eBook. Students may have to create their illustrations and audio clips in separate files. Students can assume the roles of project director, editor, narrator, graphic designer, and so on.

EVALUATE. After students have completed their eBook, students can evaluate each other's work. The teacher can provide the final evaluation and make the eBooks available in the class library.

A Recipe for Success

Lesson Description: Cookbooks are an easy way for students to share their cultural background, and they make excellent eBooks. Students are asked to research their family heritage and share a traditional family recipe. If a recipe is not available, students can research related recipes on the Internet. In addition to the recipe, students must include a photo of the final product. Students may opt to include additional photos of specific steps or food ingredients as well. As a culminating activity, students can bring their dishes to school for sharing.

DECIDE. Have students discuss with a classmate (think-pair-share) what they know about their family history (e.g., where their grandparents were born, where their grandparents' parents were born, traditions, favorite meals, and so on). Have each student complete their own KWL chart. Ask students to share some of their favorite family traditions, including food. Share with the students that they will be creating a class cookbook, highlighting traditional family recipes and interesting family facts. Discuss and list what might be considered interesting family facts. Based on the discussion, have students research and complete their KWL chart, as well as a family recipe and photo of the finished dish. Create and share the rubric that will be used to evaluate students' work. Place students in groups so they can support each other's ideas and assist when needed.

DESIGN. Provide students with templates to compose three pages: one page should provide interesting family, historical facts; one page should list the ingredients for the recipe and include a photo of the prepared dish; and one page should provide the directions for making the recipe. See Figures 12.3, 12.4 (p. 228), and 12.5 (p. 229) for examples. Students draft their work on the templates. Student groups proofread and provide suggestions to their team members' work.

DEVELOP. Once students' work has been reviewed, students use an assigned eBook application to submit their work. Calibre can be used to convert Word documents into an ePub for general distribution, or programs like iAuthor or Interact Builder can be used if you choose to make additional media elements an integral part of the project. For example, audio can be used to narrate the family history; video may be used to demonstrate various steps in the recipe. The teacher or an assigned student creates a table of contents and cover for the class cookbook.

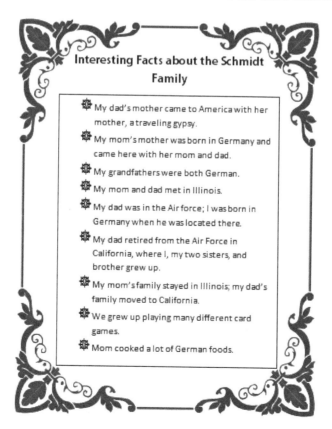

Interesting Facts about the Schmidt Family

- My dad's mother came to America with her mother, a traveling gypsy.
- My mom's mother was born in Germany and came here with her mom and dad.
- My grandfathers were both German.
- My mom and dad met in Illinois.
- My dad was in the Air force; I was born in Germany when he was located there.
- My dad retired from the Air Force in California, where I, my two sisters, and brother grew up.
- My mom's family stayed in Illinois; my dad's family moved to California.
- We grew up playing many different card games.
- Mom cooked a lot of German foods.

Figure 12.3. Interesting family facts.

Figure 12.4. Recipe ingredients and picture.

EVALUATE. The teacher evaluates each student's work based on the shared rubric. The eBook can be distributed to students to share with their families. With parent and administrator permission, the book may be used as a fund-raiser for the classroom.Round-Robin

Lesson Description: Round-robin story writing provides students with the opportunity to contribute to an already established story line and structure, while at the same time adding their own creativity and understanding of different story elements. Each student within designated teams begins a story within a certain time limit. When time is up, students rotate to and continue the story started by a classmate. This continues for several rounds, until the teacher declares the last round, where students must conclude the story. This is ideal for multiple computers, but if resources are limited, teams can be assigned to the computers on hand, with each team taking turns rotating through each person's story or adding to a story stored on a single computer. Student teams review their final products for grammar, spelling, continuity, and so on. In situations where each team member has their own computer or tablet, the group can select one of the round-robin stories to submit as their final product. The most creative, funny, or comprehensive stories can be shared and published as eBooks, and perhaps become part of a round-robin, creative writing contest among different classes.

DECIDE. Discuss round-robin writing with your students. Remind them of different story elements (e.g., character, plot, setting, conflict, climax, resolution, etc.) and the importance of story structure and cohesion. As a class, create a rubric that will be used to assess the different story elements and mechanics (e.g., spelling, punctuation, grammar) of the story. There may be an emphasis on the use of adjectives, similes, metaphors, and other writing elements as well.

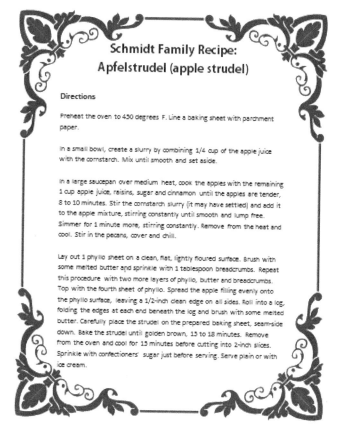

Figure 12.5. Recipe directions.

DESIGN. Create groups of four, five, or six students. If each student has access to a computer, have them each start a story and follow the round-robin procedure in their group, deciding on the "best" story that they would like to submit as a group. Otherwise, student groups can rotate through one group story.

DEVELOP. Once the parameters of the story have been discussed, student teams begin the timed round-robin process. The time provided will depend on the ability level of your students. In some cases, you may decide to pair students together as they construct their stories. Once students have completed their stories, student groups select, proofread, and submit their final story to share with the class. Stories can be created in a word processing document, saved as a PDF, and transferred to an eBook format for publication. Illustrations and other media can be added to enhance the publication.

EVALUATE. The teacher evaluates the team's selected submission based on the rubric. The eBooks can be shared with their families and, as mentioned, become part of a round-robin, creative writing contest among different classes.

Graphic Novel

Lesson Description: Graphic novels are a great way to engage reluctant readers and writers. Killeen (2013) shares how graphic novels can be used to support the Common Core State Standards, helping young students describe how characters in a story respond to major events and challenges, acknowledge differences in the points of view of characters, and use information gained from the illustrations and words to demonstrate understanding of its characters, setting, or plot. Tomasevich (2013) and Gavigan (2012) address how graphic novels have been shown to support the literacy skills of English Language Learners, special-needs students, males, and reluctant readers, and suggest graphic novels can benefit all students. Friese (2013) agrees, and notes that writing graphic novels benefits students in numerous ways as well. For example, creating graphic novels can help students visualize how to "show" a reader with words, helping students understand how excellent writers "show, not tell" their readers about characters' feelings and actions, the setting, and so on.

There are multiple topics for graphic novels, including personal accounts, a retelling of a historical event, book reports, biographies, creative stories, and so on. For this example, we will focus on creating a graphic novel that retells a historical event.

DECIDE. Asks students if they have read a graphic novel and discuss how it is similar to and different from comic strips they may read in the newspaper. Discuss basic features of comic strips (e.g., frames, pictures, captions) and how cartoonists help "show" the story through pictures. Review the important elements of a telling a story (e.g., characters, setting, plot, conflict, etc.). Provide students with examples of graphic novels, as well as time to become familiar with one of the graphic novel programs mentioned in Chapter 6 (Graphix, MakeBeliefsComix, Pixton, ToonDoo, or ComicLife) or another tool of your choice. Make sure the tool can support the requirements of the project. For example, if students are required to incorporate their own images, choose a graphic novel tool that supports importing graphics (e.g., Pixton, ToonDoo, or ComicLife). Once students have had time to explore and familiarize themselves with graphic novels and the tool, turn students' attention to the goal of the lesson: to retell a famous historical event through a graphic novel. Set parameters for the novel. For example, you may want to state that the novel must be from 15 to 20 frames, include at least three characters, and focus on an event that occurred within the last 100 years. The story should include moments leading up to the event, as well as the outcome. In addition to the parameters, share and discuss the Graphic Novel Rubric (or your own rubric), available at the end of this chapter. Place students in groups of four and have each group decide on an event they would like to retell. For younger students, you may assign them to create a novel about a particular historical hero using available clip art. For example, tools such as MakeBeliefsComix have a diverse clip art library of characters, scenes, objects, and so on that students can use to create stories about famous people (see Figure 6.18 in Chapter 6).

Provide student groups with time to research their historical event and the people involved. Have them identify the key characters that they will be using to tell their story, the setting, the event, and the outcome using the Graphic Novel Organizer at the end of this chapter.

DESIGN. After their research and organizer are approved, student groups design storyboards for their graphic novel. Students may assume particular roles, including project manager, instructional designer, graphic artist, editor, and so on.

DEVELOP. After student groups have their storyboards approved, students work together to construct their graphic novel.

EVALUATE. Novels are evaluated based on the set parameters and identified rubric. Novels may be shared online, in print, and made available in the school library.

SUMMARY

Multimedia and the Internet are changing the way students engage in textual practices. Smartphones and other mobile devices make it possible to access text and multimedia almost anywhere. In addition, these same tools make it possible to create and publish eBooks. eBooks are no longer limited to static text; new standards and software programs make it possible to create eBooks that are multimedia-rich, interactive, and accessible across a variety of devices. Interactive, multimedia eBooks can help students learn through multimodalities as well as help students express what they know in multiple ways.

BLACKLINE MASTERS

This chapter contains four blackline masters that educators may use when creating graphic novels with their students. Additional blackline masters, available in Chapters 3 and 7, may also be used to support the management and assessment of eBook activities. Blackline masters available in this chapter include:

- Graphic Novel Rubric
- Graphic Novel Organizer
- What You Should Know Rubric
- Limerick Story Rubric

REFERENCES

Friese, E. 2013. Visual narratives. *Knowledge Quest*, 41(3), 24–29.

Gavigan, K. 2012. Sequentially smart-using graphic novels across the K–12 curriculum. *Teacher Librarian*, 39(5), 20–25.

Killeen, E. 2013. Graphic novels build literacy. *Teacher Librarian*, 41(2), 57.

Tomasevich, M. 2013. Creating super learners bringing graphic novels into 6–12 instruction. *Knowledge Quest*, 41(3), 18.

Graphic Novel Rubric

CRITERIA	0	1	2	3
The novel provides a story consisted with the assignment.	The story is incomplete or does not address the assignment.	The story is difficult to follow.	The story is easy to read, but there are 1 or 2 points of confusion.	The story is clear, well organized, detailed, and easy to read.
The novel uses clear, descriptive language and captions are concise.	The language is overly simple.	The language is descriptive at times, but most is overly simple or not concise.	The majority of language is clear, descriptive, and concise.	The language is clear, descriptive, and concise.
The choice of frames, artwork, and placement of text enhance the visual appeal and clarity of the story.	The design and layout distract the reader from the story.	The design and layout support the clarity of the story in a few instances.	The design and layout support the clarity of the story in all but 1 or 2 cases.	The design and layout clearly enhance the clarity of the story.
All images are clear and work with the text to support the story.	Most of the images are unrelated to the story or are not clear.	Several images are unrelated to the story or are not clear.	1 or 2 images are not clear or do not work with the text to support the story.	Images are clear and work with the text to support the story.
The novel's theme is clear, explicit in both the visuals and the text.	The theme is not conveyed through the text or visuals.	The theme is somewhat conveyed through the text of visuals.	The theme is clearly conveyed through the text or visuals.	The theme is clearly conveyed through the text and the visuals.
Grammar, spelling, and punctuation are correct.	There are more than 5 grammar, spelling, or punctuation errors.	There are 3 to 5 grammar, spelling, or punctuation errors.	There are 1 or 2 grammar, spelling, or punctuation errors.	All grammar, spelling, and punctuation are correct.
				Total _____

From *Digital Content Creation in Schools: A Common Core Approach* by Karen S. Ivers and Ann E. Barron. Santa Barbara, CA: Libraries Unlimited. Copyright © 2015.

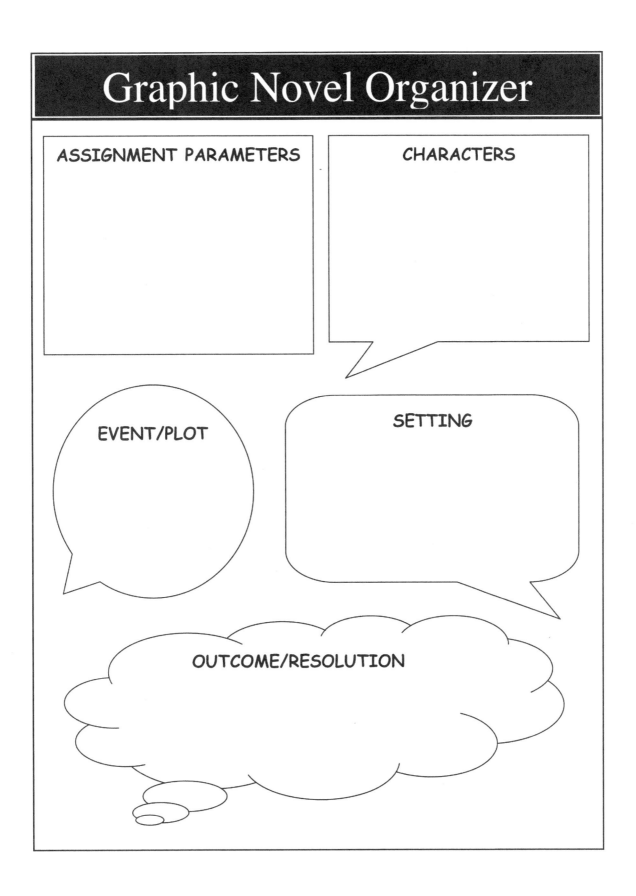

What You Should Know Rubric

CRITERIA	0	1	2	3
The eBook includes an appealing and relevant cover page, table of contents (T of C), and credits.	The eBook does not include a cover page, T of C, or credits.	The cover page, T of C, or credits is inaccurate or incomplete.	Cover page is relevant; T of C and credits are complete.	The cover page is appealing and relevant; T of C and credits are complete.
The eBook includes an engaging and accurate history of the assigned topic.	The eBook does not include the history of the given topic.	The history of the given topic has some inaccuracies or is not clear.	The eBook includes an accurate history of the given topic.	History of the assigned topic is engaging, clear and accurate.
The eBook includes accurate and thought provoking statistics about the assigned topic.	The eBook does not include statistics.	The statistics are inaccurate or not relevant.	The statistics are accurate and relevant.	The statistics are accurate, relevant and thought provoking.
The eBook includes provides, accurate, relevant and interesting facts about the assigned topic.	More than 3 of the facts are inaccurate or not relevant.	1 or 2 of the facts are inaccurate or not relevant.	Facts are accurate and relevant.	Facts are accurate, interesting, and relevant.
All images are clear and relevant to the text and the assigned topic.	More than 4 of the images are unrelated to the text or topic or are not clear.	3 or 4 images are not clear or unrelated to the text or topic.	1 or 2 images are not clear or do not support the text, relevant to the assigned topic.	Images are clear, support the text, and are relevant to the assigned topic.
Grammar, spelling, and punctuation are correct.	There are more than 5 grammar, spelling, or punctuation errors.	There are 3 to 5 grammar, spelling, or punctuation errors.	There are 1 or 2 grammar, spelling, or punctuation errors.	All grammar, spelling, and punctuation are correct.
				Total _____

Limerick Story Rubric

CRITERIA	0	1	2	3
The eBook includes a creative and relevant cover page and credits.	The eBook does not include a cover page or credits.	The cover page is not connected to the story or the credits are not complete.	The cover page is relevant; credits are complete.	The cover page is creative and relevant; credits are complete.
The eBook includes the assigned number of limericks and the limericks connect to create a clear story.	The limericks do not connect to make a clear story and number is too few.	The limericks do not connect to make a clear story or number is too few.	The number of limericks is correct, but the story is somewhat unclear.	The number of limericks is correct and they connect to create a clear story.
The eBook includes narration that matches the text and is clear and animated for each page of the story.	The eBook does not include narration.	In some cases, the narration does not match the text, is not clear, or is missing.	The narration matches the text and is clear for each page.	The narration matches the text and is clear and animated for each page.
The eBook includes provides, accurate, relevant and interesting facts about the assigned topic.	More than 3 of the facts are inaccurate or not relevant.	1 or 2 of the facts are inaccurate or not relevant.	Facts are accurate and relevant.	Facts are accurate, interesting, and relevant.
All images are clear and relevant to the text and the story.	The eBook does not contain relevant images.	3 images are not clear or are unrelated to the text.	1 or 2 images are not clear or do not support the text.	Images are clear, support the text, and are relevant to the story.
Grammar, spelling, and punctuation are correct.	There are more than 5 grammar, spelling, or punctuation errors.	There are 3 to 5 grammar, spelling, or punctuation errors.	There are 1 or 2 grammar, spelling, or punctuation errors.	All grammar, spelling, and punctuation are correct.
			Total	_____

Glossary

alternative assessment. A form of assessment other than the true or false, multiple-choice, matching, and fill-in-the-blank responses that is often associated with standardized tests. Performance-based assessment, authentic assessment, and portfolio assessment are forms of alternative assessment.

Android. An operating system designed primarily for touch screen mobile devices such as smartphones and tablet computers.

app. Short for application, a software application generally designed for smartphones and tablet computers.

authentic assessment. A method of evaluating a student's performance based on observations, performance tests, interviews, exhibitions, or portfolios. The context, purpose, audience, and constraints of the task must connect to real-world situations and problems.

authoring system. A computer program designed specifically to integrate text, images, audio, interactivity, and feedback.

AVI. A Microsoft video file format that stands for Audio Video Interleave. This audio format is used extensively on the Windows platform..

bandwidth. The transmission capacity of a telecommunications system. The greater the bandwidth, the greater the amount of digital information that can be transmitted per second.

bitmapped image. A computer image that consists of individual dots or picture elements (pixels).

Blackboard. A course management system (CMS).

blog. An online journal or communication tool that is updated frequently and intended for a specific group or the general public. Entries are posted to a single page, usually in reverse-chronological order.

branch. To move from one location of a program to another. For example, if a button initiates link to a different web page, it is said to *branch* to a web page.

bug. An error in a program.

button. An object or area of the screen used to initiate an action, such as a branch to another screen or page.

byte. Eight bits working together. A single byte can have any value from 0 to 255.

capture. The process of collecting and saving text, images, etc.

clip. A short video or audio segment.

clip art. Graphics that are distributed for use in product development.

cloud. A metaphor for the Internet when referring to cloud computing—the storing and accessing of data and programs over the Internet.

Common Core Approach. An instructional approach that emphasizes critical thinking, creativity, communication, and collaboration.

Common Core State Standards (CCSS). A set of college- and career-ready standards for kindergarten through 12th grade in English language arts/literacy and mathematics, initiated by the nation's governors and education commissioners.

compression. Reduction of data for more efficient storage and transmission; saves storage space, but may also reduce the quality of the playback.

constructivism. The belief that learning takes place through the construction of knowledge.

cooperative learning. A way of structuring student-to-student interaction so students are successful only if their group is successful. Students are held accountable for their individual learning, they receive specific instruction in the social skills necessary for the group to succeed, and they have the opportunity to discuss how well their group is working.

course management system (CMS). A comprehensive software package that facilitates the design, delivery, assessment, and management of online courses. A CMS is also called an LMS—learning management system.

DDD-E. A model for the systematic design of multimedia projects, consisting of four phases: DECIDE, DESIGN, DEVELOP, and EVALUATE.

debug. The process of correcting problems (e.g., code, grammar, and spelling) in a program.

dialog box. A window that asks a question or allows users to input information.

digital content creation. The process of using digital tools (e.g., presentation, hypermedia, web, video editors, and eBooks) with multimedia to demonstrate students' learning.

digital video. Video that is stored in bits and bytes on a computer. It can be manipulated and displayed on a computer screen.

digitizing. The process of converting an analog signal into a digital signal.

dpi (dots per inch). Refers to printing resolution of an image. Most printers can print 300–1200 dpi.

DVD (Digital Video Disc). A second generation of the original CD-ROM format. It provides up to two layers of digital information on a single-sided compact disc. It stores up to 4.7 gigabytes of text, audio, video, etc., for one layer; 8.5 gigabytes for two layers.

DVD-R. A recordable DVD disc.

DVD-RW. A recordable video disc that allows users to write to the disc many times.

eBook. An electronic book, usually read on a computer, laptop, or other mobile device.

Edmodo. Described as a "social learning platform" website for teachers, students, and parents. Teachers can post assignments, create polls for student responses, embed video clips, create learning groups, post quizzes for students to take, and create a calendar of events and assignments. Students can turn in assignments or upload assignments for their teachers to view and grade.

e-portfolio. A meaningful collection of student work in an electronic format.

ePub. A distribution and interchange format established by the International Digital Publishing Forum.

FireWire. The Apple Computer trace name for the IEEE 1394 standard that enables direct transfer of digital video between devices, such as a camcorder and computer.

flowchart. A visual depiction of the sequence and structure of a program.

fps. Frames per second. Describes the frame rate—the number of frames displayed each second.

frame. One complete video picture.

frame rate. The number of video frames displayed each second.

freeware. Software, often available for download on the Internet, that is free for anyone to use.

frequency. The number of times per second that a sound source vibrates. Frequency is expressed in hertz (Hz) or kilohertz (kHz).

full-motion video. Video frames displayed at 30 frames per second.

GIF (Graphic Interchange Format). A file format for web graphics that allows for 256 colors. It uses a lossless compression and is best used for line art and graphics with solid areas of colors. GIFs also support interlacing, transparency, and animation. GIF89a is another name for transparent or animated GIFs.

Google Apps. Free web-based applications supported by Google designed to encourage communication and collaboration.

graphic novel. Content displayed in a comic-strip format and presented as a book.

group investigation. A cooperative group technique similar to the Jigsaw method except that students do not form "expert groups." Student teams give class presentations of findings.

hertz (Hz). Unit of frequency measurement; numerically equal to cycles per second.

HTML (HyperText Markup Language). Coding language used to create hypertext documents to be posted on the Web. HTML code consists of embedded tags that specify how a block of text should appear, or that specify how a word is linked to another file on the Internet.

HTML5. The fifth revision of the HTML standard, which provides support for the latest multimedia.

HTTP (HyperText Transfer Protocol). The protocol for moving hypertext files across the World Wide Web.

hyperlink. A link from a hypertext file or document to another location or file.

hypermedia. A term used for hypertext that is not constrained to be text: it can include graphics, video and sound.

hypertext. Text displayed on a computer display or other electronic devices with references (hyperlinks) to other text that the reader can immediately access.

icon. A symbol that provides a visual representation of an action or other information. An icon or an arrow is often used to denote directional movement in hypermedia.

image. A graphic, picture, or one frame of video.

International Digital Publishing Forum. A trade and standards association for the digital publishing industry that has been set up in order to establish a reliable and complete standard for eBook publishing.

International Society for Technology in Education (ISTE). A nonprofit organization serving educators committed to empowering connected learners in a connected world.

Internet. A group of networks connecting governmental institutions, military branches, educational institutions, and commercial companies.

Internet service providers (ISPs). Organizations that provide connections to the Internet. They may be universities or private companies.

iPod. A combination portable digital media player and hard drive from Apple Computer.

iTunes. A media player, library, and mobile device management application developed by Apple Computer. It is used to play, download, and organize digital audio and video on devices running Macintosh or Microsoft Windows operating systems.

Jigsaw. A method of cooperative group learning that assigns each of its members a particular learning task. Team members meet with members of other groups to form "expert groups" to discuss and research their topic. Following research and discussion, the students return to their own teams and take turns teaching their teammates about their topic.

JPEG (Joint Photographic Experts Group). A common format for storing images (especially photographs) on the web.

kilohertz (kHz). Unit of frequency measurement; equal to 1,000 hertz.

KWL chart. A way of recording what students **k**now; what they **w**ant to find out; and what they **l**earned.

learning management system (LMS). *See* course management system.

learning together. A method of cooperative group learning that incorporates heterogeneous student groups that work on a single assignment and receive rewards based on their group product.

link. A connection from one place or medium to another. For example, buttons contain the linking information between cards.

MIDI (Musical Instrument Digital Interface). A standard for communicating musical information among computers and musical devices. *See also* general MIDI.

MIT Media Lab. An interdisciplinary research laboratory at the Massachusetts Institute of Technology devoted to projects at the convergence of technology, multimedia, and design.

mobile app. Software used on a mobile device such as a smartphone or tablet computer.

mobile device. A portable computing device such as a smartphone or tablet computer.

Moodle. An open-source course management system.

movie file. The file that is created by combining audio, video, and images.

MPEG (Moving Picture Experts Group). A common format for storing digital video files.

MP3. An audio-only compression format that can decrease the size of an audio file, but maintain a high-quality sound.

multimedia. A type of program that combines more than one media type for disseminating information. For example, a multimedia program may include text, audio, graphics, animation, and video.

object-oriented drawings. Graphics that are composed of separate geometric objects that can be layered one atop the other to create images. Also known as vector drawings or simply drawings.

objects. In hypermedia, generally refers to elements that are placed on the screen, such as buttons, fields, and graphics. Objects are components that can be manipulated and can contain links to other objects.

Open Source. A development methodology that allows users to access and modify a program's content and source code free of charge and for free distribution.

Partnership for Assessment of Readiness of College and Careers (PARCC). A group of states working together to develop a set of assessments that measure whether students are on track to be successful in college and their careers.

performance-based assessment. An assessment method whereby teachers evaluate a student's skill by asking the student to create an answer or product that demonstrates his or her knowledge or skills.

pixel. A single dot or point of an image on a computer screen. *Pixel* is a contraction of the words *picture ele*ment.

plug-and-play. A device that is automatically recognized and accessible when plugged into a computer.

PNG. Portable Network Graphics. PNG is a lossless format that supports interlacing and transparency.

podcast. Digital files that can be distributed over the Internet and played back on computers and portable media devices (e.g., cell phones, MP3 players, Apple's iPod). A podcast can be syndicated, subscribed to, and downloaded automatically when new content is added via RSS feeds.

portfolio assessment. An estimation of a student's abilities based on a systematic collection of the student's best work, records of observation, test results, and so on.

postproduction. The phase of a video project that includes editing the video.

PPI (pixels per inch). Refers to image resolution. Most monitors can display 60–120 ppi.

Project Foundry. An online learning management and student portfolio system.

preproduction. The planning phase of a video project—includes setting a goal, writing scripts, etc.

production. The phase of a video project that consists of shooting the video and compiling the media.

QuickTime. A file format that allows computers to compress and play digital video.

resolution. The number of dots or pixels that can be displayed on a computer screen. Higher resolutions create sharper images. Also refers to the sharpness or clarity of a computer screen. Displays with more lines and pixels of information have better resolution.

sampling rate. The number of intervals per second used to capture a sound when it is digitized. Sampling rate affects sound quality; the higher the sampling rate, the better the sound quality.

scanner. A hardware peripheral that takes a picture of an item and transfers the image to a computer.

screencast. A digital recording of the output of a computer screen. Also known as a video screen capture. Screencasts may contain audio, as well.

scripting language. A set of commands that is included in some icon- and menu-based development systems. The scripting language allows complex computer instructions to be created.

script. The written text of a play, movie, or broadcast.

scripts. A series of commands written in a language embedded in a hypermedia program.

sequencer. A device that records MIDI events and data.

Smarter Balanced Assessment Consortium. A state-led consortium working collaboratively to develop next-generation assessments aligned to the Common Core State Standards (CCSS) that accurately measure student progress toward college and career readiness.

smartphone. A mobile phone that is able to perform many of the functions of a computer. They typically have a relatively large screen and an operating system capable of running general-purpose applications, including accessing e-mail and the Internet.

social network. A dedicated website or other application that enables users to communicate with each other by posting information, comments, messages, images, and so on.

sound module. A peripheral for MIDI that uses an electronic synthesizer to generate the sounds of musical instruments.

storyboard. A visual representation of what will be placed on a computer screen. In addition, storyboards contain information that helps the programmer and the production specialists develop media components.

streaming. Files that can be played as they are sent over the web.

Student Teams Achievement Divisions (STAD). A cooperative group technique: Students learn something as a team, contribute to their team by improving their own past performance, and earn team rewards based on their improvements.

style guide. A set of standards for the writing and design of documents.

synthesizer. A musical instrument or device that generates sound electronically.

tablet. Short for tablet computer, a mobile computer with the display, circuitry, and battery in a single unit. Tablets are equipped with sensors, including cameras, microphone, and touch screen, with finger or stylus gestures replacing the computer mouse and keyboard.

Team Assisted Individualization (TAI). A cooperative group technique that combines cooperative learning with individualized instruction. Students are placed into groups but work at their own pace and level.

Teams Games Tournament (TGT). A cooperative group technique similar to STAD except that weekly tournaments replace weekly quizzes. Homogeneous, three-member teams formed from the existing heterogeneous groups compete against similar-ability groups to earn points for their regular, heterogeneous group.

text-to-speech synthesis. Sounds created by applying computer algorithms to text to produce spoken words.

theory of multiple intelligences. A theory proposing that there are multiple ways of knowing, suggesting that people possess several different intelligences.

timeline. A method for organizing the video clips in sequential order.

transition. Visual effects, such as dissolves or wipes, that take place as a program moves from one image or screen of information to the next.

tweet. A posting made on the social media website Twitter.

21st-century learning skills. A broad set of knowledge, skills, work habits, and character traits that are believed to be critically important to success in today's world.

Twitter. An online social networking and microblogging service that enables users to send and read short 140-character text messages, called "tweets."

Uniform Resource Locator (URL). URLs are the exact location (address) of an Internet resource, such as a web page.

upload. The process of sending a complete file to the host computer.

vector image. A computer image constructed from graphic formulae. Images that are made up of lines, boxes, and circles (such as charts) usually are vector images.

.WAV. The extension (last three letters) for sound files saved in Microsoft wave format.

Web 2.0 Tools: A new generation of tools that support using the web for creativity, collaboration, social networking, video and photo sharing, and other forms of information distribution. Web 2.0 tools include wikis, blogs, and podcasts.

web app. Software that is accessed and used online via a web browser.

web browser. A software program that can display web pages.

WebQuest. A web-based project designed to guide learners as they research a specific issue and to incorporate the results of the research into an authentic product or project.

wiki. A server program that allows users to collaboratively create and edit the content of a website using a regular web browser.

window. An area on a computer screen that displays text, graphics, messages, or documents.

Windows. A computer operating system from Microsoft.

World Wide Web (WWW). Hypermedia-based Internet information system. Graphical user interfaces allow users to click a mouse on desired menu items, accessing text, sound, pictures, or even motion video from all over the world.

Index

About the Authors

KAREN S. IVERS, PhD, is professor in the Department of Elementary and Bilingual Education at California State University, Fullerton. Her published works include numerous articles on teaching with technology and several books, including ABC-CLIO's *A Teacher's Guide to Using Technology in the Classroom*; *Multimedia Projects in Education: Designing, Producing, and Assessing*; and *Technologies for Education: A Practical Guide*. Ivers received California State University, Fullerton's first Outstanding Teaching with Innovations with Electronic Technology award and has been honored as a Distinguished Faculty Marshall for the College of Education.

ANN E. BARRON, PhD, is professor of instructional technology in the College of Education at the University of South Florida, Tampa. She has authored or coauthored more than 100 journal articles and several books, including ABC-CLIO's *Multimedia Projects in Education: Designing, Producing, and Assessing* and *Technologies for Education: A Practical Guide*. She served as executive director of the Florida Center for Instructional Technology and is a recipient of the Jerome Krivanek Distinguished Teaching Award.